The Mass Strike

THE MASS STRIKE

The Political Party and the Trade Unions

and

THE JUNIUS PAMPHLET

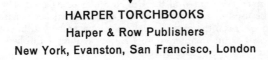

HARPER TORCHBOOKS

Harper & Row Publishers

New York, Evanston, San Francisco, London

The Mass Strike, The Political Party, and the Trade Unions was first published in pamphet form in 1906. Translated by Patrick Lavin, it was first published in English by the Marxist Educational Society in Detroit, 1925.
The Junius Pamphlet: The Crisis in the German Social Democracy was published as a Young Socialist Publication in August, 1967.

THE MASS STRIKE

First Harper TORCHBOOK Edition published 1971.

STANDARD BOOK NUMBER: 06-131583-4

CONTENTS

Editorial Note

Rosa Luxemburg and the New Left

"Who was Rosa Luxemburg?" is not an infrequent question today. Although her ideas have had perennial relevance in Europe, her works have only recently become available to American readers. *The Accumulation of Capital,* her classic analysis of imperialism, and the critical pamphlets she wrote in Germany from the beginning of the century until her death in 1919 have taken more than fifty years to achieve popular recognition here. Who was this heroine of the New Left in Europe and America whose name has momentarily honored the liberated buildings of "occupied" universities? It is generally known that she was the dissenting leader of the German Social Democrats (SPD) and a founder of the Polish and Lithuanian Social Democratic Party (SDKPIL), the *Gruppe Internationale,* the *Spartakusbund,* and the German Communist Party; and that she was the critic of Bernstein and Kautsky, of Lenin and the Bolshevik machine. She has been disparagingly called "Red Rosa," and her principles once strained under a Soviet label of "Luxemburgism"—an appeal to a specious system of political thought invented to be denounced. The latter notion was first created by Stalin in 1924, for which he was immediately criticized by Trotsky for imprecatory misstatements on her role and ideas.

As Hannah Arendt explains in *Men in Dark Times,*[1] the legend of Rosa Luxemburg has "come to life whenever a 'New Left' has come into being." Peter Nettl, in his excellent and de-

1. Hannah Arendt, *Men In Dark Times* (New York: Harcourt, Brace & World, 1969).

finitive biography[2] tell us: "Nearly every dissident group from official communism—German, French, or Russian—at once laid special and exclusive claim to the possession of Rosa Luxemburg's spirit." With the hope of the current New Left that the "movement" become truly revolutionary, it is predictable that Rosa will be given her due meed of glory and not be forgotten this time for her contributions to radical thought. For although student leaders and publicists do not yet document their tactics and rhetoric with citations from her pamphlets, there are curious parallels to her insights into situations that, with the availability now of her works, may become apparent and relevant to the *contestateurs* of the future.

The points of comparison between her life and situation and today's New Left are numerous and striking. How many draft resisters to the Vietnam war will find her an ideological colleague knowing that she spent three years in prison for lecturing (including the Junius Pamphlet written in prison) against Germany's imperialist stance in World War I? How many members of the "movement" will understand her critique of "left eletism" and her fear that the SPD was being choked by bureaucratic goals? How many freedom riders and civil rights activists will understand her warnings not to be beguiled by parliamentary reform legislation—that true social change cannot begin without the people? Despite the current notion that revolution begins at the bottom with the masses, or that theory and organization come out of action, the current dispersed adherents of *praxis* still need a theorist of her audacity—one who knew that no one "makes" a revolution. We saw in France in May, 1968 and in America in May, 1970 the resurgent appeal from the student left to the unionized workers—an appeal that was predictably disappointed but, nonetheless, echoed Rosa's hope for working-class solidarity. (Along these lines, no one can fail to notice the resurrection of the Wobbley Party in late 1970 among students at Berkeley.) Similarly, the New Left is internationally oriented toward all oppressed and recently emerged peoples of what is now called the Third World. One of the strongest points of comparison is Rosa Luxemburg's critique of anarchist bombing and terror, which she considered futile and illusory violence

2. Peter Nettl, *Rosa Luxemburg* (London: Oxford University Press, 1969).

when not coupled with truly political goals and a revolutionary program. The *Mass Strike* pamphlet makes this clear from its first pages. Furthermore, one cannot fail to notice how much Rosa was concerned with a truly political and revolutionary consciousness that it is safe to say she would never have confused it with the current hippie substitute of an expanded drug consciousness. Finally, even in her death (she was shot by Weimar police agents), her example of the life of a vanguard still speaks out.

What can Rosa Luxemburg mean for us today, for those who are revolutionary and those who are not so declared? For one thing, her independent but lucid thinking will stand as a model for all observers of the current scene. It is obvious that she used the Marxist dialectic as a model to communicate in-depth *historical* insights gained from careful analysis of situations in her own times. It is true that capitalism, imperialism, and modern technological warfare have changed since she first analyzed their collusion in the early part of this century, but to the extent these changes are significant it is still necessary for Marxists and other political commentators not to fall into vulgar and programmatic discourse merely for the sake of creating slogans and inflammatory propaganda. With the current losses of credibility and power of the governments of all major states in the world, and their turn to increasingly forceful weapons and violence that support "law and order" by fear of police aggression and terror, and with the new uses of computers, television, and the media— it is all too apparent that a model of independent, nonpartisan clear thinking and theory constructing is a paramount need. For example, today it is important not to confuse class oppression with race or sex oppression, or at least to understand how these are related.

The Junius Pamphlet and *The Mass Strike* pamphlet are Rosa's most important short works, and to recommend them today is a conscientious act, best done among friends who are, in the ancient Greek sense, fellow citizens, or in the sense of the Enlightenment, citizens of the world.

—ROBERT BLAND
The New School
1970

Part I

The Mass Strike,
The Political Party and the Trade Unions
1906

FOREWORD

In this pamphlet Rosa Luxemburg presented to the German working class an analysis of those stormy events of the Russian Revolution of 1905 which Lenin later characterized as "the dress rehearsal" for the Revolution of 1917. The characteristic feature of the period from 1895 to 1905 in the Russian Empire was the role played by the mass strike in the struggles of the Russian proletariat against capitalism and Czarist despotism: strikes in which millions took part not merely to win improvements in their standard of living but also to gain great political objectives; great mass actions which brought together and fused the various aspirations of the separate layers of the proletarian mass into one sweeping anti-capitalist movement.

The idea of the general strike was not a new one, but here in Russia for the first time it was rising up and developing in a new way, and Rosa Luxemburg attempted to bring to the notice of the German and West European workers the lessons to be learned therefrom. In England the Chartists had experimented with the general strike in 1842 to force the government to grant a general franchise; in 1893 the Swedish workers tried it out on the same question; in 1903 Dutch railwaymen began a political strike which developed into a general strike; in 1904 a wave of violent strikes swept over Italy and street fighting took place in several towns. At the time this pamphlet was written, however, the prevailing ideas concerning the general strike were either those of the Bakuninists, who at their Congress at Geneva in 1873 proclaimed the general strike as a weapon for starving out and overthrowing the bourgeoisie by a mere cessation of work which would result in a collapse of the social order, or it was regarded as a defensive weapon against reactionary attacks on working class political rights. In either case it was regarded as a weapon that could be brought out and brandished or hidden away on the orders of the leaders at their whims and fancies.

Under pressure of the events in the Russian Empire and the effect on the German workers of the object lessons in the use of the strike weapon, the German Social Democratic Party was pushed into an examination of the problems of the general strike. The Party Congress at Jena in 1905 adopted a resolution, moved by August Bebel, limiting the use of the general strike to the defense of the franchise; nevertheless here, for the first time, it took *official* notice of the general strike. The German Trade Union Congress at Cologne in 1905, on the other hand, banned even a theoretical discussion of the general strike as "playing with fire." In February 1906 the Central Committee of the Party came to a secret agreement with the Trade Union leaders to allow the implications of the Jena Resolution to remain a dead letter. Disappointed and disgusted with the attitude of the Social Democrat and Trade Union leaderships whose interest in the subject was little more than academic and little less than openly or covertly treacherous and reactionary, Rosa Luxemburg took up the task of reopening the discussion and raising it to a higher level. She had always favored the political mass strike, but her practical experience in the working class movements in Germany and her native Poland (then part of the Russian Empire), and her examination of the wide-spread mass movements of the period from 1896 to 1905 in Russia brought her to a realization of the full significance of the mass strike as the specific weapon of the proletariat in times of revolutionary ferment: "In reality the mass strike does not produce the revolution, but the revolution produces the mass strike." She placed the fruit of her knowledge and experience before the German working class in the form of this pamphlet in 1906, just before the Social Democratic Party Congress at Mannheim, expecting not so much to convert the leadership there as to develop the "revolutionary instinct" of the German workers which had led them to a renewed interest in the problems of the mass strike, under the impact of the revolutionary actions of their class brothers across the Eastern frontier.

In pointing out the lessons of the Revolution of 1905 to the

German workers, Rosa Luxemburg had to deal with the now all-too-familiar contention that the social and political conditions in Russia and in Germany were widely different, and that the methods of struggle suitable for the one country would not be suitable for the other. She points out that in spite of a parliamentary regime in Germany and a despotic regime in Russia, the legality of working class parties and trade unions in Germany and their illegality in Czarist Russia, there nevertheless exist wide layers of the proletarian mass in Germany, just as in Russia, for whom *de jure* political rights have no meaning at all, whole sections which still remain outside the trade union and party organizations, whole sections which still remain in material and cultural poverty and frustration. When and how will these millions be roused to political consciousness to make use of even the limited political rights available to them? When and how will the material level of existence of these nethermost layers be raised to the extent that would enable them to take an interest in political and cultural matters?

"In order to carry through a direct political struggle as a mass, the proletariat must first be assembled as a mass." Rosa Luxemburg's analysis shows how the social and political conditions of the Russian proletariat propelled them, without the help of any established organizations of their own, to take their fate into their own hands, and in the course of their struggle and from the lessons of that struggle to build up their own organizations and awaken and mobilize the nethermost layers. The role played by the mass strike in this self-education and self-organization of the Russian proletariat has its lessons for the international proletariat too. For in this revolutionary epoch, when the last pretenses of bourgeois democracy are being jettisoned by the ruling classes of a crumbling capitalist order, the social and political conditions of the proletarian struggle take on an international similarity and significance in spite of local variations in detail. The role of the mass strike in the education and organization of the proletariat is, therefore, not peculiar to Russia or "Russian conditions" but is determined by "an international milieu whose distinguishing characteristic is the ruin of bourgeois democracy." The lesson that Rosa Luxemburg would have us learn is that the highest common factor in the education and organization of the proletariat of all capitalist countries (whatever their stage of development and the corresponding social and political conditions) is the mass strike. She sums up her evaluation of the significance of the new development of the strike weapon by the Russian proletariat: "The mass strike is thus shown to be *not a specifically Russian product springing from absolutism, but a universal form of the proletarian class struggle resulting from the present stage of capitalist development and class relations.*"

But on the other hand, the mass strike as shown to us in the Russian Revolution is "not a crafty method discovered by subtle reasoning for the purpose of making the struggle more effective." Rosa Luxemburg warns all those opportunists and adventurers who think that the movement can be accelerated by the staging of strikes on the orders of the leaders and at their will and pleasure that "it is not by subjective criticism of the mass strike from the standpoint of *what is desirable*, but only by the objective investigation of the sources of the mass strike from the standpoint of *what is historically inevitable* that the problem can be grasped or even discussed." (Petit-bourgeois sentimentalists and moralists and their representatives of the capitalist press may also take note.) And again, she tells the German workers, "to fix beforehand the cause and the moment from and in which the mass strikes in Germany will break out is not in the power of Social Democracy, because it is not in its power to bring about historical situations by resolutions at party congresses." But what the party can and must do is "to make clear the political tendencies, when once they appear, and to formulate them as resolute and consistent tactics."

The correctness of Rosa Luxemburg's evaluation of the role of the mass strike in our revolutionary epoch, and the lessons it teaches the international working class are borne out by the historical events which followed in the Czarist Empire: first by the setting up of the Petersburg Soviet in the Revolution of 1905, and then, twelve years later, by the part played by the Soviets in the Revolution of 1917 in fusing the aspirations of the various sections of the Russian proletariat into one common class action which shattered the power of its capitalist oppressors and ushered in the world socialist revolution.

BIOGRAPHICAL NOTE

Rosa Luxemburg was born March 5th, 1871 at Zamosc in Poland. Like many others among Polish intellectual youth she was involved in the revolutionary socialist movement from her school days. At the age of eighteen she was compelled to flee the country as her activities had been discovered by the police. She entered the University of Zurich (Switzerland) in 1889. Zurich was then an important center of Polish and Russian emigration, and Rosa was soon in the thick of the emigré socialist movement. In 1893 she helped to found the Polish Social Democratic Party.

Drawn to Germany, then regarded as the center of the international working class movement, she joined the German Social Democratic Party in 1898 just at the time when Bernstein was attacking the fundamental principles of Marxism. Rosa entered the fray against revisionism with a series of articles under the title "Social Reform or Revolution."

When the 1905 revolution broke out in Russia her desire to return to her native Poland was thwarted by illness. But in December 1905 she was smuggled over the Polish frontier and into the thick of the fight. She was arrested on March 4th, 1906 and imprisoned in the Warsaw Citadel. Released in June, she retired to recuperate in Kuokkala, Finland where she wrote her pamphlet *The Mass Strike, The Political Party, and the Trade Unions* in order to interpret the lessons of the 1905 revolution for the German working class. In September 1906 she returned to Germany in time for the Social Democratic Party Congress at Mannheim.

In 1907 at the London Conference of the Russian Social Democratic Party she supported the Bolsheviks against the

7

Mensheviks on all the key problems of the Russian Revolution. In the same year at the Stuttgart Congress of the Second International, together with Lenin she introduced the revolutionary anti-war resolution which was adopted in essence by that Congress.

When war broke out in 1914 she took a revolutionary internationalist position from the outset, and this inevitably led her into jail in February 1915. From jail she collaborated in the illegally published "Spartacus Letters" and in the work of the Spartacus League. In the spring of 1916, in jail, she wrote under the pseudonym of Junius the famous pamphlet *The Crisis of Social Democracy* in which she advocated the urgent need for creating the Third International.

Freed from jail after the November 1918 Revolution in Germany, she joined with Karl Liebknecht in founding the German Communist Party, and was founder and editor of its central organ *Rote Fahne* (Red Banner). After the crushing of the 1919 uprising in Berlin Rosa Luxemburg and Karl Liebknecht were arrested on January 15th and taken to the Eden Hotel for questioning. Here Liebknecht was struck on the head with a rifle butt, then taken away in a car, given further treatment with a rifle butt and finally shot in the head. Shortly after, Rosa Luxemburg was led out of the hotel and at the door was struck to the ground with a rifle butt. Her skull was smashed by two more blows. Half dead, she was put into a car, taken a short distance and finished off with a revolver shot in the head at point-blank range. Her corpse was flung from the Lichtenstein Bridge into the Landwehr Canal from which it was not recovered until the following May.

In the words of her biographer, Paul Frolich, "her physical body will never again take its place in the struggle for social revolution, but no bonfire and no dictatorial order can destroy her ideas. They live on in the minds of her adherents and in the masses of the proletariat."

Chapter I

The Russian Revolution, Anarchism, and the General Strike

ALMOST all works and pronouncements of international Social-ism on the subject of the mass strike date from the time before the Russian revolution,[1] the first historical experiment on a very large scale with this means of struggle. It is therefore evident that they are, for the most part, out-of-date. Their standpoint is essentially that of Engels, who in 1873 wrote as follows in his criticism of the revolutionary blundering of the Bakuninists in Spain:

The general strike, in the Bakuninists' programme, is the lever which will be used for introducing the social revolution. One fine morning all the workers in every industry in a country, or perhaps in every country will cease work, and thereby compel the ruling classes either to submit in about four weeks, or to launch an attack on the workers so that the latter will have the right to defend them-selves, and may use the opportunity to overthrow the old society. The proposal is by no means new: French and Belgian Socialists have pa-raded it continually since 1848, but for all that it is of English origin. During the rapid and powerful development of Chartism among the English workers that followed the crisis of 1837, the "holy month"—a suspension of work on a national scale[2]—was preached as early as 1839, and was received with such favour that in July 1842 the fac-tory workers of the north of England attempted to carry it out. And

1. Of 1905—Ed.
2. "The Holy Month"—was the name given by the Chartist Convention of 1839 to their proposal of a general strike. (See Engles: **The Condition of the Working Class in Britain,** in Marx & Engels: **On Britain,** Moscow Edn. 1953, p. 266 et seq., and G. D. H. Cole: **The Second International,** p. 329 et seq.)

at the Congress of the Alliancists at Geneva on September 1st, 1873,[3] the general strike played a great part, but it was admitted on all sides that to carry it out it was necessary to have a perfect organization of the working class and a full war chest. And that is the crux of the question. On the one hand, the governments, especially if they are encouraged by the workers' abstention from political action, will never allow the funds of the workers to become large enough, and on the other hand, political events and the encroachments of the ruling classes will bring about the liberation of the workers long before the proletariat get the length of forming this ideal organization and this colossal reserve fund. But if they had these, they would not need to make use of the roundabout way of the general strike in order to attain their object.[4]

Here we have the reasoning that was characteristic of the attitude of international Social Democracy towards the mass strike in the following decades. It is based on the Anarchist theory of the general strike—that is, the theory of the general strike as a means of inaugurating the social revolution, in contradistinction to the daily political struggle of the working class—and exhausts itself in the following simple dilemma: either the proletariat as a whole are not yet in possession of the powerful organization and financial resources required, in which case they cannot carry through the general strike; or they are already sufficiently well organized, in which case they do not need the general strike. This reasoning is so simple and at first glance so irrefutable that, for a quarter of a century, it has rendered excellent service to the modern labor movement as a logical weapon against the Anarchist phantom and as a means of carrying the idea of political struggle to the widest circles of the workers. The enormous strides taken by the labor movement in all capitalist countries during the last twenty-five years are the most convincing evidence of the value of the tactics of political

3. "Alliancists"—During the years of the decline of the First International Bakunin and his Anarchist followers formed the "Alliance of Social Democracy" (1868). In September 1873 the Alliancists held a counter Congress to the 6th Congress of the First International. Both took place in Geneva. (See Mehring, *Karl Marx,* p. 495 et seq.)

4. Friedriech Engels, "The Bakuninists at Work" in *Der Volkstaat,* Oct. 31, Nov. 2, 5, 1873. (See Marx and Engels, *Revolution in Spain,* International Publishers, 1939, pp. 217–218.—Ed.)

struggle, which was insisted upon by Marx and Engels in opposition to Bakuninism; and German Social Democracy, in its position of vanguard of the entire international labor movement, is not in the least the direct product of the consistent and energetic application of these tactics.

The Russian revolution has now effected a radical revision of the above piece of reasoning. For the first time in the history of the class struggle it has achieved a grandiose realization of the idea of the mass strike and—as we shall discuss later—has even matured the general strike and thereby opened a new epoch in the development of the labor movement. It does not, of course, follow from this that the tactics of political struggle recommended by Marx and Engels were false, or that the criticism applied by them to Anarchism was incorrect. On the contrary, it is the same train of ideas, the same method, the Engels-Marxian tactics, which lay at the foundation of the previous practice of the German Social Democracy, which now in the Russian revolution are producing new factors and new conditions in the class struggle. The Russian revolution, which is the first historical experiment on the model of the mass strike, not merely does not afford a vindication of Anarchism, but actually means *the historical liquidation of Anarchism*. The sorry existence to which this mental tendency was condemned in recent decades by the powerful development of Social Democracy in Germany may, to a certain extent, be explained by the exclusive dominion and long duration of the parliamentary period. A tendency patterned entirely upon the "first blow" and "direct action," a tendency "revolutionary" in the most naked pitchfork sense, can only temporarily languish in the calm of the parliamentarian day and, on a return of the period of direct open struggle, can come to life again and unfold its inherent strength. Russia, in particular, appeared to have become the experimental field for the heroic deeds of Anarchism. A country in which the proletariat had absolutely no political rights and extremely weak organizations, a many-colored complex of various sections of the population, a chaos of conflicting interests, a low standard of education amongst the masses of the people, extreme brutality in the use of violence on the part of the prevailing regime—all this seemed as if created to raise Anarchism to a sudden if perhaps shortlived power. And finally, Russia was the historical birthplace of Anarchism. But the fatherland of Bakunin was to become the burial place of its teachings. Not only did and do the Anarchists in Russia not stand at the head of the mass strike movement; not only does the whole political leadership of revolutionary action and also of the mass strike lie in the hands of the Social Democratic organizations, which are bitterly opposed as "bourgeois parties" by the Russian Anarchists, or partly in the hands of such Socialist organizations as are more or less influenced by the Social Democracy and more or less approximate to it—such as the terrorist party, the "Socialist Revolutionaries"—but the Anarchists simply do not exist as a serious political tendency in the Russian revolution. Only in a small Lithuanian town with particularly difficult conditions—a confused medley of different nationalities among the workers, an extremely scattered condition of small-scale industry, a very severely oppressed proletariat —in Bialostok, there is, amongst the seven or eight different revolutionary groups a handful of half-grown "Anarchists" who promote confusion and bewilderment amongst the workers to the best of their ability; and lastly in Moscow, and perhaps in two or three other towns, a handful of people of this kidney make themselves noticeable. But apart from these few "revolutionary" groups, what is the actual role of Anarchism in the Russian revolution? It has become the sign of the common thief and plunderer; a large proportion of the innumerable thefts and acts of plunder of private persons are carried out under the name of "Anarchist-Communism"—acts which rise up like a troubled wave against the revolution in every period of depression and in every period of temporary defensive. Anarchism has become in the Russian revolution not the theory of the struggling proletariat but the ideological signboard of the counterrevolutionary lumpenproletariat, who, like a school of sharks, swarm in the wake of the battleship of the revolution. And therewith the historical career of Anarchism is wellnigh ended.

On the other hand, the mass strike in Russia has been realized not as a means of evading the political struggle of the working class, and especially of parliamentarianism, not as a means of jumping suddenly into the social revolution by means of a theatrical coup, but as a means, firstly, of creating for the proletariat the conditions of the daily political struggle and especially of parliamentarianism. The revolutionary struggle in Russia, in which mass strikes are the most important weapon is, by the working people, and above all by the proletariat, conducted for those political rights and conditions whose necessity and importance in the struggle for the emancipation of the working class Marx and Engels first pointed out, and, in opposition to Anarchism, fought for with all their might in the International.[5] Thus has historical dialectics, the rock on which the whole teaching of Marxian Socialism rests, brought it about that today Anarchism, with which the idea of the mass strike is indissolubly associated, has itself come to be opposed to the mass strike in practice; while on the contrary, the mass strike, which was combatted as the opposite of the political activity of the proletariat, appears today as the most powerful weapon of the struggle for political rights. If, therefore, the Russian revolution makes imperative a fundamental revision of the old standpoint of Marxism on the question of the mass strike, it is once again Marxism whose general methods and points of view have thereby, in a new form, carried off the prize. The Moor's beloved can die only by the hand of the Moor.

5. The First International—Ed.

Chapter II

The Mass Strike: An Historical and Not an Artificial Product

THE first revision of the question of the mass strike which results from the experience of Russia relates to the general conception of the problem. Till the present time the zealous advocates of an "attempt with the mass strike" in Germany of the stamp of Bernstein, Eisner, etc., and also the strongest opponents of such an attempt as represented in the trade union camp by, for example, Bomelburg stand, when all is said and done, on the same conception, and that is the Anarchist one. The apparent polar opposites do not mutually exclude each other but, as always, condition, and at the same time, supplement each other. For the Anarchist mode of thought is direct speculation on the "great Kladderadatsch,"[1] on the social revolution merely as an external and inessential characteristic. According to it, what is essential is the whole abstract, unhistorical view of the mass strike and of all the conditions of the proletarian struggle generally. For the Anarchist there exist only two things as material suppositions of his "revolutionary" speculations—first imagination, and second goodwill and courage to rescue humanity from the existing capitalist vale of tears. This fanciful mode of reasoning sixty years ago gave the result that the mass strike was the shortest, surest and easiest means of springing into the better social future. The same mode of reasoning re-

1. The word *Kladderadatsch* means a great noise, and is one of a large class of words in all languages formed on the principle of onomatopoeia, or imitation of natural sounds. The word is well known as the title of a satirical paper published in Berlin since 1848, the Berlin *Punch.*—Trans.

cently gave the result that the trade-union struggle was the only real "direct action of the masses" and also the only real revolutionary struggle—which, as is well known, is the latest notion of the French and Italian "Syndicalists." The fatal thing for Anarchism has always been that the methods of struggle improvised in the air were not only a reckoning without their host, that is, they were purely Utopian, but that they, while not reckoning in the least with the despised evil reality, unexpectedly became in this evil reality, practical helps to the reaction, where previously they had only been, for the most part, revolutionary speculations.

On the same ground of abstract, unhistorical methods of observation stand those today who would, in the manner of a board of directors, put the mass strike in Germany on the calendar on an appointed day, and those who, like the participants in the trade-union congress at Cologne, would by a prohibition of "propaganda" eliminate the problem of the mass strike from the face of the earth. Both tendencies proceed on the common purely Anarchistic assumption that the mass strike is a purely technical means of struggle which can be "decided" at pleasure and strictly according to conscience, or "forbidden"—a kind of pocketknife which can be kept in the pocket clasped "ready for any emergency," and according to decision, can be unclasped and used. The opponents of the mass strike do indeed claim for themselves the merit of taking into consideration the historical groundwork and the material conditions of the present situation in Germany in opposition to the "revolutionary romanticists," who hover in the air, and do not at any point reckon with the hard realities and their possibilities and impossibilities. "Facts and figures; figures and facts!" they cry, like Mr. Gradgrind in Dickens' *Hard Times.* When the trade-union opponent of the mass strike understands by the "historical basis" and "material conditions" is two things—on the one hand the weakness of the proletariat, and on the other hand, the strength of Prussian-German militarism. The inadequate organisation of the workers and the imposing Prussian bayonet—these are the facts and figures upon which these trade-union leaders base their practical policy in the given case. Now while it is quite true that the trade-union cash box and the Prussian bayonet are material and very historical phenomena, the conception based upon them is not historical materialism in Marx's sense but a policemanlike materialism in the sense of Puttkammer. The representatives of the capitalist police state reckon much, and indeed, exclusively with the occasional real power of the organized proletariat as well as with the material might of the bayonet, and from the comparative example of these two rows of figures the comforting conclusion is always drawn that the revolutionary labor movement is produced by individual demagogues and agitators; and that therefore there is in the prisons and bayonets an adequate means of subduing the unpleasant "passing phenomena."

The class-conscious German workers have at last grasped the humor of the policemanlike theory that the whole modern labor movement is an artificial, arbitrary product of a handful of conscienceless "demagogues and agitators."

It is exactly the same conception, however, that finds expression when two or three worthy comrades unite in a voluntary column of night-watchmen in order to warn the German working class against the dangerous agitation of a few "revolutionary romanticists" and their "propaganda of the mass strike"; or when, on the other side, a noisy indignation campaign is engineered by those who, by means of "confidential" agreements between the executive of the party and the general commission of the trade unions, believe they can prevent the outbreak of the mass strike in Germany. If it depended on the inflammatory "propaganda" of revolutionary romanticists or on confidential or public decisions of the party direction, then we should not even yet have had in Russia a single serious mass strike. In no country in the world—as I pointed out in March 1905 in the *Sachische Arbeiterzeitung*—was the mass strike so little "propagated" or even "discussed" as in Russia. And the isolated examples of decisions and agreements of the Russian party executive which really sought to proclaim the mass strike of their own accord—as, for example, the last attempt in August of this year after the dissolution of the Duma—are almost valueless. If, therefore, the Russian revolution teaches us anything, it teaches above all that the mass strike is not artificially "made," not "decided" at random, not "propagated," but that it is an historical phenomenon which, at a given moment, results from social conditions

with historical inevitability. It is not therefore by abstract speculations on the possibility or impossibility, the utility or the
injuriousness of the mass strike, but only by an examination of
those factors and social conditions out of which the mass strike
grows in the present phase of the class struggle—in other words,
it is not by *subjective criticism* of the mass strike from the standpoint of what is desirable, but only by *objective investigation*
of the sources of the mass strike from the standpoint of what is
historically inevitable, that the problem can be grasped or even
discussed.

In the unreal sphere of abstract logical analysis, it can be
shown with exactly the same force on either side that the mass
strike is absolutely impossible and sure to be defeated, and that
it is possible and that its triumph cannot be questioned. And
therefore the value of the evidence shown on each side is exactly
the same—and that is nil. Therefore the fear of the "propaga-
tion" of the mass strike which has even led to formal anathemas
against the persons alleged to be guilty of this crime, is solely
the product of the droll confusion of persons. It is just as impossible to "propagate" the mass strike as an abstract means of
struggle as it is to propagate the "revolution." "Revolution" like
"mass strike" signifies nothing but an external form of the class
struggle which can have sense and meaning only in connection
with definite political situations.

If anyone were to undertake to make the mass strike generally
as a form of proletarian action the object of methodical agitation, and to go house-to-house canvassing with this "idea" in
order to gradually win the working class to it, it would be as idle
and profitless and absurd an occupation as it would be to seek
to make the idea of the revolution or of the fight at the barricades the object of a special agitation. The mass strike has now
become the center of the lively interest of the German and the
international working class because it is a new form of struggle,
and as such is the sure symptom of a thorough-going internal
revolution in the relations of the classes and in the conditions of
the class struggle. It is a testimony to the sound revolutionary
instinct and to the quick intelligence of the mass of the German
proletariat that, in spite of the obstinate resistance of their trade-
union leaders, they are applying themselves to this new problem

with such keen interest. But it does not meet the case, in the presence of this interest and of this fine, intellectual thirst and desire for revolutionary deeds on the part of the workers, to treat them to abstract mental gymnastics on the possibility or impossibility of the mass strike; they should be enlightened on the development of the Russian revolution, the international significance of that revolution, the sharpening of class antagonisms in Western Europe, the wider political perspectives of the class struggle in Germany, and the role and the tasks of the masses in the coming struggles. Only in this form will the discussion on the mass strike lead to the widening of the intellectual horizon of the proletariat, to the sharpening of their way of thinking, and to the steeling of their energy.

Viewed from this standpoint however, the criminal proceedings desired by the enemies of "revolutionary romanticism" appear in all their absurdity because, in treating of the problem, one does not adhere strictly to the text of the Jena resolution.[2] The "practical politicians" agree to this resolution if need be because they couple the mass strike chiefly with the fate of universal suffrage, from which it follows that they can believe two things—first, that the mass strike is of a purely defensive character, and second, that the mass strike is even subordinate to Parliamentarianism, that is, has been turned into a mere appendage of Parliamentarianism. But the real kernel of the Jena resolution in this connection is that in the present position of Germany an attempt on the part of the prevailing reaction on the Parliamentary vote would in all probability be the moment for the introduction of, and the signal for, a period of stormy political struggles in which the mass strike as a means of struggle in Germany might well come into use for the first time. But to seek to narrow and to artificially smother the social importance and to limit the historical scope of the mass strike as a phenomenon and as a problem of the class struggle by the wording of a congress resolution, is an undertaking which for short-sightedness can only be compared with the veto on discussion of the

2. The Congress of the Social Democratic Party of Germany held at Jena in 1905 decided generally in favor of the general strike, leaving the matter, however, vague.

trade union congress at Cologne.[3] In the resolution of the Jena Congress German Social Democracy has officially taken notice of the fundamental change which the Russian revolution has effected in the international conditions of the proletarian class struggle, and its capacity for revolutionary development and its power of adaptability to the new demands of the coming phase of the class struggle. Therein lies the significance of the Jena resolution. As for the practical application of the mass strike in Germany, history will decide that as it decided it in Russia— history in which German Social Democracy with its decisions is, it is true, an important factor, but at the same time, only *one* factor amongst many.

3. The Cologne Congress of Trade Unions also held in 1905 decided against the mass strike. The next year, a compromise was reached between the leaders of the Party and those of the trade unions whereby a mass-strike decision would be taken only after consultation with the trade unions, and with their consent. This decision, taken against the background of the Russian revolution, clearly indicated that the majority leaders of the German Social Democracy learned nothing from historical events.

Chapter III

Development of the Mass Strike Movement in Russia

The mass strike, as it appears for the most part in the discussion in Germany, is a very clear and simply thought out, sharply sketched, isolated phenomenon. It is the political mass strike exclusively that is spoken of. What is meant by it is a single grand rising of the industrial proletariat springing from some political motive of the highest importance, undertaken on the basis of an opportune and mutual understanding on the part of the controlling authorities of the party and of the trade unions, carried through in the spirit of party discipline and in perfect order, and in still more perfect order brought to the directing committees at a signal given at the proper time, by which committees the regulation of support, the cost, the sacrifice—in a word, the whole material balance of the mass strike—is exactly determined in advance.

Now, when we compare this theoretical scheme with the real mass strike as it appeared in Russia five years ago, we are compelled to say that this representation which, in the German discussion occupies the central position, hardly corresponds to a single one of the many mass strikes that have taken place, and on the other hand that the mass strike in Russia displays such a multiplicity of the most varied forms of action that it is altogether impossible to speak of "the" mass strike, of an abstract schematic mass strike. All the factors of the mass strike, as well as its character, are not only different in the different towns and districts of the country, but its general character has often changed in the course of the revolution. The mass strike has passed through a definite history in Russia, and is passing still further through it. Who, therefore, speaks of the mass strike in Russia must, above all things, keep its history before his eyes.

The present official period, so to speak, of the Russian revolution is justly dated from the rising of the proletariat on January 22, 1905, when the demonstration of 200,000 workers ended in a frightful bloodbath before the Czar's palace. The bloody massacre in St. Petersburg was, as is well known, the signal for the outbreak of the first gigantic series of mass strikes which spread over the whole of Russia within a few days and which carried the call to action of the revolution from St. Petersburg to every corner of the Empire and among the widest sections of the proletariat. But the St. Petersburg rising of January 22 was only the critical moment of a mass strike which the proletariat of the Czarist capital had previously entered upon in January 1905. This January mass strike was without doubt carried through under the immediate influence of the gigantic general strike which in December 1904 broke out in the Caucasus, in Baku, and for a long time kept the whole of Russia in suspense. The events of December in Baku were on their part only the last and powerful ramification of those tremendous mass strikes which, like a periodical earthquake, shook the whole of south Russia, and whose prologue was the mass strike in Batum in the Caucasus in March 1902. This first mass strike movement in the continuous series of present revolutionary eruptions is, finally, separated by five or six years from the great general strike of the textile workers in St. Petersburg in 1896 and 1897, and if this movement is apparently separated from the present revolution by a few years of apparent stagnation and strong reaction, every one who knows the inner political development of the Russian proletariat to their present stage of class consciousness and revolutionary energy will realize that the history of the present period of the mass struggles begins with those general strikes in St. Petersburg. They are therefore important for the problems of the mass strike because they already contain, in the germ, all the principal factors of later mass strikes.

Again, the St. Petersburg general strike of 1896 appears as a purely economic partial wage struggle. Its causes were the intolerable working conditions of the spinners and weavers in

St. Petersburg: a working day of thirteen, fourteen or fifteen hours, miserable piece-work rates, and a whole series of contemptible chicaneries on the part of the employers. This condition of things, however, was patiently endured by the workers for a long time till an apparently trivial circumstance filled the cup to overflowing. The coronation of the present Czar, Nicholas II, which had been postponed for two years through fear of the revolutionaries, was celebrated in May 1896, and on that occasion the St. Petersburg employers displayed their patriotic zeal by giving their workers three days compulsory holidays, for which, curious to relate, they did not desire to pay their employees. The workers, angered at this, began to move. After a conference of about three hundred of the intelligent workers in the Ekaterinhof Garden a strike was decided upon, and the following demands were formulated: first, payment of wages for the coronation holidays, second, a working day of ten hours; third, increased rates for piece-work. This happened on May 24th. In a week every weaving and spinning establishment was at a standstill, and 40,000 workers were in the general strike. Today this event, measured by the gigantic mass strike of the revolution may appear a little thing. In the political polar rigidity of the Russia of that time a general strike was something unheard of; it was even a complete revolution in miniature. There began, of course, the most brutal persecution. About one thousand workers were arrested and the general strike was suppressed.

Here already we see all the fundamental characteristics of the later mass strikes. The next occasion of the movement was wholly accidental, even unimportant, its outbreak elementary; but in the success of the movement the fruits of the agitation extending over several years of the Social Democracy were seen, and in the course of the general strike the Social Democratic agitators stood at the head of the movement, directed it, and used it to stir up revolutionary agitation. Further the strike was outwardly a mere economic struggle for wages, but the attitude of the government and the agitation of the Social Democracy made it a political phenomenon of the first rank. The strike was suppressed; the workers suffered a "defeat." But in January of the following year the textile workers of St. Petersburg repeated the general strike once more and achieved this time a remarkable success: the legal introduction of a working day of eleven hours throughout the whole of Russia. What was nevertheless a much more important result was this: since that first general strike of 1896 which was entered upon without a trace of organization or of strike funds, an intensive trade union fight began in Russia proper which spread from St. Petersburg to the other parts of the country and opened up entirely new vistas to Social Democratic agitation and organization, and by which in the apparently death-like peace of the following period the revolution was prepared by underground work.

The outbreak of the Caucasian strike in March 1902 was apparently as accidental and as much due to purely economic [partial] causes (although produced by quite other factors) as that of 1896. It was connected with the serious industrial and commercial crisis which in Russia was the precursor of the Japanese war and which, together with it, was the most powerful factor of the nascent revolutionary ferment. The crisis produced an enormous mass of unemployment which nourished the agitation among the proletarian masses, and therefore the government, to restore tranquility amongst the workers, undertook to transport the "superfluous hands" in batches to their respective home districts. One such measure, which was to affect about four hundred petroleum workers called forth a mass protest in Batum, which led to demonstrations, arrests, a massacre, and finally to a political trial in which the purely economic and [partial] affair suddenly became a political and revolutionary event. The reverberation of the wholly "fruitless" expiring and suppressed strike in Batum was a series of revolutionary mass demonstrations of workers in Nijni Novgorod, Saratov and other towns, and therefore a mighty surge forward of the general wave of the revolutionary movement.

Already in November 1902 the first genuine revolutionary echo followed in the shape of a general strike at Rostov-on-Don. Disputes about the rates of pay in the workshops of the Vladicaucasus Railway gave the impetus to this movement. The management sought to reduce wages and therefore the Don Committee of the Social Democracy issued a proclamation with a summons to strike for the following demands: a nine-hour day, increase of wages, abolition of fines, dismissal of obnoxious engineers, etc. Entire railway workshops participated in the strike. Presently all other industries joined in and suddenly an unprecedented state of affairs prevailed in Rostov: all industrial work was at a standstill, and every day mammoth meetings of from 15,000 to 20,000 were held in the open air, sometimes surrounded by a cordon of Cossacks, at which for the first time Social Democratic popular speakers appeared publicly, inflammatory speeches on Socialism and political freedom were delivered and received with immense enthusiasm, and revolutionary appeals were distributed by tens of thousands of copies. In the midst of rigid absolutist Russia the proletariat of Rostov won for the first time the right of assembly, and freedom of speech by storm. It goes without saying that there was a massacre here. The disputes over wages in the Vladicaucasus Railway workshops grew in a few days into a political general strike and a revolutionary street battle. As an echo to this there followed immediately a general strike at the station of Tichoretzkaia on the same railway. Here also a massacre took place and also a trial, and thus even Tichoretzkaia has taken its place in the indissoluble chain of the factors of the revolution.

The spring of 1903 gave the answer to the defeated strikes in Rostov and Tichoretzkaia; the whole of South Russia in May, June and July was aflame. Baku, Tiflis, Batum, Elizavetgrad, Odessa, Kiev, Nicholaiev and Ekaterinoslav were in a general strike in the literal meaning of those words. But here again the movement did not arise on any preconceived plan from one to another; it flowed together from individual points in each one from a different cause and in a different form. The beginning was made by Baku where several partial wage struggles in individual factories and departments culminated in a general strike. In Tiflis the strike was begun by 2000 commercial employees who had a working day of from six o'clock in the morning to eleven at night. On the fourth of July they all left their shops and made a circuit of the town to demand from the proprietors of the shops that they close their premises. The victory was complete; the commercial employees won a working day of from eight in the morning to eight in the evening, and they were immediately joined by all the factories, workshops and offices, etc. The newspapers did not appear, and tramway traffic could not be carried on under military protection. In Elisavetgrad on July 4 a strike began in all the factories with purely economic demands. These were mostly conceded, and the strike ended on the 14th. Two weeks later however it broke out again. The bakers this time gave the word and they were joined by the bricklayers, the joiners, the dyers, the mill workers, and finally all factory workers. In Odessa the movement began with a wage struggle in the course of which the "legal" workers' union, founded by government agents according to the program of the famous gendarme Zubatov, was developed. Historical dialectics had again seized the occasion to play one of its malicious little pranks. The economic struggles of the earlier period (among them the great St. Petersburg general strike of 1896) had misled Russian Social Democracy into exaggerating the importance of so-called "economics," and in this way the ground had been prepared among the workers for the demagogic activities of Zubatov. After a time, however, the great revolutionary stream turned round the little ship with the false flag, and compelled it to ride right at the head of the revolutionary proletarian flotilla. The Zubatovian unions gave the signal for the great general strike in Odessa in the spring of 1904, as for the general strike in St. Petersburg in January 1905. The workers in Odessa, who were not to be deceived by the appearance of friendliness on the part of the government for the workers, and of its sympathy with purely economic strikes, suddenly demanded proof by example, and compelled the Zubatovian "workers union" in a factory to declare a strike for very moderate demands. They were immediately thrown on the streets, and when they demanded the protection of the authorities which was promised them by their leader, the gentleman vanished and left the workers in the wildest excitement. The Social Democrats at once placed themselves at the head of affairs, and the strike movement extended to other factories. On the first of July 2500 dockers struck work for an increase of wages from eighty kopeks to two roubles, and the shortening of the working day by half an hour. On the 16th of July the seamen joined the movement. On the 13th the tramway staff began a strike. Then a meeting took place of all the strikers, seven or eight thousand men; they formed a procession which went from factory to factory, growing like an avalanche, and presently a crowd of from 40,000 to 50,000 betook themselves to the docks in order to bring all work there to a standstill. A general strike soon reigned throughout the whole city. In Kiev a strike began in the railway workshops on July 21. Here also the immediate cause was miserable conditions of labor, and wage demands were presented. On the following day the foundry men followed the example. On July 23 an incident occurred which gave the signal for the general strike. During the night two delegates of the railwaymen were arrested. The strikers immediately demanded their release, and as this was not conceded, they decided not to allow trains to leave the town. At the station all the strikers with their wives and families sat down on the railway track—a sea of human beings. They were threatened with rifle salvoes. The workers bared their breasts and cried "Shoot"! A salvo was fired into the defenseless seated crowd, and thirty to forty corpses, among them those of women and children, remained on the ground. When this became known the whole town of Kiev went on strike immediately. The corpses of the murdered workers were raised on high by the crowd and carried round in a mass demonstration. Meetings, speeches, arrests, isolated street fights—Kiev was in the midst of the revolution. The movement was soon at an end. But the printers had won a shortening of the working day of one hour and a wage increase of one rouble; in a yeast factory the eight-hour day was introduced; the railway workshops were closed by order of the Ministry; other departments continued partial strikes for their demands. In Nicholaiev the general strike broke out under the immediate influence of the news from Odessa, Baku, Batum and Tiflis, in spite of the opposition of the Social Democratic Committee who wanted to postpone the outbreak of the movement till the time came when the military should have left the town for manoeuvres. The masses refused to hold back; one factory made a beginning, the strikes went from one workshop to another, the resistance of the military only poured oil on the fire. Mass processions with revolutionary songs were formed which were taken part in by all workers, employees, tramways officials, men and women. The cessation of work was complete. In Ekaterinoslav the bakers came out on strike on August 5, the men in the railway workshops on the 7th, and then all the other factories on August 8. Tramway traffic stopped, and the newspapers did not appear. Thus the colossal general strike in south Russia came into being in the summer of 1903. By many small channels of partial economic struggles and little "accidental" occurrences it flowed rapidly to a raging sea, and changed the entire south of the Czarist empire for some weeks into a bizarre revolutionary workers' republic. "Brotherly embraces, cries of delight and of enthusiasm, songs of freedom, merry laughter, humor and joy, were seen and heard in the crowd of many thousands of persons which surged through the town from morning till evening. The mood was exalted; one could almost believe that a new, better life was beginning on the earth. A most solemn and at the same time an idyllic, moving spectacle." . . . So wrote at the time the correspondent of the Liberal *Osvoboshdenye*[1] of Peter Struve.

The year 1904 brought with it war, and for a time, an interval of quiet in the mass strike movement. At first a troubled wave of "patriotic" demonstrations arranged by the police authorities spread over the country. The "liberal" bourgeois society was for the time being struck to the ground by the Czarist official chauvinism. But soon the Social Democrats took possession of the arena; revolutionary workers' demonstrations were opposed to the demonstrations of the patriotic lumpenproletariat which were organized under police patronage. At last the shameful defeats of the Czarist army woke the liberal society from its lethargy; then began the era of democratic congresses, banquets, speeches, addresses and manifestos. Absolutism, temporarily suppressed through the disgrace of the war, gave full scope to these gentlemen, and by and by they saw everything in rosy colors. For six months bourgeois liberalism occupied the center of the stage, and the proletariat remained in the shadows. But after a long depression absolutism again roused itself, the camarilla gathered all its strength and by a single powerful movement of the Cossack's heel the whole liberal movement was driven into a corner. Banquets, speeches and congresses were prohibited out of hand as "intolerable presumption," and liberalism suddenly found itself at the end of its tether. But

1. Emancipation—Ed.

exactly at the point where liberalism was exhausted, the action of the proletariat began. In December 1904 the great general strike, due to unemployment, broke out in Baku; the working class was again on the field of battle. Action began as speech was forbidden and rendered impossible. In Baku for some weeks in the midst of the general strike the Social Democrats ruled as absolute masters of the situation; and the peculiar events of December in the Caucasus would have caused an immense sensation if they had not been so quickly put in the shade by the rising tide of the revolution which they had themselves set in motion. The fantastic confused news of the general strike in Baku had not reached all parts of the Czarist empire when in January 1905 the mass strike in St. Petersburg broke out.

Here also as is well known, the immediate cause was trivial. Two men employed at the Putilov works were discharged on account of their membership in the legal Zubatovian union. This measure called forth a solidarity strike on January 16 of the whole of the 12,000 employees in this works. The Social Democrats seized the occasion of the strike to begin a lively agitation for the extension of the demands and set forth demands for the eight-hour day, the right of combination, freedom of speech and of the press, etc. The unrest among the Putilov workers communicated itself quickly to the remainder of the proletariat, and in a few days 140,000 workers were on strike. Joint conferences and stormy discussions led to the proletarian charter of bourgeois freedom, with the eight-hour day at its head, with which 200,000 workers led by Father Gapon on January 22nd marched to the Czar's palace. The conflict of the two Putilov workers who had been subjected to disciplinary punishment had changed within a week into the prologue of the most violent revolution of modern times.

The events that followed upon this are well known; the bloodbath in St. Petersburg called forth gigantic mass strikes and a general strike in the months of January and February in all the industrial centers and towns in Russia. Poland, Lithuania, the Baltic provinces, the Caucasus, Siberia, from north to south and east to west. On closer inspection, however, it can be seen that the mass strike was appearing in other forms than those of the previous period. Everywhere at that time the Social Democratic organizations went ahead with appeals; everywhere revolutionary solidarity with the St. Petersburg proletariat was expressly stated as the cause and aim of the general strike; everywhere, at the same time, there were demonstrations, speeches, conflicts with the military. But even here there was no predetermined plan, no organized action, because the appeals of the parties could scarcely keep pace with the spontaneous risings of the masses; the leaders had scarcely time to formulate the watchwords of the onrushing crowd of the proletariat. Further, the earlier mass and general strikes had originated from coalescing wage struggles which, in the general temper of the revolutionary situation and under the influence of the Social Democratic agitation, rapidly became political demonstrations; the economic factor and the scattered condition of trade unionism were the starting point, all-embracing class action and political direction the result. The movement was now reversed. The general strikes of January and February broke out as unified revolutionary actions to begin with under the direction of the Social Democrats; but this action soon fell into an unending series of local [partial] economic strikes in separate districts, towns, departments and factories. Throughout the spring of 1905 and into the middle of the summer there fermented throughout the whole of the immense empire an uninterrupted economic strike of almost the entire proletariat against capital—a struggle which caught on the one hand all the petit-bourgeois and liberal professions (commercial employees, technicians, actors and members of artistic professions), and on the other hand penetrated to the domestic servants, the minor police officials and even to the stratum of the lumpenproletariat, and simultaneously surged from the towns to the country districts and even knocked at the iron gates of the military barracks.

This is a gigantic, many-colored picture of a general arrangement of labor and capital which reflects all the complexity of social organization and of the political consciousness of every section and of every district. The whole long scale runs from the regular trade-union struggle of a picked and tested troop of the proletariat drawn from large-scale industry, to the formless protest of a handful of rural proletarians, and to the first slight stirrings of an agitated military garrison; from the well-educated and elegant revolt in cuffs and white collars in the counting house of a bank to the shy-bold murmurings of a clumsy meeting of dissatisfied policemen in a smoke-grimed, dark and dirty guardroom.

According to the theory of the lovers of "orderly and well-disciplined" struggles, according to plan and scheme, according to those especially who always ought to know better from afar "how it should have been done," the decay of the great political general strike of January 1905 into a number of economic struggles was probably "a great mistake" which crippled that action and changed it into a "straw fire."[2] But Social Democracy in Russia, which had taken part in the revolution but had not "máde" it, and which had even to learn its law from its course itself, was at the first glance put out of countenance for a time by the apparently fruitless ebb of the storm-flood of the general strike. History, however, which had made that "great mistake" thereby accomplished, heedless of the reasonings of its officious schoolmaster, a gigantic work for the revolution which was as inevitable as it was, in its consequences, incalculable.

The sudden general rising of the proletariat in January under the powerful impetus of the St. Petersburg events was outwardly a political act of the revolutionary declaration of war on absolutism. But this first general direct action reacted inwardly all the more powerfully as it for the first time awoke class feeling and class consciousness in millions upon millions as if by an electric shock. And this awakening of class feeling expressed itself forthwith in the circumstances that the proletarian mass, counted by millions, quite suddenly and sharply came to realize how intolerable was that social and economic existence which they had patiently endured for decades in the chains of capitalism. Thereupon there began a spontaneous general shaking of and tugging at these chains. All the innumerable sufferings of the modern proletariat reminded them of the old bleeding wounds. Here was the eight-hour day fought for, there piece work was resisted, here were brutal foremen "driven off" in a sack on a handcar. At another place infamous systems of fines were fought against, everywhere better wages were striven for

2. A type of passing ardor.—Trans.

and here and there the abolition of home-work. Backward de-graded occupations in large towns, small provincial towns, which had hitherto dreamed in an idyllic sleep, the village with its legacy from feudalism—all these, suddenly awakened by the January lightning, bethought themselves of their rights and now sought feverishly to make up for their previous neglect. The economic struggle was not really a decay here, or a dissipation of action, but merely change of front, a sudden and natural alteration of the first general engagement with absolutism, in a general reckoning with capital, which in keeping with its charac-ter, assumed the form of individual, scattered wage struggles. Political class action was not broken in January by the decay of the general strike into economic strikes, but the reverse; after the possible content of political action in the given situation and at the given stage of the revolution was exhausted, it broke, or rather changed, into economic action.

In point of fact, what more could the general strike in January have achieved? Only complete thoughtlessness could expect that absolutism could be destroyed at one blow by a single "long-drawn" general strike after the Anarchist plan. Absolutism in Russia must be overthrown by the proletariat. But in order to be able to overthrow it the proletariat require a high degree of political education, of class consciousness and organization. All these conditions cannot be fulfilled by pamphlets and leaflets, but only by the living political school, by the fight and in the fight, in the continuous course of the revolution. Further, ab-solutism cannot be overthrown at any desired moment in which only adequate "exertion" and "endurance" are necessary. The fall of absolutism is merely the outer expression of the inner social and class development of Russian society. Before abso-lutism can, and may be overthrown, the bourgeois Russia must be formed in its interior, in its modern class divisions. That re-quires the drawing together of the various social layers and in-terests, besides the education of the proletarian revolutionary parties, and not less of the liberal, radical, petit-bourgeois, conservative and reactionary parties; it requires self-conscious-ness, self-knowledge and the class consciousness not merely of the layers of the people, but also of the layers of the bourgeoisie. But this also can be achieved and come to fruition in no way but in the struggle, in the process of the revolution itself, through the actual school of experience, in collision with the proletariat as well as with one another, in incessant mutual friction. This class division and class maturity of bourgeois society, as well as its action in the struggle against absolutism, is on the one hand, hampered and made difficult by the peculiar leading role of the proletariat and on the other hand, is spurred on and accelerated. The various undercurrents of the social process of the revolution cross one another, check one another, and increase the internal contradictions of the revolution, but in the end accelerate and thereby render still more violent its eruptions.

This apparently simple and purely mechanical problem may therefore be stated thus: the overthrow of absolutism is a long, continuous social process, and its solution demands a complete undermining of the soil of society; the uppermost part be placed lowest and the lowermost part highest, the apparent "order" must be changed to a chaos, and the apparently "anarchistic" chaos must be changed into a new order. Now in this process of the social transformation of the old Russia, not only the January lightning of the first general strike but also the spring and summer thunderstorms that followed it, played an indispensable part. The embittered general relations of wage labor and capital contributed in equal measure to the drawing together of the various layers of the people and those of the bourgeoisie, to the class consciousness of the revolutionary proletariat and to that of the liberal and conservative bourgeoisie. And just as the urban wage struggle contributed to the formation of a strong monarchist industrial party in Moscow, so the conflagration of the violent rural rising in Livonia led to the rapid liquidation of the famous aristocratic-agrarian Zemstvo-Liberalism.

But at the same time, the period of the economic struggles of the spring and summer of 1905 made it possible for the urban proletariat, by means of active Social Democratic agitation and direction, to assimilate later all the lessons of the January prologue and to grasp clearly all the further tasks of the revolution. There was connected with this too, another circumstance of an enduring social character: *a general raising of the standard of life of the proletariat,* economic, social and intellectual. The January strikes of 1905 ended victoriously almost throughout. As proof of this, some data from the enormous, and still for the most part inaccessible, mass of material may be cited here relating to a few of the most important strikes carried through in Warsaw alone by the Social Democrats of Poland and Lithuania. In the great factories of the metal industry of Warsaw: Lilpop Ltd., Ran & Lowenstein, Rudzki and Co., Borman, Schwede and Co., Handtke, Gerlach and Pulst, Geisler Bros., Eberherd, Wolski and Co., Konrad and Yarnuszkiewicz Ltd., Weber and Daehu, Ewizdzinski and Co., Wolonoski Wire Works, Gostynski and Co. Ltd., Rrun and Son, Frage Norblin, Werner, Buch, Kenneberg Bros., Labor, Dittunar Lamp Factory, Serkowski, Weszk —twenty-two factories in all the workers won, after a strike of from four to five weeks (from January 25 and 26) a nine-hour day, a twenty-five per cent increase of wages, and obtained various smaller concessions. In the large workshops of the timber industry of Warsaw, namely Karmanski, Damieki, Gromel, Szerbinskik, Tremerowski, Horn, Devensee, Tworkowski, Daab and Martens—twelve workshops in all—the strikes had won the nine-hour day by the 23rd of February; they were not satisfied with this, but insisted upon the eight-hour day, which they also won, together with an increase of wages, after a further strike of a week. The entire bricklaying industry began a strike on February 27 and demanded, in conformity with the watchword of Social Democracy, the eight-hour day; they won the ten-hour day on March 11 together with an increase of wages for all categories, regular payment of wages weekly, etc. The painters, the cartwrights, the saddlers and the smiths all won the eight-hour day without decrease of wages. The telephone workshops struck for ten days and won the eight-hour day and an increase of wages of from ten to fifteen per cent. The large linen-weaving establishment of Hielle and Dietrich (10,000 workers) after a strike lasting nine weeks, obtained a decrease of the working day of one hour and a wage increase of from five to ten per cent. And similar results in endless variation were to be seen in all the older branches of industry in Warsaw, Lodz and Sosnovitz.

In Russia proper the eight-hour day was won in December 1904 by a few categories of oil workers in Baku; in May 1905 by the sugar workers of the Kiev district; in January 1905 in all the printing works in Samara (where at the same time an increase of piece-work rates was obtained and fines were abolished); in February in the factory in which medical instruments for the army are manufactured, in a furniture factory and in the cartridge factory in St. Petersburg. Further, the eight-hour day was introduced in the mines at Vladivostock, in March in the government mechanical workshops dealing with government stock, and in May among the employees of the Tiflis electric town railway. In the same month a working day of eight and a half hours was introduced in the large cotton-weaving factory of Morosov (and at the same time the abolition of night work and a wage increase of eight per cent were won); in June an eight-hour day in a few oil works in St. Petersburg and Moscow; in July a working day of eight and a half hours among the smiths at the St. Petersburg docks; and in November in all the private printing establishments of the town of Orel (and at the same time an increase of time rates of twenty per cent and piece-work rates of one hundred per cent, as well as the setting up a conciliation board in which workers and employer were equally represented).

The nine-hour day was obtained in all the railway workshops (in February), in many government, military and naval workshops, in most of the factories of the town of Berdiansk, in all the printing works of the towns of Poltava and Musk; nine and a half hours in the shipyards, mechanical workshops and foundries in the town of Nicholayev in June, after a general strike of waiters in Warsaw in many restaurants and cafes (and at the same time a wage increase of from twenty to forty per cent, with a two-week holiday every year).

The ten-hour day won in almost all the factories of the towns of Lodz, Sosnovitz, Riga, Kovno, Oval, Dorfat, Minsk, Kharkov, in the bakeries of Odessa, among the mechanics in Kishinev, at a few smelting works in St. Petersburg, in the match factories of Kovno (with an increase of wages of ten per cent), in all the government marine workshops, and among all the dockers.

The wage increases were in general smaller than the shortening of hours but always more significant: in Warsaw in the middle of March 1905 a general increase of wages of fifteen per cent was fixed by the municipal factories department; in the center of the textile industry, Ivanovo-Vosnosensk, the wage increase amounted to from seven to fifteen per cent, in Kovno the increase affected seventy-three per cent of the workers. A fixed minimum wage was introduced in some of the bakeries in Odessa, in the Neva shipbuilding yards in St. Petersburg, etc.

It goes without saying that these concessions were withdrawn again, here and there. This however, was only the cause of renewed strife and led to still more bitter struggles for revenge, and thus the strike period of the spring of 1905 has of itself become the prologue to an endless series of everspreading and interlacing economic struggles which have lasted to the present day. In the period of the outward stagnation of the revolution, when the telegraph carried no sensational news from the Russian theatre of war to the outside world, and when the West European laid aside his newspaper in disappointment with the remark that there "was nothing doing" in Russia, the great underground work of the revolution was in reality being carried on without cessation, day by day and hour by hour in the very heart of the empire. The incessant intensive economic struggle effected, by rapid and abbreviated methods, the transition of capitalism from the stage of primitive accumulation and of patriarchal unmethodical methods of working, to a highly modern, civilized one. At the present time the actual working day in Russian industry leaves behind not only Russian factory legislation (that is the legal working day of eleven hours) but even the actual conditions of Germany. In most departments of large-scale industry in Russia the ten-hour day prevails, which in Germany is declared in social legislation to be an unattainable goal. And what is more, that longed-for "industrial constitutionalism," for which there is so much enthusiasm in Germany, and for the sake of which the advocates of opportunist tactics would keep every keen wind from the stagnant waters of their all-suffering Parliamentarianism, has already been born, together with political "constitutionalism," in the midst of the revolutionary storm, from the revolution itself! In actual fact it is not merely a general raising of the standard of life, or of the cultural level of the working class that has taken place. The material standard of life as a permanent stage of well-being has no place in the revolution. Full of contradictions and contrasts it brings simultaneously

surprising economic victories, and the most brutal acts of revenge on the part of the capitalists; today the eight-hour day,
and tomorrow wholesale lockouts and actual starvation for the
millions. The most precious, because lasting, thing in this rapid
ebb and flow of the wave is its mental sediment: the intellectual,
cultural growth of the proletariat, which proceeds by fits and
starts, and which offers an inviolable guarantee of their further
irresistible progress in the economic as in the political struggle.
And not only that. Even the relations of the worker to the employer are turned round; since the January general strike and
the strikes of 1905 which followed upon it, the principle of the
capitalist "mastery of the house" is de facto abolished. In the
large factories of all important industrial centers the establishment of workers' committees has, as if by itself, taken place,
with which alone the employer negotiates and which decide all
disputes. And finally another thing the apparently "chaotic"
strikes and the "disorganised" revolutionary action after the January general strike is becoming the starting point of a feverish
work of organization. Dame History, from afar, smilingly hoaxes
the bureaucratic lay figures who keep grim watch at the gate
over the fate of the German trade unions. The firm organizations, which as the indispensable hypothesis for an eventual
German mass strike should be fortified like an impregnable
citadel—these organisations are in Russia, on the contrary, already born from the mass strike. And while the guardians of
the German trade unions for the most part fear that the organizations will fall in pieces in a revolutionary whirlwind like rare
porcelain, the Russian revolution shows us the exactly opposite
picture; from the whirlwind and the storm, out of the fire and
glow of the mass strike and the street fighting rise again, like
Venus from the foam, fresh, young, powerful, buoyant trade
unions.

Here again a little example however, which is typical of the
whole empire. At the second conference of the Russian trade
unions which took place at the end of February 1906 in St.
Petersburg, the representative of the Petersburg trade unions,
in his report on the development of trade union organizations
of the Czarist capital said:

January 22nd, 1905, which washed away the Gapon union, was a turning point. The workers in large numbers have learned by experience to appreciate and understand the importance of organization, and that only they themselves can create these organizations. The first trade union—that of the printers—originated in direct connection with the January movement. The commission appointed to work out the tariffs framed the statutes, and on July 19th the union began its existence. Just about this time the union of office workers and bookkeepers was called into existence. In addition to those organizations, which existed almost openly, there arose from January to October 1906 semi-legal and illegal trade unions. To the former belonged, for example, the union of chemists' assistants and commercial employees. Among the illegal unions special attention must be drawn to the watchmakers' union, whose first secret session was held on April 24th. All attempts to convene a general open meeting were shattered on the obstinate resistance of the police and the employers in the form of the Chamber of Commerce. This mischance has not prevented the existence of the union. It held secret meetings of members on June 9th and August 14th, apart from the sessions of the executive of the union. The tailors' and tailoresses' union was founded in 1905 at a meeting in a wood at which seventy tailors were present. After the question of forming the union was discussed a commission was appointed which was entrusted with the task of working out the statutes. All attempts of the commission to obtain a legal existence for the union were unsuccessful. Its activities were confined to agitation and the enrolling of new members in the individual workshops. A similar fate was in store for the shoemakers' union. In July a secret night meeting was convened in a wood near the city. Over 100 shoemakers attended; a report was read on the importance of trade unionism, on its history in Western Europe and its tasks in Russia. It was then decided to form a trade union; a commission of twelve was appointed to work out the statutes and call a general meeting of shoemakers. The statutes were drawn up, but in the meantime it had not been found possible to print them nor had the general meeting been convened.

These were the first difficult beginnings. Then came the October days, the second general strike, the Czar's manifesto of October 30 and the brief "constitution period." The workers threw themselves with fiery zeal into the waves of political freedom in order to use it forthwith for the purpose of the work of organization. Besides daily political meetings, debates and the formation of clubs, the development of trade unionism was immediately taken in hand. In October and November *forty* new trade unions appeared in St. Petersburg. Presently a "central bureau," that is a trade union council, was established, various trade union papers appeared, and since November a central organ has also been published, *The Trade Union*. What was reported above concerning Petersburg was also true on the whole of Moscow and Odessa, Kiev and Nichola, Saratov and Voronezh, Samara and Nizhni-Novgorod, and all the larger towns of Russia, and in still higher degree of Poland. The trade unions of different towns seek contact with one another and conferences are held. The end of the "constitution period," and the return to reaction in December 1905, put a stop for the time being to the open widespread activity of the trade unions, but did not however, altogether extinguish them. They operate as organizations in secret and occasionally carry on quite open wage struggles. A peculiar mixture of the legal and illegal condition of trade union life is being built up, corresponding to the highly contradictory revolutionary situation. But in the midst of the struggle the work of organization is being more widely extended, in a thoroughgoing, not to say pedantic fashion. The trade unions of the Social Democracy of Poland and Lithuania, for example, which at the last congress (in July 1906) were represented by five delegates from a membership of 10,000 are furnished with the usual statutes, printed membership cards, adhesive stamps, etc. And the same bakers and shoemakers, engineers and printers of Warsaw and Lodz who in June 1905 stood on the barricades and in December only awaited the word from Petersburg to begin street fighting, find time and are eager, between one mass strike and another, between prison and lockout, and under the conditions of a siege, to go into their trade union statutes and discuss them earnestly. These barricade fighters of yesterday and tomorrow have indeed more than once at meetings severely reprimanded their leaders and threatened them with withdrawal from the party because the unlucky trade union membership cards could not be printed quickly enough—in secret printing works under incessant police persecution. This zeal and this earnestness continue to this day. For example, in the first two weeks of July 1906 fifteen new trade unions appeared in Ekaterinoslav, six in Kostroma, several in Kiev, Poltava, Smolensk, Tscherkassy, Proskurvo, down to the most insignificant provincial towns. In the session of the Moscow trade union council of June 4 this year, after the acceptance of the reports of individual trade union delegates, it was decided "that the trade unions should discipline their members and restrain from street rioting because the time is not considered opportune for the mass strike. In the face of possible provocation on the part of the government care should be taken that the masses do not stream out in the streets." Finally, the Council decided that if at any time one trade union began a strike the others should hold back from any wages movement. Most of the economic struggles are now directed by the trade unions.[3]

Thus the great economic struggle which proceeded from the January general strike and which has not ceased to the present day, has formed a broad background of the revolution from which, in ceaseless reciprocal action with the political agitation and the external events of the revolution there ever arise here and there now isolated explosions, and now great general actions of the proletariat. Thus there flame up against this background the following events one after the other; at the May

3. In the first two weeks of June 1906 alone the following wage struggles were conducted: by the printers in Petersburg, Moscow, Odessa, Minsk, Vilna, Aratov, Mogilev, and Tambov, for an eight-hour day and Sunday holiday; a general strike of seamen in Odessa, Nicholaiev, Kertch, in the Crimea, in the Caucasus, in the Volga Fleet, in Warsaw and Plock for the recognition of the trade union and the release of the arrested workers delegates; by the dockers in Saratov, Nicholaiev, Tsaritzin, Archangel, Nizhni-Novgorod and Rubinsk. The bakers struck in Kiev, Archangel, Bialystok, Vilna, Odessa, Kharkov, Brest Litovsk, Radom, and Tiflis; the agricultural workers in the districts of Verchne-Dneprovski, Vorosovsk and Simferopol, in the governments of Podolsk, Tula and Kurak, in the districts of Koslov and Lipovet, in Finland, in the government of Kiev and in the district of Elizavetgrad. In this period almost all branches of industry in several towns struck work simultaneously, as Saratov, Archangel, Kertch, and Krementchug. In Bachmut there was a strike of colliers of the whole district. In other towns the wages movement in the same two weeks seized all branches of industry, one after another, as in Kiev, Petersburg, Warsaw and Moscow and in the entire district of Ivanovo-Voznosensk. Object of the strikers everywhere: shortening of the working day, Sunday holiday and wage increases. *Most of the strikes ran a victorious course.* It is emphasised in the local reports that some strata of the workers were affected who took part for the first time in a wage movement.

Day demonstration there was an unprecedented, absolute general strike in Warsaw which ended in a bloodly encounter between the defenseless crowd and the soldiers. At Lodz, in June a mass outing which was scattered by the soldiers led to a demonstration of 100,000 workers at the funeral of some of the ·victims of the brutal soldiery and to a renewed encounter with the military, and finally, on June 23, 24, and 25th, passed into the first barricade fight in the Czarist empire. Similarly in June the first great revolt of the sailors of the Black Sea Fleet exploded in the harbor at Odessa from a trifling incident on board the armored vessel *Potemkin* which reacted immediately on Odessa and Nicholaiev in the form of a violent mass strike. As a further echo, the mass strike and the sailors' revolts followed in Kronstadt, Libau and Vladivostok.

In the month of October the grandiose experiment of St. Petersburg was made with the introduction of the eight-hour day. The general council of workers delegates decided to achieve the eight-hour day in a revolutionary manner. That means that on the appointed day all the workers of Petersburg should inform their employers that they were not willing to work more than eight hours a day, and should leave their places of work at the end of eight hours. The idea was the occasion of lively agitation, was accepted by the proletariat with enthusiasm and carried out, but very great sacrifices were not thereby avoided. Thus for example, the eight-hour day meant an enormous fall in wages for the textile workers who had hitherto worked eleven hours and that on a system of piece work. This, however, they willingly accepted. *Within a week the eight-hour day prevailed in every factory and workshop in Petersburg,* and the joy of the workers knew no bounds. Soon, however, the employers, stupefied at first, prepared their defenses; everywhere they threatened to close their factories. Some of the workers consented to negotiate and obtained here a working-day of ten hours and there one of nine hours. The elite of the Petersburg proletariat, however, the workers in the large government engineering establishments, remained unshaken, and a lockout ensued which threw from 45,000 to 50,000 men on the streets for a month. At the settlement the eight-hour day movement was carried into the general strike of December which the great lockout had hampered to a great extent.

Meanwhile, however, the second tremendous general strike throughout the whole empire followed in October as a reply to the project of the Bulygin Duma[4]—the strike to which the railwaymen gave the summons. This second great action of the proletariat already bears a character essentially different from that of the first one in January. The element of political consciousness already plays a much bigger role. Here also, to be sure the immediate occasion for the outbreak of the mass strike was a subordinate and apparently accidental thing: the conflict of the railwaymen with the management over the pension fund. But the general rising of the industrial proletariat which followed upon it was conducted in accordance with clear political ideas. The prologue of the January strike was a procession to the Czar to ask for political freedom: the watchword of the October strike ran away with the constitutional comedy of Czarism! And thanks to the immediate success of the general strike, to the Czar's manifesto of October 30, the movement does not flow back on itself (as in January) but rushes over outwardly in the eager activity of newly acquired political freedom. Demonstrations, meetings, a young press, public discussions and bloody massacres as the end of the story, and thereupon new mass strikes and demonstrations—such is the stormy picture of the November and December days. In November, at the instance of the Social Democrats in Petersburg the first demonstrative mass strike is arranged as a protest demonstration against the bloody deeds and the proclamation of a state of siege in Poland and Livonia. The fermentation after the brief constitutional period and the gruesome awakening finally leads in December to the outbreak of the third general mass strike

4. The Bulygin Duma—Russia's first parliament—was announced on August 19, 1905. It was to be a mere advisory body of representatives of the landlords and the big bourgeoisie. The events of October prevented the convening of this body, and Count Witte, the premier in the period of the October general strike and the first Soviets, by the Czar's Manifesto of October 30, convened the Witte Duma with restricted franchise granted to the workers. In June 1906, this "liberal" period ended and the reactionary Stolypin government emerged.

throughout the empire. This time its course and its outcome are altogether different from those in the two earlier cases. Political action does not change into economic action (as in January), but it no longer achieves a rapid victory (as in October). The attempts of the Czarist camarilla with real political freedom are no longer made, and revolutionary action therewith, for the first time, and along its whole length, knocked against the strong wall of the physical violence of absolutism. By the logical internal development of progressive experience the mass strike this time changes into an open insurrection, to armed barricades, and street fighting in Moscow. The December days in Moscow close the first eventful year of the revolution as the highest point in the ascending line of political action and of the mass strike movement.

The Moscow events show a typical picture of the logical development and at the same time of the future of the revolutionary movement on the whole: their inevitable close in a general open insurrection, which again on its part cannot come in any other way than through the school of a series of preparatory partial insurrections, which therefore meantime end in partial outward "defeats" and considered individually, may appear to be "premature."

The year 1906 brings the elections to the Duma and the Duma incidents. The proletariat, from a strong revolutionary instinct and clear knowledge of the situation, boycotts the whole Czarist constitutional farce; and liberalism again occupies the center of the stage for a few months. The situation of 1904 appears to have come again, a period of speeches instead of acts, and the proletariat for a time walk in the shadow in order to devote themselves the more diligently to the trade union struggle and the work of organization. The mass strikes are no longer spoken of, while the clattering rockets of liberal rhetoric are fired off day after day. At last the iron curtain is torn down, the actors are dispersed, and nothing remains of the liberal rockets but smoke and vapor. An attempt of the Central Committee of the Russian Social Democracy to call forth a mass strike as a demonstration for the Duma and the reopening of the period of liberal speechmaking falls absolutely flat. The role of the political mass strike alone is exhausted, but at the same time, the transition of the mass strike into a general popular rising is not yet accomplished. The liberal episode is past, the proletarian episode is not yet begun. The stage remains empty for the time being.

Chapter IV

The Interaction of the Political and the Economic Struggle

We have attempted in the foregoing to sketch the history of the mass strike in Russia in a few strokes. Even a fleeting glance at this history shows us a picture which in no way resembles that usually formed by the discussions in Germany on the mass strike. Instead of the rigid and hollow scheme of an arid political action carried out by the decision of the highest committees and furnished with a plan and panorama, we see a bit of pulsating life of flesh and blood, which cannot be cut out of the large frame of the revolution but is connected with all parts of the revolution by a thousand veins.

The mass strike, as the Russian revolution shows it to us, is such a changeable phenomenon that it reflects all phases of the political and economic struggle, all stages and factors of the revolution. Its adaptability, its efficiency, the factors of its origin are constantly changing. It suddenly opens new and wide perspectives of the revolution when it appears to have already arrived in a narrow pass and where it is impossible for anyone to reckon upon it with any degree of certainty. It flows now like a broad billow over the whole kingdom, and now divides into a gigantic network of narrow streams; now it bubbles forth from under the ground like a fresh spring and now is completely lost under the earth. Political and economic strikes, mass strikes and partial strikes, demonstrative strikes and fighting strikes, general strikes of individual branches of industry and general strikes in individual towns, peaceful wage struggles and street massacres, barricade fighting—all these run through one another, run side by side, cross one another, flow in and over one another—it is ceaselessly moving, a changing sea of phenomena. And the law of motion for these phenomena is clear: it does not lie in the mass strike itself nor in its technical details, but in the political and social proportions of the forces of the revolution. The mass strike is merely the form of the revolutionary struggle and every disarrangement of the relations of the contending powers, in party development and in class division, in the position of the counterrevolution—all this immediately influences the action of the strike in a thousand invisible and scarcely controllable ways. But strike action itself does not cease for a single moment. It merely alters its forms, its dimensions, its effect. It is the living pulse-beat of the revolution and at the same time its most powerful driving wheel. In a word, the mass strike, as shown to us in the Russian revolution, is not a crafty method discovered by subtle reasoning for the purpose of making the proletarian struggle more effective, *but the method of motion of the proletarian mass,* the phenomenal form of the proletarian struggle in the revolution.

Some general aspects may now be examined which may assist us in forming a correct estimate of the problem of the mass strike.

1. It is absurd to think of the mass strike as one act, one isolated action. The mass strike is rather the indication, the rallying idea, of a whole period of the class struggle lasting for years, perhaps for decades. Of the innumerable and highly varied mass strikes which have taken place in Russia during the last four years the scheme of the mass strike was a purely political movement, begun and ended after a cut and dried plan, a short single act of one variety only and that a subordinate variety—pure demonstration strike. In the whole course of the five-year period we see in Russia only a few demonstration strikes which, be it noted, were generally confined to single towns. Thus the annual May Day general strike in Warsaw and Lodz in Russia proper on the First of May has not yet been celebrated to any appreciable extent by abstention from work—the mass strike in Warsaw on September 11, 1905, as a memorial service in honor of the executed Martin Kasprzak; the Petersburg protest demonstration against the declaration of a state of siege in Poland

and Livonia in November 1905; that of January 22, 1906 in Warsaw, Lodz, Czentochon and in the Dombrowa coal basin, as well as, in part, those in a few Russian towns as anniversary celebrations of the Petersburg bloodbath; in addition, in July 1906 a general strike in Tiflis as demonstration of sympathy with soldiers sentenced by court-martial on account of the military revolt; and finally from the same cause in September 1906, during the deliberations of the court-martial in Reval. All the above great and partial mass strikes and general strikes were not demonstration strikes but fighting strikes, and as such they originated for the most part spontaneously, in every case from specific local accidental causes, without plan and undesignedly, and grew with elemental power into great movements, and then they did not begin an "orderly retreat," but turned now into economic struggles, now into street fighting, and now collapsed of themselves.

In this general picture the purely political demonstration strike plays quite a subordinate role—isolated small points in the midst of a mighty expanse. Thereby, temporarily considered, the following characteristic discloses itself: the demonstration strikes which, in contradistinction to the fighting strikes, exhibit the greatest mass of party discipline, conscious direction and political thought, and therefore must appear as the highest and most mature form of the mass strike, play in reality the greatest part in the *beginnings* of the movement. Thus for example, the absolute cessation of work on May 1, 1905 in Warsaw as the first instance of a decision of the Social Democrats carried throughout in such an astonishing fashion, was an experience of great importance for the proletarian movement in Poland. In the same way the sympathetic strike of the same year in Petersburg made a great impression as the first experiment on conscious systematic mass action in Russia. Similarly the "trial mass strike" of the Hamburg comrades on January 17, 1906 will play a prominent part in the history of the future German mass strike as the first vigorous attempt with the much disputed weapon, and also a very successful and convincingly striking test of the fighting temper and the lust for battle of the Hamburg working class. And just as surely will the period of the mass strike in Germany, when it has once begun in real earnest, lead itself to a real, general cessation of work on May First. The May Day festival may naturally be raised to a position of honor as the first great demonstration under the aegis of the mass struggle. In this sense the "lame horse," as the May Day festival was termed at the trade-union congress at Cologne, has still a great future before it and an important part to play in the proletarian class struggle in Germany. But with the development of the earnest revolutionary struggle the importance of such demonstration diminishes rapidly. It is precisely those factors which objectively facilitate the realization of the demonstration strike after a preconceived plan and at the party's word of command —namely, the growth of political consciousness and the training of the proletariat—make this kind of mass strike impossible; to-day the proletariat in Russia, the most capable vanguard of the masses, does not want to know about mass strikes; the workers are no longer in a mood for jesting and will now think only of a serious struggle with all its consequences. And when, in the first great mass strike in January 1905, the demonstrative element, not indeed in an intentional but more in an instinctive spontaneous form, still played a great part, on the other hand, the attempt of the central committee of the Russian Social Democrats to call a mass strike in August as a demonstration for the dissolved Duma, was shattered by, among other things, the positive disinclination of the educated proletariat to engage in weak half-actions and mere demonstrations.

2. When, however, we have in view the less important strike of the demonstrative kind, instead of the fighting strike as it represents in Russia today the actual vehicle of proletarian action, we see still more clearly that it is impossible to separate the economic and the political factors from one another. Here also the reality deviates from the theoretical scheme, and the pedantic representation in which the pure political mass strike is logically derived from the trade union general strike as the ripest and highest stage, but at the same time is kept distinct from it, is shown to be absolutely false. This is expressed not merely in the fact that the mass strikes, from that first great wage struggle of the Petersburg textile workers in 1896–97 to the last great mass strike in December 1905, passed imperceptibly from the economic field to the political, so that it is almost

impossible to draw a dividing line between them. Again, every one of the great mass strikes repeats, so to speak, on a small scale, the entire history of the Russian mass strike, and begins with a pure economic, or at all events, a partial trade union conflict, and runs through all the stages to the political demonstration. The great thunderstorm of mass strikes in South Russia in 1902 and 1903 originated, as we have seen, in Baku from a conflict arising from the disciplinary punishment of the unemployed, in Rostov from disputes about wages in the railway workshops, in Tiflis from a struggle of the commercial employees for reduction of working hours, in Odessa from a wage dispute in one single small factory. The January mass strike of 1905 developed from an internal conflict in the Putilov works, the October strike from the struggle of the railway workers for a pension fund, and finally the December strike from the struggle of the postal and telegraph employees for the right of combination. The progress of the movement on the whole is not expressed in the circumstances that the economic initial stage is omitted, but much more in the rapidity with which all the stages to the political demonstration are run through and in the extremity of the point to which the strike moves forward.

But the movement on the whole does not proceed from the economic to the political struggle, not even the reverse. Every great political mass action, after it has attained its political highest point, breaks up into a mass of economic strikes. And that applies not merely to each of the great mass strikes, but also to the revolution as a whole. With the spreading, clarifying and involution of the political struggle the economic struggle not merely does not recede, but extends, organizes and becomes involved in equal measure. Between the two there is the most complete reciprocal action.

Every new onset and every fresh victory of the political struggle is transformed into a powerful impetus for the economic struggle extending at the same time its external possibilities and intensifying the inner urge of the workers to better their position, and their desire to struggle. After every foaming wave of political action a fructifying deposit remains behind from which a thousand stalks of economic struggle shoot forth. And conversely, the workers' condition of ceaseless economic struggle with the capitalists keeps their fighting energy alive in every political interval; it forms, so to speak the permanent fresh reservoir of the strength of the proletarian classes, from which the political fight ever renews its strength and at the same time leads the indefatigable economic sappers of the proletariat at all times, now here and now there, to isolated sharp conflicts, out of which political conflicts on a large scale unexpectedly explode.

In a word, the economic struggle is the transmitter from one political center to another; the political struggle is the periodic fertilization of the soil for the economic struggle. Cause and effect here continually change places; and thus the economic and the political factor in the period of the mass strike, now widely removed, completely separated or even mutually exclusive, as the theoretical plan would have them, merely form the two interlacing sides of the proletarian class struggle in Russia. And *their unity* is precisely the mass strike. If the sophisticated theory purposes to make a clever logical dissection of the mass strike for the purpose of getting at the "purely political mass strike," it will by this dissection, as with any other, not perceive the phenomenon in its living essence, but will kill it altogether.

3.   Finally, the events in Russia show us that the mass strike is inseparable from the revolution. The history of the Russian mass strikes is the history of the Russian revolution. When, to be sure, the representatives of our German opportunism hear of "revolution," they immediately think of bloodshed, street fighting or powder and shot, and the logical conclusion thereof is: the mass strike leads inevitably to the revolution, therefore we dare not have it. In actual fact we see in Russia that almost every mass strike in the long run leads to an encounter with the armed guardians of Czarist order, and therein the so-called political strikes exactly resemble the larger economic struggle. The revolution, however, is something other and something more than bloodshed. In contradiction to the police interpretation, which views the revolution exclusively from the standpoint of street disturbances and rioting, that is, from the standpoint of "disorder," the interpretation of scientific Socialism sees in the revolution above all a thorough-going internal reversal of social class relations. And from this standpoint an altogether different

connection exists between revolution and mass strike in Russia
from that contained in the commonplace conception that the
mass strike generally ends in bloodshed.

We have seen above the inner mechanism of the Russian mass
strike which depends upon the ceaseless reciprocal action of
the political and economic struggles. But this reciprocal action
is conditioned during the revolutionary period. Only in the
sultry air of the period of revolution can any [partial] little
conflict between labor and capital grow into a general explosion.
In Germany the most violent, most brutal collisions between
the workers and employers take place every year and every day
without the struggle overleaping the bounds of the individual
departments or individual towns concerned, or even those of
the individual factories. Punishment of organized workers in
Petersburg and unemployment as in Baku, wage struggles as in
Odessa, struggles for the right of combination as in Moscow,
are the order of the day in Germany. No single one of these
cases however, changes suddenly into a common class action.
And when they grow into isolated mass strikes, which have
without question a political coloring, they do not bring about a
general storm. The general strike of the Dutch railwaymen,
which died away in spite of the warmest sympathy, in the
midst of the complete impassivity of the proletariat of the country, affords a striking proof of this.

And conversely, only in the period of the revolution, when the
social foundations and the walls of the class society are shaken
and subjected to a constant process of disarrangement, any
political class action of the proletariat can arouse from their
passive condition in a few hours whole sections of the working
class who have hitherto remained unaffected, and this is immediately and naturally expressed in a stormy economic struggle.
The worker, suddenly aroused to activity by the electric shock
of political action, immediately seizes the weapon lying nearest
his hand for the fight against his condition of economic slavery:
the stormy gesture of the political struggle causes him to feel
with unexpected intensity the weight and the pressure of his
economic chains. And while, for example, the most violent
political struggle in Germany—the electoral struggle or the Par-

liamentary struggle on the customs tariff—exercised a scarcely perceptible direct influence upon the course and the intensity of the wage struggles being conducted at the same time in Germany, every political action of the proletariat in Russia immediately expresses itself in the extension of the area and the deepening of the intensity of the economic struggle.

The revolution thus first creates the social conditions in which this sudden change of the economic struggle into the political and of the political struggle into the economic is possible, a change which finds its expression in the mass strike. And if the vulgar scheme sees the connection between mass strike and revolution only in bloody street encounters with which the mass strikes conclude, a somewhat deeper look into the Russian events shows an exactly opposite connection: in reality the mass strike does not produce the revolution, but the revolution produces the mass strike.

4. It is sufficient, in order to comprehend the foregoing, to obtain an explanation of the question of the conscious direction and initiative in the mass strike. If the mass strike is not an isolated act but a whole period of the class struggle, and if this period is identical with a period of revolution, it is clear that the mass strike cannot be called at will, even when the decision to do so may come from the highest committee of the strongest Social Democratic party. As long as the Social Democracy has not the power to stage and countermand revolutions according to its fancy, even the greatest enthusiasm and impatience of the Social Democratic troops will not suffice to call into being a real period of mass strike as a living, powerful movement of the people. On the basis of a decision of the party leadership and of party discipline a single short demonstration may well be arranged similar to the Swedish mass strike, or to the latest Austrian strike, or even to the Hamburg mass strike of January 17. These demonstrations, however, differ from an actual period of revolutionary mass strikes in exactly the same way that the well-known demonstrations in foreign ports during a period of strained diplomatic relations differ from a naval war. A mass strike born of pure discipline and enthusiasm will, at best, merely play the role of an episode, of a symptom of the

fighting mood of the working class upon which, however, the conditions of a peaceful period are reflected. Of course, even during the revolution mass strikes do not exactly fall from heaven. They must be brought about in some way or another by the workers. The resolution and determination of the workers also play a part and indeed the initiative and the wider direction naturally fall to the share of the organized and most enlightened kernel of the proletariat. But the scope of this initiative and this direction, for the most part, is confined to application to individual acts, to individual strikes, when the revolutionary period is already begun, and indeed, in most cases, is confined within the boundaries of a single town. Thus, for example, we have seen the Social Democrats have already on several occasions successfully issued a direct summons for a mass strike in Baku, in Warsaw, in Lodz and in Petersburg. But this succeeds much less frequently when applied to general movements of the whole proletariat. Further, there are quite definite limits set to initiative and conscious direction. During the revolution it is extremely difficult for any directing organ of the proletarian movement to foresee and to calculate which occasions and factors can lead to explosions and which cannot. Here also initiative and direction do not consist in issuing commands according to one's inclinations, but in the most adroit adaptability to the given situation, and the closest possible contact with the mood of the masses. The element of spontaneity, as we have seen, plays a great part in all Russian mass strikes without exception, be it as a driving force or as a restraining influence. This does not occur in Russia, however, because Social Democracy is still young or weak, but because in every individual act of the struggle so very many important economic, political and social, general and local, material and psychical, factors react upon one another in such a way that no single act can be arranged and resolved as if it were a mathematical problem. The revolution, even when the proletariat with the Social Democrats at their head appear in the leading role, is not a maneuver of the proletariat in the open field, but a fight in the midst of the incessant crashing, displacing, and crumbling of the social foundation. In short, in the mass strikes in Russia the element of spontaneity plays such a predominant part, not because the Russian proletariat are "uneducated," but because revolutions do not allow anyone to play the schoolmaster with them.

On the other hand, we see in Russia that the same revolution which rendered the Social Democrats' command of the mass strike so difficult, and which struck the conductor's baton from, or pressed it into, their hand at all times in such a comical fashion—we see that it resolved of itself all those difficulties of the mass strike which, in the theoretical scheme of German discussion, are regarded as the chief concern of the "directing body": the question of "provisioning," "discovery of cost," and "sacrifice." It goes without saying that it does not resolve them in the way that they would be resolved in a quiet, confidential discussion between the higher directing committees of the labor movement, the members sitting pencil in hand. The "regulation" of all these questions consists in the circumstance that the revolution brings such an enormous mass of people upon the stage that any computation or regulation of the cost of the movement such as can be effected in a civil process, appears to be an altogether hopeless undertaking. The leading organizations in Russia certainly attempt to support the direct victims to the best of their ability. Thus, for example, the brave victims of the gigantic lockout in St. Petersburg, which followed upon the eight-hour day campaign, were supported for weeks. But all these measures are, in the enormous balance of the revolution, but as a drop in the ocean. At the moment that a real, earnest period of mass strikes begins, all these "calculations" of "cost" become merely projects for exhausting the ocean with a tumbler. And it is a veritable ocean of frightful privations and sufferings which is brought by every revolution to the proletarian masses. And the solution which a revolutionary period makes of this apparently invincible difficulty consists in the circumstance that such an immense volume of mass idealism is simultaneously released that the masses are insensible to the bitterest sufferings. With the psychology of a trade unionist who will not stay off his work on May Day unless he is assured in advance of a definite amount of support in the event of his being victimized, neither revolution nor mass strike can be made. But in the storm of the revolutionary period even the proletarian is transformed from a provident *pater familias* demanding support into a "revolutionary romanticist," for whom even the highest good, life itself, to say nothing of material well-being, possesses but little in comparison with the ideals of the struggle.

If, however, the direction of the mass strike in the sense of command over its origin, and in the sense of the calculating and reckoning of the cost, is a matter of the revolutionary period itself, the directing of the mass strike becomes, in an altogether different sense, the duty of Social Democracy and its leading organs. Instead of puzzling their heads with the technical side, with the mechanism of the mass strike, the Social Democrats are called upon to assume *political* leadership in the midst of the revolutionary period.

To give the cue for and the direction to the fight; to so regulate the tactics of the political struggle in its every phase and at its every moment that the entire sum of the available power of the proletariat which is already released and active will find expression in the battle array of the party; to see that the tactics of the Social Democrats are decided according to their resoluteness and acuteness, and that they never fall below the level demanded by the actual relations of forces, but rather rise above it—that is the most important task of the directing body in a period of mass strikes. And this direction changes of itself, to a certain extent, into technical direction. Consistent, resolute, progressive tactic on the part of the Social Democrats produces in the masses a feeling of security, self-confidence and desire for struggle; vacillating weak tactics, based on an underestimation of the proletariat, has a crippling and confusing effect upon the masses. In the first case mass strikes break out "of themselves" and "opportunely"; in the second case they remain ineffective amid direct summonses of the directing body to mass strikes. And of both the Russian revolution affords striking examples.

Chapter V

Lessons of the Working Class Movement in Russia Applicable to Germany

LET us now see how far all these lessons which can be learned from the Russian mass strikes are applicable to Germany. The social and political conditions, the history and status of the labor movement, are widely different in Germany and Russia. At first sight the inner law of the Russian mass strikes as sketched above may appear to be solely the product of specifically Russian conditions which need not be taken into account by the German proletariat. Between the political and the economic struggle in the Russian revolution there is a very close internal connection; their unity becomes an actual fact in the period of mass strikes. But is not that simply a result of Russian absolutism? In a state in which every form and expression of the labor movement is forbidden, in which the simplest strike is a political crime, it must logically follow that every economic struggle will become a political one.

Further, when contrariwise, the first outbreak of the political revolution has drawn after it a general reckoning of the Russian working class with the employers, that is likewise a simple result of the circumstances that the Russian worker has hitherto had a very low standard of life, and has never yet engaged in a single economic struggle for an improvement of his condition. The proletariat in Russia has first, to a certain extent, to work their way out of these miserable conditions, and what wonder that they eagerly availed themselves, with the eagerness of youth, of the first means to that end as soon as the revolution brought the first fresh breeze into the heavy air of absolutism? And finally, the stormy revolutionary course of the Russian mass strike as well as their preponderant spontaneous, elementary character is explained on the one hand by the political backwardness of Russia, by the necessity of first overthrowing the oriental despotism, and on the other hand, by the want of organization and of discipline of the Russian proletariat. In a country in which the working class has had thirty years experience of political life, a strong Social Democratic party of 3,000,000 members and a quarter of a million picked troops organized in trade unions, neither the political struggle nor the mass strike can possibly assume the same stormy and elemental character as in a semi-barbarous state which has just made the leap from the Middle Ages into the modern bourgeois order. This is the current conception amongst those who would read the stage of maturity of the social conditions of a country from the text of the written laws.

Let us examine the questions in their order. To begin with, it is going the wrong way about the matter to date the beginning of the economic struggle in Russia only from the outbreak of the revolution. As a matter of fact, the strikes and wage disputes in Russia proper were increasingly the order of the day since the nineties of the last century, and in Russian Poland even since the eighties, and had eventually won civic rights for the workers. Of course, they were frequently followed by brutal police measures, but nevertheless they were daily phenomena. For example, in both Warsaw and Lodz as early as 1891, there was a considerable strike fund, and the enthusiasm for trade unionism in those years had even created that "economic" illusion in Poland for a short time which a few years later prevailed in Petersburg and the rest of Russia.[1]

1. Comrade Roland-Holst, therefore, commits an error of fact when, in the preface to the Russian edition of her book on the mass strike, she says: "The proletariat in Russia were, almost since the first appearance of large industry, acquainted with the mass strike, for the simple reason that partial strikes proved to be impossible under the political oppression of absolutism" (see Neue Zeit, No. 33 [1906]). The opposite was rather the case. The man who submitted the report of the Petersburg trade union council at the second congress of the Russian trade unions in Feb. 1906 said at the beginning of his report: "By the composition of the conference which I see before me it is not necessary for me to emphasize the fact that our trade union movement is

In the same way there is a great deal of exaggeration in the notion that the proletarian in the Czarist empire had the standard of life of a pauper before the revolution. The layer of the workers in large industries in the great towns who had been the most active and jealous in the economic as in the political struggle are, as regards the material conditions of life, on a scarcely lower plane than the corresponding layer of the German proletariat, and in some occupations as high wages are to be met with in Russia as in Germany, and here and there, even higher. And as regards the length of the working day, the difference in the large-scale industries in the two countries is here and there insignificant. The notion of the presumed material and cultural condition of helotry of the Russian working class is similarly without justification in fact. This notion is contradicted, as a little reflection will show, by the facts of the revolution itself and the prominent part that was played therein by the proletariat. With paupers no revolution of this political maturity and cleverness of thought can be made, and the industrial workers of St. Petersburg and Warsaw, Moscow and Odessa, who stand in the forefront of the struggle, are culturally and mentally much nearer to the West European type than is imagined by those who regard bourgeois parliamentarism and methodical trade union practice as the indispensable, or even the only, school of culture for the proletariat. The modern large capitalist development of Russia and the intellectual influence exerted

---

not due to the "Liberal" period of Prince Sviatopolk-Mirski (in 1906–R.L.) or to January 22nd, as some people endeavour to prove. The trade union movement has much deeper roots: it is indissolubly bound up with the past of our labour movements. Our trade unions are simply new forms of organisation for the direction of those economic struggles which the Russian proletariat have already waged for decades. Without going deeply into history we may say that the economic struggle of the Petersburg workers has assumed more or less organised forms since the memorable strikes of 1896 and 1897. The direction of this struggle is happily combined with the direction of the political struggle, the work of that Social Democratic organisation which was called the 'St. Petersburg Union of Struggle for the Liberation of the Working Class' and which, after the conference in March 1898 became the 'St. Petersburg Committee of the Russian Social Democratic Labour Party'. There is a complicated system of factory, district and, suburban organisations created which connect the centres with the working masses by innumerable threads which make it possible to reach the workers on all occasions by means of leaflets. The possibility is thereby created of supporting and directing strikes.

for a decade and a half of Social Democracy, which has encouraged and directed the economic struggle, have accomplished an important piece of cultural work without the outward guarantees of the bourgeois legal order.

The contrast, however, grows less when, on the other hand, we look a little further into the actual standard of life of the German working class. The great political mass strikes in Russia have from the first aroused the widest layers of the proletariat and thrown them into a feverish economic struggle. But are there not in Germany whole unenlightened sections among the workers to which the warm light of the trade unions has hitherto scarcely penetrated, whole layers which up to the present have never attempted, or vainly attempted, to raise themselves out of their social helotry by means of daily wage struggles?

Let us consider *the poverty of the miners*. Already in the quiet working day, in the cold atmosphere of the parliamentary monotony of Germany—as also in other countries, and even in the El Dorado of trade unionism, Great Britain—the wage struggle of the mine workers hardly ever expresses itself in any other way than by violent eruptions from time to time in mass strikes of typical, elemental character. This only shows that the antagonism between labor and capital is too sharp and violent to allow of its crumbling away in the form of quiet systematic, partial trade union struggles. The misery of the miners, with its eruptive soil which even in "normal" times is a storm center of the greatest violence, must immediately explode in a violent economic socialist struggle, with every great political mass action of the working class, with every violent sudden jerk which disturbs the momentary equilibrium of everyday social life. Let us take further the case of the *poverty of the textile workers*. Here also the bitter, and for the most part fruitless, outbreaks of the wage struggle which raged through Vogtland[2] every few years, give but a faint idea of the vehemence with which the great agglomerate mass of helots of trusted textile capital must explode during a political convulsion, during a powerful, daring mass action of the German proletariat. Again

2. An old district of Germany in the Southwest of the Kingdom of Saxony. —Trans.

let us take the *poverty of the home workers, of the ready-made clothing workers, of the electricity workers,* veritable storm centers in which violent economic struggles will be the more certain to break out with every political atmospheric disturbance in Germany; the less frequently the proletariat take up the struggle in tranquil times, and the more unsuccessfully they fight at any time, the more brutally will capital compel them to return, gnashing their teeth to the yoke of slavery.

Now, however, whole great categories of the proletariat have to be taken into account which, in the "normal" course of things in Germany, cannot possibly take part in a peaceful economic struggle for the improvement of their condition and cannot possibly avail themselves of the right of combination. First and foremost we give the example of the glaring poverty of the *railway and the postal employees.* For these government workers there exist Russian conditions in the midst of the parliamentary constitutional state of Germany, that is to say, Russian conditions as they existed only before the revolution, during the untroubled splendor of absolutism. Already in the great October strike of 1905 the Russian railwaymen in the then formally absolutist Russia were, as regards the economic and social freedom of their movement, head and shoulders above the Germans. The Russian railway and postal employees won the de facto right of combination in the storm, and if momentarily trial upon trial and victimization were the rule they were powerless to affect the inner unity of the workers. However, it would be an altogether false psychological reckoning if one were to assume, with the German reaction, that the slavish obedience of the German railway and postal employees will last forever, that it is a rock which nothing can wear away. When even the German trade union leaders have become accustomed to the existing conditions to such an extent that they, untroubled by an indifference almost without parallel in the whole of Europe, can survey with complete satisfaction the results of the trade union struggle in Germany, then the deep-seated, long-suppressed resentment of the uniformed state slaves will inevitably find vent with a general rising of the industrial workers. And when the industrial vanguard of the proletariat by means of mass strikes grasp at new political rights or attempt to defend existing ones, the great army of railway and postal employees must of necessity bethink themselves of their own special disgrace, and at last rouse themselves for their liberation from the extra share of Russian absolutism which is specially reserved for them in Germany.

The pedantic conception which would unfold great popular movements according to plan and recipe regards the acquisition of the right of combination for the railway workers as necessary before anyone will "dare to think" of a mass strike in Germany. The actual and natural course of events can only be the opposite of this: only from a spontaneous powerful mass strike action can the right of combination for the German railway workers, as well as for the postal employees, actually be born. And the problems which in the existing conditions of Germany are insoluble will suddenly find their solution under the influence and the pressure of a universal political mass action of the proletariat.

And finally, the greatest and most important: *the poverty of the land workers.* If the British trade unions are composed exclusively of industrial workers, agricultural poverty is quite understandable in view of the specific character of the British national economy, and of the unimportant part that agriculture plays on the whole in the economic life of Britain. In Germany, a trade union organization, be it ever so well constructed, if it comprises only industrial workers, and is inaccessible to the great army of land workers, will give only a weak, partial picture of the conditions of the proletariat. But again it would be a fatal illusion to think that conditions in the country are unalterable and immovable and that the indefatigable educational work of the Social Democrats, and still more, the whole internal class politics of Germany, does not continually undermine the outward passivity of the agricultural workers and that any great general class action of the German proletariat, for whatever object undertaken, may not also draw the rural proletariat into the conflict.

Similarly, the picture of the alleged economic superiority of the German over the Russian proletariat is considerably altered when we look away from the tables of the industries and departments organized in trade unions and bestow a look upon those great groups of the proletariat who are altogether outside the trade union struggle, or whose special economic condition does not allow of their being forced into the narrow framework of the daily guerrilla warfare of the trade unions. We see there one important sphere after another, in which the sharpening of antagonisms has reached the extreme point, in which inflammable material in abundance is heaped up, in which there is a great deal of "Russian absolutism" in its most naked form, and in which economically the most elementary reckonings with capital have first to be made.

In a general political mass strike of the proletariat, then, all these outstanding accounts would inevitably be presented to the prevailing system. An artificially arranged demonstration of the urban proletariat, taking place once, a mere mass strike action arising out of discipline, and directed by the conductor's baton of a party executive, could therefore leave the broad masses of the people cold and indifferent. But a powerful and reckless fighting action of the industrial proletariat, born of a revolutionary situation, must surely react upon the deeper-lying layers, and ultimately draw all those into a stormy general economic struggle who, in normal times, stand aside from the daily trade union fight.

But when we come back to the organized vanguard of the German industrial proletariat, on the other hand, and keep before our eyes the objects of the economic struggle which have been striven for by the Russian working class, we do not at all find that there is any tendency to look down upon the things of youth, as the oldest German trade unions had reason to do. Thus the most important general demand of the Russian strikes since January 22—the eight-hour day—is certainly not an unattainable platform for the German proletariat, but rather in most cases, a beautiful, remote ideal. This applies also to the struggle for the "mastery of the household" platform, to the struggle for the introduction of workers' committees into all the factories, for the abolition of piecework, for the abolition of home work in handicraft, for the complete observance of Sunday rest, and for the recognition of the right of combination. Yes, on closer inspection all the economic objects of struggle of the Russian proletariat are also for the German proletariat very real, and touch a very sore spot in the life of the workers.

It therefore inevitably follows that the pure political mass strike, which is operated with for preference, is, in Germany, a mere lifeless theoretical plan. If the mass strikes result, in a natural way from a strong revolutionary ferment, in a determined political struggle of the urban workers, they will equally, naturally, and exactly as in Russia, change into a whole period of elementary, economic struggles. The fears of the trade union leaders, therefore, that the struggle for economic interests in a period of stormy political strife, in a period of mass strikes, can simply be pushed aside and suppressed rest upon an utterly baseless, schoolboy conception of the course of events. A revolutionary period in Germany would so alter the character of the trade union struggle and develop its potentialities to such an extent that the present guerrilla warfare of the trade unions would be child's play in comparison. And on the other hand, from this elementary economic tempest of mass strikes, the political struggle would derive always new impetus and fresh strength. The reciprocal action of economic and political struggle which is the mainspring of present-day strikes in Russia, and at the same time the regulating mechanism, so to speak, of the revolutionary action of the proletariat, would result also in Germany, and quite as naturally from the conditions themselves.

Chapter VI

Cooperation of Organized and Unorganized Workers Necessary for Victory

In connection with this, the question of organization in relation to the problem of the mass strike in Germany assumes an essentially different aspect.

The attitude of many trade union leaders to this question is generally summed up in the assertion: "We are not yet strong enough to risk such a hazardous trial of strength as a mass strike." Now this position is so far untenable that it is an insoluble problem to determine the time, in a peaceful fashion by counting heads, when the proletariat are "strong enough" for any struggle. Thirty years ago the German trade unions had 50,000 members. That was obviously a number with which a mass strike on the above scale was not to be thought of. Fifteen years later the trade unions were four times as strong, and counted 237,000 members. If, however, the present trade union leaders had been asked at the time if the organization of the proletariat was then sufficiently ripe for a mass strike, they would assuredly have replied that it was still far from it and that the number of those organized in trade unions would first have to be counted by millions. Today the number of trade unionists already runs into the second million, but the views of the leaders are still exactly the same, and may very well be the same to the end. The tacit assumption is that the entire working class of Germany, down to the last man and the last woman, must be included in the organization before it "is strong enough" to risk a mass action, which then, according to the old formula, would probably be represented as "superfluous." This theory is nevertheless absolutely Utopian, for the simple reason that it suffers from an internal contradiction, that it goes in a vicious circle. Before the workers can engage in any direct class struggle they must all be organised. The circumstances, the conditions, of capitalist development and of the bourgeois state, make it impossible that, in the normal course of things, without stormy class struggles, certain sections—and these the greatest, the most important, the lowest and the most oppressed by capital, and by the state— can be organized at all. We see even in Britain, which has had a whole century of indefatigable trade union effort without any "disturbances"—except at the beginning in the period of the Chartist movement—without any "romantic revolutionary" errors or temptations, it has not been possible to do more than organize a minority of the better-paid sections of the proletariat.

On the other hand the trade unions, like all fighting organizations of the proletariat, cannot permanently maintain themselves in any other way than by struggle, and that not struggle of the same kind as the war between the frogs and the mice[1] in the stagnant waters of the bourgeois Parliamentary period, but struggle in the troubled revolutionary periods of the mass strike. The rigid, mechanical-bureaucratic conception cannot conceive of the struggle save as the product of organization at a certain stage of its strength. On the contrary the living, dialectical explanation makes the organization arise as product of the struggle. We have already seen a grandiose example of this phenomenon in Russia, where a proletariat almost wholly unorganised created a comprehensive network of organizational appendages in a year and a half of stormy revolutionary struggle. Another example of this kind is furnished by the history of the German unions. In the year 1878 the number of trade union members amounted to 50,000. According to the theory of the present day trade union leaders this organization, as stated above, was not nearly "strong enough" to enter upon a violent political struggle. The German trade unions however, weak as they were at the time, did take up the struggle—namely the struggle against the Anti-Socialist

---

1. An allusion to the "Batrachomyomachy" (The Battle of the Frogs and the Mice), a Greek parody of the Iliad.—Trans.

Law[2]—and showed that they were "strong enough", not only to emerge victorious from the struggle, but to increase their strength five-fold: in 1891, after the repeal of the Anti-Socialist Law, their membership was 277,659. It is true that the methods by which the trade unions conquered in the struggle against the Anti-Socialist Law, do not correspond to the ideal of a peaceful, bee-like, uninterrupted process: they first went into the fight absolutely in ruins, to rise again on the next wave and to be born anew. But this is precisely the specific method of growth corresponding to the proletarian class organizations: to be tested in the struggle and to go forth from the struggle with increased strength.

On a closer examination of German conditions and of the condition of the different sections of the working class, it is clear that the coming period of stormy political mass struggles will not bring the dreaded, threatening downfall of the German trade unions, but on the contrary, will open up hitherto unsuspected prospects of the extension of their sphere of power—an extension that will proceed rapidly by leaps and bounds. But the question has still another aspect. The plan of undertaking mass strikes as a serious political class action with organized workers only is absolutely hopeless. If the mass strike, or rather, mass strikes, and the mass struggle are to be successful they must become a real *people's movement*, that is, the widest sections of the proletariat must be drawn into the fight. Already in the Parliamentary form the might of the proletarian class struggle rests not on the small organized group, but on the surrounding periphery of the revolutionary-minded proletariat. If the Social Democrats were to enter the electoral battle with their few hundred thousand organized members alone they would condemn themselves to futility. And although it is the tendency of Social Democracy wherever possible to draw the whole great army of its voters into the party organization, its mass of voters after thirty years experience of Social Democracy, is not in-

2. The Anti-Socialist Law was introduced in Germany by Bismarck in 1878 for a period of two and a half years: assemblies and even literary works on socialism were forbidden on pain of deportation. The law was extended till 1890 when the Reichstag refused to renew it further. In this period the Party recorded a three-fold increase in membership.

creased through the growth of the party organization, but on
the contrary, the new sections of the proletariat, won for the
time being through the electoral struggle, are the fertile soil
for the subsequent seed of organization. Here the organization
does not supply the troops for the struggle, but the struggle, in
an ever growing degree, supplies recruits for the organization.
In a much greater degree does this obviously apply to direct
political mass action than to the Parliamentary struggle. If the
Social Democrats, as the organized nucleus of the working class,
are the most important vanguard of the entire body of the
workers and if the political clarity, the strength, and the unity
of the labor movement flow from this organization, then it is
not permissible to visualize the class movement of the proletariat
as a movement of the organized minority. Every real, great class
struggle must rest upon the support and cooperation of the
widest masses, and a strategy of class struggle which does not
reckon with this cooperation, which is based upon the idea of
the finely stage-managed march out of the small well-trained
part of the proletariat is foredoomed to be a miserable fiasco.

Mass strikes, and political mass struggles cannot, therefore,
possibly be carried through in Germany by the organized workers alone, nor can they be appraised by regular "direction" from
the central committee of a party. In this case, again—exactly as
in Russia—they depend not so much upon "discipline" and
"training" and upon the most careful possible regulation beforehand of the questions of support and cost, as upon a real revolutionary, determined class action, which will be able to win and
draw into the struggle the widest circles of the unorganized
workers, according to their mood and their conditions.

The overestimate and the false estimate of the role of organizations in the class struggle of the proletariat is generally reinforced, by the underestimate of the unorganized proletarian
mass and of their political maturity. In a revolutionary period,
in the storm of great unsettling class struggles, the whole educational effect of the rapid capitalist development and of Social
Democratic influences first shows itself upon the widest sections
of the people, of which, in peaceful times the tables of the
organized, and even election statistics, give only a faint idea.

We have seen that in Russia, in about two years a great general action of the proletariat can forthwith arise from the smallest partial conflict of the workers with the employers, from the most insignificant act of brutality of the government organs. Everyone, of course, sees and believes that, because in Russia "the revolution" is there. But what does that mean? It means that class feeling, the class instinct, is alive and very active in the Russian proletariat, so that immediately they regard every partial question of any small group of workers as a general question, as a class affair, and quick as lightening they react to its influence as a unity. While in Germany, France, Italy and Holland the most violent trade union conflicts call forth hardly any general action of the working class—and when they do, only the organized part of the workers moves—in Russia the smallest dispute raises a storm. That means nothing else however, than that at present—paradoxical as it may sound—the class instinct of the youngest, least trained, badly educated and still worse organized Russian proletariat is immeasurably stronger than that of the organized, trained and enlightened working class of Germany or of any other West European country. And that is not to be reckoned a special virtue of the "young, unexhausted East" as compared with the "sluggish West," but is simply a result of direct revolutionary mass action. In the case of the enlightened German worker the class consciousness implanted by the Social Democrats is *theoretical and latent:* in the period ruled by bourgeois Parliamentarianism it cannot, as a rule, actively participate in a direct mass action; it is the ideal sum of the 400 parallel actions of the electoral sphere during the election struggle, of the many partial economic strikes and the like. In the revolution when the masses themselves appear upon the political battle field this class consciousness becomes *practical and active.* A year of revolution has therefore given the Russian proletariat that "training" which thirty years of Parliamentary and trade union struggle cannot artificially give to the German proletariat. Of course, this living, active class feeling of the proletariat will considerably diminish in intensity, or rather change into a concealed and latent condition, after the close of the period of revolution and the erection of a bourgeois-parliamentary constitutional state. And just as surely, on the other hand, will the living revolutionary class feeling, capable of

action, affect the widest and deepest layers of the proletariat in
Germany in a period of strong political engagement, and that
the more rapidly and more deeply, the more energetically the
educational work of Social Democracy is carried on among
them. This educational work and the provocative and revolutionizing effect of the whole present policy of Germany will
express itself in the circumstances that all those groups which at
present in their apparent political stupidity remain insensitive
to all the organizing attempts of the Social Democrats and of
the trade unions will suddenly follow the flag of Social Democracy in a serious revolutionary period. Six months of a revolutionary period will complete the work of the training of these
as yet unorganized masses which ten years of public demonstrations and distribution of leaflets would be unable to do. And
when conditions in Germany have reached the critical stage for
such a period, the sections which are today unorganized and
backward will, in the struggle, prove themselves the most radical, the most impetuous element, and not one that will have to
be dragged along. If it should come to mass strikes in Germany,
it will almost certainly not be the best organized workers—and
most certainly not the printers—who will develop the greatest
capacity for action, but the worst organized or totally unorganized—the miners, the textile workers, and perhaps even the land
workers.

In this way we arrive at the same conclusions in Germany in
relation to the peculiar tasks of *direction*, in relation to the role
of Social Democracy in mass strikes, as in our analysis of events
in Russia. If we now leave the pedantic scheme of demonstrative
mass strikes artificially brought about by order of parties and
trade unions, and turn to the living picture of a peoples' movement arising with elementary energy, from the culmination of
class antagonisms and the political situation—a movement which
passes, politically as well as economically, into mass struggles
and mass strikes—it becomes obvious that the task of Social
Democracy does not consist in the technical preparation and
direction of mass strikes, but, first and foremost, in the *political
leadership* of the whole movement.

The Social Democrats are the most enlightened, most class-
conscious vanguard of the proletariat. They cannot and dare

not wait, in a fatalist fashion, with folded arms for the advent of the "revolutionary situation," to wait for that which in every spontaneous peoples' movement, falls from the clouds. On the contrary, they must now, as always, hasten the development of things and endeavour to accelerate events. This they cannot do, however, by suddenly issuing the "slogan" for a mass strike at random at any odd moment, but first and foremost, by making clear to the widest layers of the proletariat the *inevitable advent* of this revolutionary period, the inner *social factors* making for it and the *political consequences* of it. If the widest proletarian layer should be won for a political mass action of the Social Democrats, and if vice versa, the Social Democrats should seize and maintain the real leadership of a mass movement, should they become, in a *political sense*, the rulers of the whole movement, then they must, with the utmost clearness, consistency and resoluteness, inform the German proletariat of their tactics and aims in the period of coming struggle.

Chapter VII

The Role of the Mass Strike
in the Revolution

WE have seen that the mass strike in Russia does not represent an artificial product of premeditated tactics on the part of the Social Democrats, but a natural historical phenomenon on the basis of the present revolution. Now what are the factors which in Russia have brought forth this new phenomenal form of the revolution?

The Russian revolution has for its next task the abolition of absolutism and the creation of a modern bourgeois-parliamentary constitutional state. It is exactly the same in form as that which confronted Germany at the March revolution, and France at the great revolution at the end of the eighteenth century. But the condition, the historical milieu, in which these formally analogous revolutions took place, are fundamentally different from those of present-day Russia. The most decisive difference is the circumstance that between those bourgeois revolutions of the West and the present bourgeois revolution in the East, the whole cycle of capitalist development has run its course. And this development had seized not only the West European countries, but also absolutist Russia. Large-scale industry with all its consequences—modern class divisions, sharp social contrasts, modern life in large cities and the modern proletariat—has become in Russia the prevailing form, that is, in social development the decisive form of production. The remarkable, contradictory, historical situation results from this that the bourgeois revolution, in accordance with its formal tasks will, in the first place, be carried out by a modern class-conscious proletariat, and in an international milieu whose distinguishing characteristic is the ruin of bourgeois democracy. It is not the bourgeoisie that is now the leading revolutionary element as in the earlier revolutions of the West, while the proletarian masses, disorganised amongst the petit-bourgeoisie, furnishes material for the army of the bourgeoisie, but on the contrary, it is the class-conscious proletariat that is the leading and driving element, while the big-bourgeois sections are partly directly counterrevolutionary, partly and weakly liberal, and only the rural petit-bourgeoisie and the urban petit-bourgeois intelligentsia are definitely oppositional and even revolutionary minded. The Russian proletariat, however, who are destined to play the leading part in the bourgeois revolution, enters the fight free from all illusions of bourgeois democracy, with a strongly developed consciousness of their own specific class interests, and at a time when the antagonism between capital and labor has reached its height. This contradictory situation finds expression in the fact that in this formally bourgeois revolution, the antagonism of the bourgeois society to absolutism is governed by the antagonism of the proletariat to bourgeois society, that the struggle of the proletariat is directed simultaneously and with equal energy against both absolutism and capitalist exploitation, and that the program of the revolutionary struggle concentrates with equal emphasis on political freedom, the winning of the eight-hour day, and a human standard of material existence for the proletariat. This two-fold character of the Russian revolution is expressed in that close union of the economic with the political struggle and in their mutual interaction which we have seen is a feature of the Russian events and which finds its appropriate expression in the mass strike.

In the earlier bourgeois revolutions where on the one hand, the political training and the leadership of the revolutionary masses were undertaken by the bourgeois parties, and where on the other hand, it was merely a question of overthrowing the old government, the brief battle at the barricades was the appropriate form of the revolutionary struggle. Today, when the working classes are being enlightened in the course of the revolutionary struggle, when they must marshall their forces and lead themselves, and when the revolution is directed as much against the old state power as against capitalist exploitation, the mass strike appears as the natural means of recruiting the widest proletarian layers for the struggle, as well as being at the same time a means of undermining and overthrowing the old state power and of stemming capitalist exploitation. The urban industrial proletariat is now the soul of the revolution in Russia. But in order to carry through a direct political struggle as a mass, the proletariat must first be assembled as a mass, and for this purpose they must come out of factory and workshop, mine and foundry, must overcome the decay to which they are condemned under the daily yoke of capitalism. The mass strike is the first natural, impulsive form of every great revolutionary struggle of the proletariat and the more highly developed the antagonism is between capital and labor, the more effective and decisive must mass strikes become. The chief form of previous bourgeois revolutions, the fight at the barricades, the open conflict with the armed power of the state, is in the revolution of today only the culminating point, only a moment on the process of the proletarian mass struggle. And therewith in the new form of the revolution there is reached that civilizing and mitigating of the class struggle which was prophesied by the opportunists of German Social Democracy—the Bernsteins, Davids, etc. It is true that these men saw the desired civilizing and mitigating of the class struggle in the light of petit-bourgeois-democratic illusions— they believed that the class struggle would shrink to an exclusively parliamentary contest and that street fighting would simply be done away with. History has found the solution in a deeper and finer fashion: in the advent of revolutionary mass strikes, which, of course, in no way replaces brutal street fights or renders them unnecessary, but which reduces them to a moment in the long period of political struggle, and which at the same time unites with the revolutionary period an enormous cultural work in the most exact sense of the words: the material and intellectual elevation of the whole working class through the "civilizing" of the barbaric forms of capitalist exploitation.

The mass strike is thus shown to be not a specifically Russian product, springing from absolutism but a universal form of the proletarian class struggle resulting from the present stage of capitalist development and class relations. From this standpoint the three bourgeois revolutions—the great French revolution, the German revolution of March,[1] and the present Russian revolution—form a continuous chain of development in which the fortunes and the end of the capitalist century are to be seen. In the great French revolution the still wholly underdeveloped internal contradictions of bourgeois society gave scope for a long period of violent struggles, in which all the antagonisms which first germinated and ripened in the heat of the revolution raged unhindered and unrestrained in a spirit of reckless radicalism. A century later the revolution of the German bourgeoisie, which broke out midway in the development of capitalism, was already hampered on both sides by the antagonism of interests and the equilibrium of strength between capital and labor, and was smothered in a bourgeois-feudal compromise, and shortened to a brief miserable episode ending in words. Another half century, and the present Russian revolution stands at a point of the historical path which is already over the summit, which is on the other side of the culminating point of capitalist society, at which the bourgeois revolution cannot again be smothered by the antagonism between bourgeoisie and proletariat, but, will, on the contrary, expand into a new lengthy period of violent social struggles, at which the balancing of the account with absolutism appears a trifle in comparison with the many new accounts which the revolution itself opens up. The present revolution realizes in the particular affairs of absolutist Russia the general results of international capitalist development, and appears not so much as the last successor of the old bourgeois revolutions as the forerunner of the new series of proletarian revolutions of the West. *The most backward country of all, just because it has been so unpardonably late with its bourgeois revolution, shows ways and methods of further class struggle to the proletariat of Germany and the most advanced capitalist countries.*

Accordingly it appears, when looked at in this way, to be entirely wrong to regard the Russian revolution as a fine play, as something specifically "Russian," and at best to admire the heriosm of the fighting men, that is, the last accessories of the

---

1. 1848.—Ed.

struggle. It is much more important that the German workers should learn to look upon the Russian revolution *as their own affair*, not merely as a matter of international solidarity with the Russian proletariat, but first and foremost, as a *chapter of their own social and political history*. Those trade union leaders and parliamentarians who regard the German proletariat as "too weak" and German conditions "as not ripe enough" for revolutionary mass struggles, have obviously not the least idea that the measure of the degree of ripeness of class relations in Germany and of the power of the proletariat does not lie in the statistics of German trade unionism or in election figures, but— in the events of the Russian revolution. Exactly as the ripeness of French class antagonisms under the July monarchy and the June battle of Paris was reflected in the German March revolution, in its course and its fiasco, so today the ripeness of German class antagonisms is reflected in the events and in the power of the Russian revolution. And while the bureaucrats of the German labor movement rummage in their office drawers for information as to their strength and maturity, they do not see that that for which they seek is lying before their eyes in a great historical revolution, because, historically considered, the Russian revolution is a reflex of the power and the maturity of the international, and therefore in the first place, of the German labor movement.

It would therefore be a too pitiable and grotesquely insignificant result of the Russian revolution if the German proletariat should merely draw from it the lesson—as is desired by Comrades Frohme, Elm, and others—of using the extreme form of the struggle, the mass strike, and so weaken themselves as to be merely a reserve force in the event of the withdrawal of the Parliamentary vote, and therefore a passive means of Parliamentary defensive. When the Parliamentary vote is taken from us there we will resist. That is a self-evident decision. But for this it is not necessary to adopt the heroic pose of a Danton as was done, for example, by Comrade Elm in Jena; because the defense of the modest measure of Parliamentary right already possessed is less a heaven-storming innovation, for which the frightful hecatombs of the Russian revolution were first necessary as a means of encouragement, than the simplest and first duty of every opposition party. But the mere defensive can never exhaust the policy of the proletariat in a period of revolution. And if it is, on the one hand, difficult to predict with any degree of certainty whether the destruction of universal suffrage would cause a situation in Germany which would call forth an immediate mass strike action, so on the other hand, it is absolutely certain that when we in Germany enter upon the period of stormy mass actions, it will be impossible for the Social Democrats to base their tactics upon a mere parliamentary defensive. To fix beforehand the cause and the moment from and in which the mass strikes in Germany will break out is not in the power of Social Democracy, because it is not in its power to bring about historical situations by resolutions at party congresses. But what it can and must do is to make clear the political tendencies when they once appear, and to formulate them as a resolute and consistent tactics. Man cannot keep historical events in check while making recipes for them. But he can see in advance their apparently calculable consequences and arrange his mode of action accordingly.

The first threatening political danger with which the German proletariat have concerned themselves for a number of years, is a coup d'état of the reaction which will wrest from the wide masses of the people the most important political right—universal suffrage. In spite of the immense importance of this possible event it is, as we have already said, impossible to assert with certainty that an open popular movement would immediately break out after the coup d'état, because today innumerable circumstances and factors have to be taken into account. But when we consider the present extreme acuteness of conditions in Germany, and on the other hand, the manifold international reactions of the Russian revolution and of the future rejuvenated Russia, it is clear that the collapse of German politics which would ensue from the repeal of universal suffrage could not alone call a halt to the struggle for this right. This coup d'état would rather draw after it, in a longer or shorter period and with elementary power, a great general political reckoning of the insurgent and awakened mass of the people—a reckoning with bread usury, with artificially caused dearness of meat, with expenditure on a boundless militarism and "navalism," with the corruption of colonial policy, with the national disgrace of the Konigsberg trial, with the cessation of social reform, with the discharging of railway workers, the postal officials and the land workers, with the tricking and mocking of the miners, with the judgement of Lobtau and the whole system of class justice, with the brutal lockout system—in short, with the whole thirty-year-old oppression of the combined dominion of Junkerdom and large trusted capital.

But if once the ball is set rolling then Social Democracy, whether it wills it or not, can never again bring it to a standstill. The opponents of the mass strike are in the habit of denying that the lessons and examples of the Russian revolution can be a criterion for Germany because, in the first place, in Russia the great step must first be taken from an Oriental despotism to a modern bourgeois legal order. The formal distance between the old and the new political order is said to be a sufficient explanation of the vehemence and the violence of the revolution in Russia. In Germany we have long had the most necessary forms and guarantees of a constitutional state, from which it follows that such an elementary raging of social antagonisms is impossible here. Those who speculate thus forget that in Germany when it once comes to the outbreak of open political struggles, even the historically determined goal will be quite different from that in Russia today. Precisely because the bourgeois legal order in Germany has existed for a long time, because therefore, it has had time to completely exhaust itself and to draw to an end, because bourgeois democracy and liberalism have had time to die out—because of this there can no longer be any talk of a *bourgeois* revolution in Germany. And therefore in a period of open political popular struggles in Germany the last historical necessary goal can only be the *dictatorship of the proletariat*. The distance, however, of this task from the present conditions of Germany is still greater than that of the bourgeois legal order from Oriental despotism, and therefore, the task cannot be completed at one stroke, but must similarly be accomplished during a long period of gigantic social struggles.

But is there not a gross contradiction in the picture we have drawn? On the one hand it means that in an eventual future period of political mass action the most backward layers of the German proletariat—the land workers, the railwaymen, and the postal slaves—will first of all win the right of combination, and that the worst excrescences of exploitation must first be removed, and on the other hand, the political task of this period is said to be the conquest of power by the proletariat! On one hand, economic, trade union struggles for the most immediate interests, for the material elevation of the working class; on the other hand, the ultimate goal of Social Democracy! Certainly these are great contradictions, but they are not contradictions due to our reasoning, but contradictions due to capitalist development. It does not proceed in a beautiful straight line but in a lightning-like zigzag. Just as the various capitalist countries represent the most varied stages of development, so within each country the different layers of the same working class are represented. But history does not wait patiently till the backward countries, and the most advanced layers have joined together so that the whole mass can move symmetrically forward like a compact column. It brings the best prepared parts to explosion as soon as conditions there are ripe for it, and then in the storm of the revolutionary period, lost ground is recovered, unequal things are equalized, and the whole pace of social progress changed at one stroke to the double-quick.

Just as in the Russian revolution all the grades of development and all the interests of the different layers of workers are united in the Social Democratic program of the revolution, and the innumerable partial struggles united in the great common class action of the proletariat, so will it also be in Germany when the conditions are ripe for it. And the task of Social Democracy will then be to regulate its tactics, not by the most backward phases of development but by the most advanced.

Chapter VIII

Need for United Action of
Trade Unions and Social Democracy

THE most important desideratum which is to be hoped for from the German working class in the period of great struggles which will come sooner or later is, after complete resoluteness and consistency of tactics, the utmost capacity for action, and therefore the utmost possible unity of the leading Social Democratic part of the proletarian masses. Meanwhile the first weak attempts at the preparation of great mass actions have discovered a serious drawback in this connection: the total separation and independence of the two organizations of the labor movement, the Social Democracy and the trade unions.

It is clear on a closer consideration of the mass strikes in Russia as well as of the conditions in Germany itself that any great mass action, if it is not confined to a mere one-day demonstration, but is intended to be a real fighting action, cannot possibly be thought of as a so-called political mass strike. In such an action in Germany the trade unions would be implicated as much as the Social Democrats. Not because the trade union leaders imagine that the Social Democrats, in view of their smaller organization, would have no other resources than the cooperation of one and a quarter million trade unionists and without them would be unable to do anything, but because of a much more deep-lying motive: because every direct mass action of the period of open class struggles would be at the same time both political and economic. If in Germany, from any cause and at any time, it should come to great political struggles, to mass strikes, then at that time an era of violent trade union struggles would begin in Germany, and events would not stop to inquire whether the trade union leaders had given their consent to the movement or not. Whether they stand aside or endeavor to resist the movement, the result of their attitude will only be that the trade union leaders, like the party leaders in the analogous case, will simply be swept aside by the rush of events, and the economic and the political struggles of the masses will be fought out without them.

As a matter of fact the separation of the political and the economic struggle and the independence of each is nothing but an artificial product of the Parliamentarian period, even if historically determined. On the one hand in the peaceful, "normal" course of bourgeois society, the economic struggle is split into a multitude of individual struggles in every undertaking and dissolved in every branch of production. On the other hand the political struggle is not directed by the masses themselves in a direct action, but in correspondence with the form of the bourgeois state, in a representative fashion, by the presence of legislative representation. As soon as a period of revolutionary struggles commences, that is, as soon as the masses appear upon the scene of conflict, the breaking up of the economic struggle into many parts, as well as the indirect Parliamentary form of the political struggle ceases; in a revolutionary mass action the political and the economic struggle are one, and the artificial boundary between trade union and Social Democracy as two separate, wholly independent forms of the labor movement, is simply swept away. But what finds concrete expression in the revolutionary mass movement finds expression also in the Parliamentary period as an actual state of affairs. There are no two different class struggles of the working class, an economic and a political one, but only *one* class struggle, which aims at one and the same time at the limitation of capitalist exploitation within bourgeois society, and at the abolition of exploitation together with bourgeois society itself.

When these two sides of the class struggle are separated from one another for technical reasons in the Parliamentary period, there they do not form two parallel concurrent actions, but merely two phases, two stages of the struggle for emancaption of the working class. The trade union struggle embraces the immediate interests, and the Social Democratic struggle the future interests, of the labor movement. The Communists, says the Communist Manifesto, represent, as against various group interests, national or local, of the proletariat, the common interests of the proletariat as a whole, and in the various stages of development of the class struggle, they represent the interests of the whole movement, that is, the ultimate goal—the liberation of the proletariat. The trade unions represent only the group interests and only one stage of development of the labor movement. Social Democracy represents the working class and the cause of its liberation as a whole. The relation of the trade unions to Social Democracy is therefore a part of the whole, and when, among the trade union leaders, the theory of "equal authority" of trade unions and Social Democracy finds so much favor, it rests upon a fundamental misconception of the essence of trade unionism itself and of its role in the general struggle for freedom of the working class.

This theory of the parallel action of Social Democracy and the trade unions and of their "equal authority" is nevertheless not altogether without foundation, but has its historical roots. It rests upon the illusion of the peaceful, "normal" period of bourgeois society, in which the political struggle of Social Democracy appears to be consumed in the parliamentary struggle. The parliamentary struggle, however, the counterpart of the trade union struggle, is equally with it, a fight conducted exclusively on the basis of the bourgeois social order. It is by its very nature political reform work, as that of the trade unions is economic reform work. It represents political work for the present, as trade unions represent economic work for the present. It is, like them, merely a phase, a stage of development in the complete process of the proletarian class struggle whose ultimate goal is as far beyond the parliamentarian struggle as it is beyond the trade union struggle. The parliamentary struggle is, in relation to Social Democratic policy, also a part of the whole, exactly as trade union work is. Social Democracy today comprises the parliamentary and the trade union struggle in one class struggle aiming at the abolition of the bourgeois social order.

The theory of the "equal authority" of trade unions and Social Democracy is likewise not a mere theoretical misunderstanding, not a mere case of confusion but an expression of the well-known tendency of that opportunist wing of Social Democracy which reduces the political struggle of the working class to the parliamentary contest, and desires to change Social Democracy from a revolutionary proletarian party into a petit-bourgeois reform one.[1] If Social Democracy should accept the theory of the "equal authority" of the trade unions it would thereby accept, indirectly and tacitly, that transformation which has long been striven for by the representatives of the opportunist tendency.

In Germany, however, there is such a shifting of relations within the labor movement as is impossible in any other country.

1. As the existence of such a tendency within German Social Democracy is generally denied, one must be grateful for the candor with which the opportunist trend has recently formulated its real aims and wishes. At a party meeting in Mayence on Sept. 10, 1909, the following resolution, proposed by Dr. David, was carried:

"Whereas the Social Democratic Party interprets the term 'revolution' not in the sense of violent overthrow but in the peaceful sense of development, that is, the gradual realization of a new economic principle, the public party meeting at Mayence repudiates every kind of 'revolutionary romance.'

"The meeting sees in the conquest of political power nothing but the winning over of the majority of the people to the ideas and demands of the Social Democracy; a conquest which cannot be achieved by means of violence, but only by the revolutionizing of the mind by means of intellectual propaganda and practical reform work in all spheres of political, economic and social life.

"In the conviction that Social Democracy flourishes far better when it employs legal means than when it relies on illegal means and revolution, the meeting repudiates '*Direct Mass Action*' as a tactical principle, and holds fast to the principle of 'parliamentary reform action,' that is, it desires that the Party in the future as in the past shall earnestly endeavour *to achieve its aims by legislation and gradual organized development.*

"The indispensable condition for this reformist method of struggle is that *the possibility of participation of the dispossessed masses of the people in the legislation* of the empire and of the individual states shall not be lessened but *increased to the fullest possible extent.* For this reason, the meeting declares it to be an incontestable right of the working class to withhold their labor for a longer or shorter period to ward off attacks on their legal rights and to gain further rights, when all other means fail.

"But as the political mass strike can only be victoriously carried through when kept within *strictly legal limits* and when the strikers give no reasonable excuse to the authorities to resort to armed force, the meeting perceives the only necessary and real preparation for the exercise of this method of struggle in the further extension of the political, trade union and cooperative organizations. Because only in this way can the conditions be created among the wide masses of the people which can guarantee the successful prosecution of a mass strike: conscious discipline and adequate economic support."

The theoretical conception according to which the trade unions are merely a part of Social Democracy finds its classic expression in Germany in fact, in actual practice, and that in three directions. First, the German trade unions are a direct product of Social Democracy; it was Social Democracy which created the beginnings of the present trade union movement in Germany and which enabled it to attain such great dimensions, and it is Social Democracy which supplies it to this day with its leaders and the most active promoters of its organization. Second, the German trade unions are a product of Social Democracy also in the sense that Social Democratic teaching is the soul of trade union practice, as the trade unions owe their superiority over all bourgeois and denominational trade unions to the idea of the class struggle; their practical success, their power, are a result of the circumstance that their practise is illuminated by the theory of scientific socialism and they are thereby raised above the level of a narrow-minded socialism. The strength of the "practical policy" of the German trade unions lies in their insight into the deeper social and economic connections of the capitalist system; but they owe this insight—entirely to the theory of scientific socialism upon which their practise is based. Viewed in this way, any attempt to emancipate the trade unions from the Social Democratic theory in favor of some other "trade union theory" opposed to Social Democracy is from the standpoint of the trade unions themselves and of their future, nothing but an attempt to commit suicide. The separation of trade union practise from the theory of scientific socialism would mean to the German trade unions the immediate loss of all their superiority over all kinds of bourgeois trade unions, and their fall from their present height to the level of unsteady groping and mere dull empiricism.

Thirdly and finally, the trade unions are, although their leaders have gradually lost sight of the fact, even as regards their numerical strength, a direct product of the Social Democratic movement and the Social Democratic agitation. It is true that in many districts trade union agitation precedes Social Democratic agitation, and that everywhere trade union work prepares the way for party work. From the point of view of effect party and trade unions assist each other to the fullest extent. But when the picture of the class struggle in Germany is looked at as a whole and its more deep-seated associations, the proportions are considerably altered. Many trade union leaders are in the habit of looking down triumphantly from the proud height of their membership of one and a quarter millions on the miserable organized members of the Social Democratic Party, not yet half a million strong, and of recalling the time, ten or twelve years ago, when those in the ranks of Social Democracy were pessimistic as to the prospects of trade union development. They do see that between these two things—the large number of organised trade unionists and the small number of organized Social Democrats—*there exists in a certain degree a direct causal connection.* Thousands and thousands of workers do not join the party organizations precisely because they join the trade unions. According to the theory all the workers must be doubly organized, must attend two kinds of meetings, pay double contributions, read two kinds of workers' papers, etc. But for this it is necessary to have a higher standard of intelligence and of that idealism which, from a pure feeling of duty to the labor movement, is prepared for the daily sacrifice of time and money, and finally, a higher standard of that passionate interest in the actual life of the Party which can only be engendered by membership of the party organisation. All this is true of the most enlightened and intelligent minority of Social Democratic workers in the large towns, where party life is full and attractive and where the workers' standard of living is high. Among the wider sections of the working masses in the large towns, however, as well as in the provinces, in the smaller and the smallest towns where local political life is not an independent thing but a mere reflex of the course of events in the capital, where consequently, party life is poor and monotonous, and where finally, the economic standard of life of the workers is, for the most part, miserable, it is very difficult to secure the double form of organization.

For the Social Democratically-minded worker from the masses the question will be solved by joining his trade union. The immediate interests of his economic struggle which are conditioned by the nature of the struggle itself cannot be advanced in any other way than by membership of a trade union organization. The contribution which he pays, often amid considerable sacrifice of his standard of living, bring him immediate, visible results. His Social Democratic inclinations, however, enable him to participate in various kinds of work without belonging to a special party organization; by voting at parliamentary elections, by attendance at Social Democratic public meetings, by following the reports of Social Democratic speeches in representative bodies, and by reading the party press. Compare in this connection the number of Social Democratic electors or the number of subscribers to *Vorwarts* with the number of organized party members in Berlin! And what is most decisive, the Social Democratically-minded average worker who as a simple man can have no understanding of the intricate and fine "two-soul theory" so called, feels that he is, even in the trade union *Social Democratically* organized. Although the central committees of the unions have no official party label, the workman from the masses in every city and town sees at the head of his trade union as the most active leaders, those colleagues whom he knows also as comrades and Social Democrats in public life, now as Reichstag, Landtag or local representatives, now as trusted men of the Social Democracy, members of election committees, party editors and secretaries, or merely as speakers and agitators. Further, he hears expressed in the agitational work of his trade union much the same ideas, pleasing and intelligible to him, of capitalist exploitation, class relations, etc., as those that have come to him from Social Democratic agitation. Indeed, the most and best loved of the speakers at trade union meetings are those same Social Democrats.

Thus everything combines to give the average class-conscious worker the feeling that he, in being organized in his trade union, is also a member of his labor party and is Social Democratically organized, *and therein lies the peculiar recruiting strength of the German trade unions.* Not because of the appearance of neutrality, but because of the Social Democratic reality of their being have the central unions been enabled to attain their present strength. This is simply through the coexistence of the various unions—Catholic, Hirsch-Dunker,[2] etc.—founded by bourgeois parties by which it was sought to establish the neces-

2. Unions under "liberal" leadership.—Ed.

sity for that political "neutrality." When the German worker who has full freedom of choice to attach himself to a Christian, Catholic, Evangelical or Freethinking trade union, chooses none of these but the "free trade union" instead, or leaves one of the former to join the latter, he does so only because he considers that the central unions are the avowed organizations of the modern class struggle, or, what is the same thing in Germany, that they are Social Democratic trade unions. In a word the appearance of "neutrality," which exists in the minds of many trade union leaders, does not exist for the mass of organized trade unionists. And that is the good fortune of the trade union movement. If the appearance of "neutrality," that alienation and separation of the trade unions from Social Democracy, really and truly becomes a reality in the eyes of the proletarian masses, then the trade unions would immediately lose all their advantages over competing bourgeois unions, and therewith their recruiting power, their living fire. This is conclusively proved by facts which are generally known. The appearance of party-political "neutrality" of the trade unions could, as a means of attraction, render inestimable service in a country in which Social Democracy itself has no credit among the masses, in which the odium attached to a workers' organization injures it in the eyes of the masses rather than advantages it—where, in a word, the trade unions must first of all recruit their troops from a wholly unenlightened, bourgeois-minded mass.

The best example of such a country was, throughout the whole of the last century, and is to a certain extent today—Great Britain. In Germany, however, party relations are altogether different. In a country in which Social Democracy is the most powerful political party, in which its recruiting power is represented by an army of over three million proletarians, it is ridiculous to speak of the deterrent effect of Social Democracy and of the necessity for a fighting organization of the workers to ensure political neutrality. The mere comparison of the figures of Social Democratic voters with the figures of the trade union organizations in Germany is sufficient to prove to the most simple-minded that the trade unions in Germany do not, as in England, draw their troops from the unenlightened bourgeois-minded mass, but from the mass of proletarians already aroused by the Social

Democracy and won by it to the idea of the class struggle. Many trade union leaders indignantly reject the idea—a requisite of the "theory of neutrality"—and regard the trade unions as a recruiting school for Social Democracy. This apparently insulting, but in reality, highly flattering presumption is in Germany reduced to mere fancy by the circumstance that the positions are reversed; it is the Social Democracy which is the recruiting school for the trade unions. Moreover, if the organizational work of the trade unions is for the most part of a very difficult and troublesome kind it is, with the exception of a few cases and some districts, not merely because on the whole, the soil has not been prepared by the Social Democratic plough, but also because the trade union seed itself and the sower as well must also be "red," Social Democratic, before the harvest can prosper. But when we compare in this way the figures of trade union strength, not with those of the Social Democratic organizations but—which is the only correct way—with those of the mass of Social Democratic voters, we come to a conclusion which differs considerably from the current view of the matter. The fact then comes to light that the "free trade unions" actually represent today but a minority of the class-conscious workers of Germany, that even with their one and a quarter million organized members they have not yet been able to draw into their ranks one half of those already aroused by Social Democracy.

The most important conclusion to be drawn from the facts above cited is that the *complete unity* of the trade union and the Social Democratic movements which is absolutely necessary for the coming mass struggles in Germany *is actually here,* and that it is incorporated in the wide mass which forms the basis at once of Social Democracy and trade unionism, and in whose consciousness both parts of the movement are mingled in a mental unity. The alleged antagonism between Social Democracy and trade unions shrinks to an antagonism between Social Democracy and a certain part of the trade union officials, which is, however, at the same time an antagonism within the trade unions between this part of the trade union leaders and the proletarian mass organized in trade unions.

The rapid growth of the trade union movement in Germany in the course of the last fifteen years, especially in the period of great economic prosperity from 1895 to 1900 has brought with it a great independence of the trade unions, a specializing of their methods of struggle, and finally the introduction of a regular trade union officialdom. All these phenomena are quite understandable and natural historical products of the growth of the trade unions in this fifteen-year period, and of the economic prosperity and political calm of Germany. They are, although inseparable from certain drawbacks, without doubt an historically necessary evil. But the dialectics of development also brings with it the circumstance that these necessary means of promoting trade union growth become, on the contrary, obstacles to its further development at a certain stage of organization and at a certain degree of ripeness of conditions.

The specialization of professional activity as trade union leaders, as well as the naturally restricted horizon which is bound up with disconnected economic struggles in a peaceful period, leads only too easily, amongst trade union officials, to bureaucratism and a certain narrowness of outlook. Both, however, express themselves in a whole series of tendencies which may be fateful in the highest degree for the future of the trade union movement. There is first of all the overvaluation of the organization, which from a means has gradually been changed into an end in itself, a precious thing, to which the interests of the struggles should be subordinated. From this also comes that openly admitted need for peace which shrinks from great risks and presumed dangers to the stability of the trade unions, and further, the overvaluation of the trade union method of struggle itself, its prospects and its successes. The trade union leaders, constantly absorbed in the economic guerrilla war whose plausible task it is to make the workers place the highest value on the smallest economic achievement, every increase in wages and shortening of the working day, gradually lose the power of seeing the larger connections and of taking a survey of the whole position. Only in this way can one explain why many trade union leaders refer with the greatest satisfaction to the achievements of the last fifteen years, instead of, on the contrary, emphasizing the other side of the medal; the simultaneous and immense reduction of the proletarian standard of life by land usury, by the whole tax and customs policy, by landlord rapacity which has increased house rents to such an exorbitant extent, in short, by all the objective tendencies of bourgeois policy which have largely neutralized the advantages of the fifteen years of trade union struggle. From the *whole* Social Democratic truth which, while emphasizing the importance of the present work and its absolute necessity, attaches the chief importance to the criticism and the limits to this work the *half* trade union truth is taken which emphasizes only the positive side of the daily struggle. And finally, from the concealment of the objective limits drawn by the bourgeois social order to the trade union struggle, there arises a hostility to every theoretical criticism which refers to these limits in connection with the ultimate aims of the labor movement. Fulsome flattery and boundless optimism are considered to be the duty of every "friend of the trade union movement." But as the Social Democratic standpoint consists precisely in fighting against uncritical trade union optimism, as in fighting against uncritical parliamentary optimism, a front is at last made against the Social Democratic theory: men grope for a "new trade union theory," that is, a theory which would open an illimitable vista of economic progress to the trade union struggle within the capitalist system, in opposition to the Social Democratic doctrine. Such a theory has indeed existed for some time—the theory of Professor Sombart which was promulgated with the express intention of driving a wedge between the trade unions and the Social Democracy in Germany, and of enticing the trade unions over to the bourgeois position.

In close connection with these theoretical tendencies is a revolution in the relations of leaders and rank and file. In place of the direction by colleagues through local committees, with their admitted inadequacy, there appears the businesslike direction of the trade union officials. The initiative and the power of making decisions thereby devolve upon trade union specialists, so to speak, and the more passive virtue of discipline upon the mass of members. This dark side of officialdom also assuredly conceals considerable dangers for the party, as from the latest innovation, the institution of local party secretariats, it can quite easily result, if the Social Democratic mass is not careful that these secretariats may remain mere organs for carrying out decisions and not be regarded in any way the appointed bearers of the initiative and of the direction of local party life. But by the nature of the case, by the character of the political struggle, there are narrow bounds drawn to bureaucratism in Social Democracy as in trade union life. But here the technical specializing of wage struggles as, for example, the conclusion of intricate tariff agreements and the like frequently means that the mass of organized workers are prohibited from taking a "survey of the whole industrial life," and their incapacity for taking decisions is thereby established. A consequence of this conception is the argument with which every theoretical criticism of the prospects and possibilities of trade union practise is tabooed and which alleges that it represents a danger to the pious trade union sentiment of the masses. From this the point of view has been developed that it is only by blind, childlike faith in the efficacy of the trade union struggle that the working masses can be won and held for the organization. In contradistinction to Social Democracy which bases its influence on the unity of the masses amid the contradictions of the existing order and in the complicated character of its development, and on the critical attitude of the masses to all factors and stages of their own class struggle, the influence and the power of the trade unions are founded upon the upside down theory of the incapacity of the masses for criticism and decision. "The faith of the people must be maintained"—that is the fundamental principle, acting upon which many trade union officials stamp as attempts on the life of this movement all criticisms of the objective inadequacy of trade unionism. And finally, a result of this specialization and this bureaucratism amongst trade union officials is the great independence and the "neutrality" of the trade unions in relation to Social Democracy. The extreme independence of the trade union organization has resulted as a natural condition from its growth, as a relation which has grown out of the technical division of work between the political and the trade union forms of struggle. The "neutrality" of the German trade unions, on its part, arose as a product of the reactionary trade union legislation of the Prusso-German police state. With time, both aspects of their nature have altered. From the condition of political "neutrality" of the trade unions imposed by the police a theory of their voluntary neutrality has been evolved as a necessity founded upon the alleged nature of the trade union struggle itself. And the technical independence of the trade unions which should rest upon the division of work in the unified Social Democratic class struggle, the separation of the trade unions from Social Democracy, from its views and its leadership, has been changed into the so-called "equal authority" of trade unions and Social Democracy.

This appearance of separation and equality of trade unions and Social Democracy is, however, incorporated chiefly in the trade union officials, and strengthened through the managing apparatus of the trade unions. Outwardly, by the coexistence of a complete staff of trade union officials, of a wholly independent central committee, a numerous professional press, and finally, of a trade union congress, the illusion is created of an exact parallel with the managing apparatus of the Social Democracy, the party executive, the party press and the party conference. This illusion of equality between Social Democracy and the trade union has led to, amongst other things, the monstrous spectacle that, in part, quite analogous agendas are discussed at Social Democratic conferences and trade union congresses, and that on the same questions different, and even diametrically opposite, decisions are taken. From the natural division of work between the party conference, which represents the general interests and tasks of the labor movement, and the trade union congress (which deals with the much narrower sphere of social questions and interests) the artificial division has been made of a pretended trade union and a Social Democratic outlook in relation to *the same* general questions and interests of the labor movement.

Thus the peculiar position has arisen that this same trade union movement which below, in the wide proletarian masses, is absolutely one with Social Democracy, parts abruptly from it above, in the superstructure of management, and sets itself up as an independent great power. The German labor movement therefore assumes the peculiar form of a double pyramid whose base and body consist of one solid mass but whose apices are wide apart.

It is clear from this presentation of the case in what way

alone in a natural and successful manner that compact unity of the German labor movement can be attained which, in view of the coming political class struggles and of the peculiar interest of the further development of the trade unions, is indispensably necessary. Nothing could be more perverse or more hopeless than to desire to attain the unity desired by means of sporadic and periodical negotiations on individual questions affecting the labor movement between the Social Democratic Party leadership and the trade union central committees. It is just the highest circles of both forms of the labor movement which as we have seen incorporate their separation and self-sufficiency, which are themselves, therefore, the promoters of the illusion of the "equal authority" and of the parallel existence of Social Democracy and trade unionism. To desire the unity of these through the union of the party executive and the general commission is to desire to build a bridge at the very spot where the distance is greatest and the crossing most difficult. Not above, among the heads of the leading directing organisations and in their federative alliance, but below, among the organized proletarian masses, lies the guarantee of the real unity of the labor movement. In the consciousness of the million trade unionists, the Party and the trade unions are actually *one*, they represent in different forms the *Social Democratic* struggle for the emancipation of the proletariat. And the necessity automatically arises therefrom of removing any causes of friction which have arisen between the Social Democracy and a part of the trade unions, of adapting their mutual relation to the consciousness of the proletarian masses, that is, *of rejoining the trade unions to Social Democracy.* The synthesis of the real development which led from the original incorporation of the trade unions to their separation from Social Democracy will thereby be expressed, and the way will be prepared for the coming period of great proletarian mass struggles during the period of vigorous growth, of both trade unions and Social Democracy, and their reunion, in the interests of both, will become a necessity.

It is not, of course, a question of the merging of the trade union organization in the party, but of the restoration of the unity of Social Democracy and the trade unions which corresponds to the actual relation between the labor movement as a whole and its partial trade union expression. Such a revolution will inevitably call forth a vigorous opposition from a part of the trade union leadership. But it is high time for the working masses of Social Democracy to learn how to express their capacity for decision and action, and therewith to demonstrate their ripeness for that time of great struggles and great tasks in which they, the masses, will be the actual chorus and the directing bodies will merely act the "speaking parts," that is, will only be the interpreters of the will of the masses.

The trade union movement is not that which is reflected in the quite understandable *but irrational illusion* of a minority of the trade union leaders, but that which lives in the consciousness of the mass of proletarians who have been won for the class struggle. In this consciousness the trade union movement is a part of Social Democracy. "And what it is, that it should dare to appear."

Written in Kuokkala, Finland, autumn 1906.

GLOSSARY OF NAMES

Bakunin, Mikhail (1814–1876) Of Russian origin, he was a contemporary and antagonist of Marx in the First International. The founder of the Anarchist movement.

Bernstein, Eduard (1850–1932) Of German Jewish origin. Member of the German Social Democracy. From 1896 developed the revisionist theory of "evolutionary socialism." From 1902 to 1928 a member of the German Reichstag, though not continuously. During the War a pacifist-centrist.

David, Eduard (1863–1930) Right-wing member of the German Social Democracy; revisionist and supporter of the Kaiser in the First World War. Minister without portfolio, 1919 to 1920. First president of the National Assembly.

Gapon, Father Georgiy Appolonovich (1870–1906) Russian priest and Czarist Police spy. Organized Assembly of Russian Factory Workers in 1904. On January 22, 1905 led the march to the Winter Palace after secretly writing to the Czar. However, the massacre of Bloody Sunday took place. Escaped abroad but failed in his efforts to unify all anti-Czarist parties. Tried to smuggle arms into Russia. Hanged by Social Revolutionaries whom he tried to recruit to spying in April 1906.

Kasprzak, Martin Polish revolutionary, friend and mentor of Rosa Luxemburg. Spent most of his life in prison and ended it on the gallows.

Roland-Holst, Henrietta (b. 1869) Dutch writer and Marxist: left-wing member of Social Democracy. Organizer of women's unions. Member of the Zimmerwald Left. In 1916 joined Left Socialist Party, in 1918 the Communist Party. In 1924 formed the Independent Communist Party, finally became a Christian Socialist and retired from politics.

Struve, Peter B. (b. 1870) A Social Democrat in the 1890's. Economist and Russian legal Marxist. Liberal till 1905, then Right Wing

Cadet. After the 1917 Revolution became a Minister in the counter-revolutionary White Guard Government of Denikin and Wrangel.

Zubatov, Sergei Vasilievich (d. 1917) Police chief under General Trepov. Organized the break up of the First Congress of Russian Social Democracy, Minsk 1898. Brought Russian police methods up to date by introducing finger printing, photography and the secret service. At the turn of the century he was head of the Moscow Okhrana. In May 1901 formed the Moscow Society for Mutual Aid for Workingmen in the mechanical industries in an attempt to prevent workers moving to the Social Democracy. Within five days of formation it mobilized 50,000 workers. He organized Jews separately in the Jewish Independent Workers Party in 1901. The movement spread to South Russia in 1902, and with partial successes in winning demands found itself heading mass strikes in 1903. Removed from office under pressure of imperialist interests in 1903. Committed suicide after Czar's abdication in 1917.

Part II

The Junius Pamphlet:
The Crisis in the German Social Democracy February–April 1915

EDITOR'S NOTE

The Crisis in the German Social Democracy was begun in prison by Rosa Luxemburg in February 1915 (she had been arrested on the 19th), and completed in April. The manuscript was smuggled out.

When she was released, in January 1916, she found the manuscript untouched on her table. It was published only a year after its completion in April 1916, in Switzerland, and was secretly distributed in Germany.

In her absence, but largely due to her efforts, the German revolutionaries who were able to meet, gathered at Karl Liebknecht's flat in Berlin, and on New Year's Day 1916 they launched the "International Group," which was later to be known as "Spartacusbund" and emerge as the Communist Party of Germany on January 1, 1919.

At this meeting the pamphlet was adopted as the statement of policy of the "International Group" and the *Theses on the War and the International* as their programatic document. Rosa Luxemburg had wanted to put her name to it, but was dissuaded from doing so as it would certainly have earned her another long term in prison. She therefore published her booklet under the pseudonym "Junius." This by-line had been used earlier in England in letters attacking the Ministry of the Duke of Grafton appearing in the London *Public Advertiser* from 1769 to 1772. The letters caused quite a stir at the time, but the author's identity has never been definitely established. He probably took the name from Lucius Junius Brutus, a legendary Roman patriot of uncertain date, some centuries B.C., who, it is claimed, had led a republican revolution in classical Rome.

Notwithstanding this precaution, Rosa Luxemburg was ar-

rested again on July 10, 1916 and was released from prison only
in 1918, by the November Revolution in Germany.

The 'Juniusbrochure,' as the pamphlet was soon to be known,
had an immediate effect, and not in Germany alone.

Lenin, without knowing the identity of the author, was enthusiastic:

"Written in a very lively style, Junius' pamphlet has undoubtedly
played and will continue to play an important role in the struggle
against the ex-Social Democratic Party of Germany, which has deserted to the bourgeoisie and the Junkers, and we extend our hearty
congratulations to the author. . . .

"On the whole, the Junius pamphlet is a splendid Marxist work, and
its defects are, in all probability, to a certain extent accidental. . . ."
(*Collected Works XXII*, pp. 305–6)

In retrospect, Paul Frolich, Rosa Luxemburg's biographer
writes: "Today it is still more than a historical document: it is
the thread of Ariadne in the labyrinth of our times. . . ."

*   *   *

Our edition follows the English translation published by the
Socialist Publication Society, New York, 1918, under the names
of Karl Liebknecht, Rosa Luxemburg and Franz Mehring.

The original German edition had as an appendix Rosa Luxemburg's *Theses on the War and the International*, also written
in prison and adopted as a programatic document by the "International Group."

The theses are published here, following the text in the *Fourth
International* (Amsterdam, Winter 1959–1960). (See also Gankin
& Fischer, *The Bolsheviks and the World War*, Stanford, 1940,
p. 394 et seq.)

The notes and the glossary of names were added to this edition by Young Socialist Publications.

Chapter I

The scene has thoroughly changed. The six weeks' march[1] to Paris has become world drama. Mass murder has become a monotonous task, and yet the final solution is not one step nearer. Capitalist rule is caught in its own trap, and cannot ban the spirit that it has invoked.

Gone is the first mad delirium. Gone are the patriotic street demonstrations, the chase after suspicious looking automobiles, the false telegrams, the cholera-poisoned wells. Gone the mad stories of Russian students who hurl bombs from every bridge of Berlin, or Frenchmen flying over Nuremberg;[2] gone the excesses of a spy-hunting populace, the singing throngs, the coffee shops with their patriotic songs; gone the violent mobs, ready to denounce, ready to persecute women, ready to whip themselves into a delirious

1. **Count Alfred von Schlieffen** (1893–1913) Chief of Staff of the Imperial German Army 1891–1906, drew up a plan (since named after him) for the capture of Paris in six weeks, based on the estimated six weeks required for Russia to mobilize. Drawn up in 1899, the plan was continually revised by him till retirement. Slightly modified, it was put into operation on August 4, 1914. The first few days went according to plan, but calculations were upset by unexpected Belgian and French resistance.

2. Official and semi-official rumors were circulated in the first few days of August 1914 in justification of Germany's declaration of war: August 2: Russian troops had crossed into Germany; French airmen had bombed Nuremburg; a French doctor had poisoned the wells at Montsigny, suburb of Metz, and been shot; French flour dealer had poisoned some flour. August 3: French cavalry had violated the frontier at two points; French infantry had fired across the Alsatian frontier; two Frenchmen had been shot while trying to blow up a tunnel on the Moselle railroad. As a result, on August 4, the British Embassy was attacked and a number of Russian "spies" were assaulted and some trampled to death.

frenzy over every wild rumor; gone the atmosphere of ritual murder, the Kishinev[3] air that left the policeman at the corner as the only remaining representative of human dignity.

The show is over. The curtain has fallen on trains filled with reservists, as they pull out amid the joyous cries of enthusiastic maidens. We no longer see their laughing faces, smiling cheerily from the train windows upon a war-mad population. Quietly they trot through the streets, with their sacks upon their shoulders. And the public, with a fretful face, goes about its daily task.

Into the disillusioned atmosphere of pale daylight there rings a different chorus; the hoarse croak of the hawks and hyenas of the battlefield. Ten thousand tents, guaranteed according to specifications, 100,000 kilos of bacon, cocoa powder, coffee substitute, cash on immediate delivery. Shrapnel, drills, ammunition bags, marriage bureaus for war widows, leather belts, war orders—only serious propositions considered. And the cannon fodder that was loaded upon the trains in August and September is rotting on the battlefields of Belgium and the Vosges, while profits are springing, like weeds, from the fields of the dead.

Business is flourishing upon the ruins. Cities are turned into shambles, whole countries into deserts, villages into cemeteries, whole nations into beggars, churches into stables; popular rights, treaties, alliances, the holiest words and the highest authorities have been torn into scraps; every sovereign by the grace of God is called a fool, an unfaithful wretch, by his cousin on the other side;[4] every diplomat calls his colleague in the enemy's country a desperate criminal; each government looks upon the other as the evil genius of its people, worthy only of the contempt of the world. Hunger revolts in Venetia, in Lisbon, in Moscow, in Singapore; pestilence in Russia, misery and desperation is everywhere.

3. A pogrom atmosphere. In April 1903, during the Feast of the Passover, Kishinev in South Russia, presently capital of Soviet Moldavia, was the scene of a particularly atrocious pogrom: 45 Jews were killed, 600 injured, 1500 Jewish homes looted with the connivance, if not the actual participation, of Czarist officialdom.

4. Thanks to Queen Victoria of England, all royal families in Europe were related by blood and marriage. Among her grandchildren were George V of England, Wilhelm II of Germany, Czarina Alexandra of Russia, Queen Maud of Norway, Queen Eva of Spain and Queen Marie of Rumania.

Shamed, dishonored, wading in blood and dripping with filth, thus capitalist society stands. Not as we usually see it, playing the roles of peace and righteousness, of order, of philosophy, of ethics —but as a roaring beast, as an orgy of anarchy, as a pestilential breath, devastating culture and humanity—so it appears in all its hideous nakedness.

And in the midst of this orgy a world tragedy has occurred; the capitulation of the Social Democracy.[5] To close one's eyes to this fact, to try to hide it, would be the most foolish, the most dangerous thing that the international proletariat could do. "The Democrat [i.e., the revolutionary middle-class]," says Karl Marx, "emerges from the most shameful downfall as spotlessly as he went innocently into it. With the strengthened confidence that he must win, he is more than ever certain that he and his party need no new principles, that events and conditions must finally come to meet them." His mistakes are as gigantic as his problems. No firmly fixed plan, no orthodox ritual that holds good for all times shows him the path that he must travel. Historical experience is his only teacher, his Via Dolorosa[6] to freedom is covered not only with unspeakable suffering, but with countless mistakes. The goal of his journey, his final liberation, depends entirely upon the proletariat, on whether *it* understands to learn from *its* own mistakes. Self-criticism, cruel, unsparing criticism that goes to the very root of the evil is life and breath for the proletarian movement. The catastrophe into which the world has thrust the socialist proletariat is an unexampled misfortune for humanity. But socialism is lost only if the international proletariat is unable to measure the depths of the catastrophe and refuses to understand the lesson that it teaches.

The last forty-five years in the development of the labor movement are at stake. The present situation is a closing of its accounts, a summing-up of the items of half a century of work. In

5. On August 4th, 1914 (a few hours after German armies had violated the neutrality of Belgium and Luxemburg), the vote for war credits came up in the Reichstag, and the entire Social Democratic fraction voted for the credits. The date marks the collapse of the German Social Democracy and the 2nd International.

6. **Via Dolorosa:** "Path of Sorrow," Christ's road to Calvary.

the grave of the Paris Commune[7] lies buried the first phase of the
European labor movement and the First International. Instead of
spontaneous revolution, revolts, and barricades, after each of
which the proletariat relapsed once more into its dull passiveness,
there came the systematic daily struggle, the utilization of bourgeois parliamentarism, mass organization, the welding of the
economic with the political struggle, of socialist ideals with the
stubborn defense of most immediate interests. For the first time
the cause of the proletariat and its emancipation were led by the
guiding star of scientific knowledge. In place of sects and schools,
Utopian undertakings and experiments in every country, each
altogether and absolutely separate from each other, we found a
uniform, international, theoretical basis that united the nations.
The theoretical works of Marx gave to the working class of the
whole world a compass by which to fix its tactics from hour to
hour, in its journey toward the one unchanging goal.

  The bearer, the defender, the protector of this new method was
the German Social Democracy. The war of 1870[8] and the downfall of the Paris Commune had shifted the center of gravity of

  7. Following France's defeat in the war of 1870–71, the workers of Paris
seized power. On March 28th 1871, the Paris Commune was declared. It was
drowned in blood May 21–28, 1871. Some 20,000 to 30,000 Communards, including women and children were killed, 270 executed after "trial," 400
jailed, 7000 transported from the country. The Commune marked the end of
monarchy in France and the beginning of the Third Republic.
  8. The rulers of both France and German wanted war. In May 1869 the
Empress Eugenie had declared that only a war would save the Bonaparte
dynasty. In September 1869, an agreement was reached between Austria, Italy
and France. On 2 July 1870, the Provisional Government of Spain promulgated the candidature of Prince Leopold of Hohenzollern to succeed Queen
Isabella who had been deposed in September 1868. On 6 July, France protested and six days later, the candidature was withdrawn. On 7 July, the
French Ambassador to Germany, Benedetti, demanded an apology from the
Kaiser and an understanding that a Hohenzollern would never again aspire to
the Spanish throne. The Kaiser was at Ems taking the waters. Bismarck re-
drafted the Kaiser's reply, the now famous Ems despatch, making war inevitable. On 19 July 1870, France declared war. Prussia, having neutralized
England and Russia, scored immediate victories: August 4th at Wissenburg,
August 6th at Worth. On 27 October, 175,000 troops under Marshal Bazaine
were surrounded at Metz. The main army under Marshal MacMahon and
the Emperor Napoleon III himself surrendered at Sedan on 2 September
1870. Paris fell after a four-month siege, 19th September to 28th January
1871. By the Peace of Frankfurt (10th May 1871) France lost Alsace-Lor-

the European labor movement to Germany. Just as France was the classic country of the first phase of the proletarian class struggle, as Paris was the torn and bleeding heart of the European working class of that time, so the German working class became the vanguard of the second phase. By innumerable sacrifices in the form of agitational work it has built up the strongest, the model organization of the proletariat, has created the greatest press, has developed the most effective educational and propaganda methods. It has collected under its banners the most gigantic labor masses, and has elected the largest representative groups to its national parliament.

The German Social Democracy has been generally acknowledged to be the purest incarnation of Marxian Socialism. It has held and wielded a peculiar prestige as teacher and leader in the Second International. Friedrich Engels wrote in his famous foreword to Marx's *Class Struggles in France*: "Whatever may occur in other countries, the German Social Democracy occupies a particular place and, for the present at least, has therefore a particular duty to perform. The two million voters that it sends to the ballot boxes, and the young girls and women who stand behind them as non-voters, are numerically the greatest, the most compact mass, the most decisive force of the proletarian international army." The German Social Democracy was, as the *Wiener Arbeiter-Zeitung*[9] wrote on August 5, 1914, the jewel of the organization of the class-conscious proletariat. In its footsteps the French, the Italian, and the Belgian Social Democracies, the labor movements of Holland, Scandinavia, Switzerland and United States followed more or less eagerly. The Slav nations, the Russians, and the Social Democrats of the Balkans looked up to the German movement in boundless, almost unquestioning ad-

---

raine, Moselle, Haut Rhine, Bas Rhine and had to pay an indemnity of five thousand million francs.

The victory of Prussia brought about the union of Germany under Prussian hegemony. Wilhelm I was crowned Emperor of Germany at Versailles on 18th January 1871. The defeat of France led to the Paris Commune and the end of French monarchy. (See Note 7.)

9. **The Wiener Arbeiter Zeitung** was the central organ of the Austrian Social Democracy, founded in Vienna 1889 and a daily from 1895.

miration. In the Second International the German Social Democracy was the determining factor. In every Congress, in the
meetings of the International Socialist Bureau,[10] everything
waited upon the opinion of the German group.

Particularly in the fight against militarism and war the position
taken by the German Social Democracy has always been decisive. "We Germans cannot accept that," was usually sufficient to
determine the orientation of the International. Blindly confident,
it submitted to the leadership of the much admired, mighty
German Social Democracy. It was the pride of every socialist, the
horror of the ruling classes of all countries.

And what happened in Germany when the great historical
crisis came? The deepest fall, the mightiest cataclysm. Nowhere
was the organization of the proletariat made so completely sub-
servient to imperialism. Nowhere was the state of siege so un-
complainingly borne. Nowhere was the press so thoroughly
gagged, public opinion so completely choked off; nowhere was
the political and industrial class struggle of the working class so
entirely abandoned as in Germany.

But the German Social Democracy was not only the strongest
body, it was the thinking brain of the International as well. Therefore the process of self-analysis and appraisement must begin in
its own movement, with its own case. It is in honor bound to lead
the way to the rescue of international socialism, to proceed with
the unsparing criticism of its own shortcomings.

No other party, no other class in capitalist society can dare to
expose its own errors, its own weaknesses before the whole world
in the clear mirror of reason, for the mirror would reflect the
historical fate that is hidden behind it. The working class can
always look truth in the face even when this means bitterest
self-accusation; for its weakness was but an error and the inexorable laws of history give it strength and assure its final
victory.

This unsparing self-criticism is not only a fundamental necessity, but the highest duty of the working class as well. We have

10. **The International Socialist Bureau** was the Executive Committee of the
Second International, established by decision of the Paris Congress of 1900
with headquarters in Brussels.

on board the highest treasure of humanity, and the proletariat is their ordained protector. While capitalist society, shamed and dishonored, rushes through the bloody orgy to its doom, the international proletariat will gather the golden treasures that were allowed to sink to the bottom in the wild whirlpool of the world war in the moment of confusion and weakness.

One thing is certain. It is a foolish delusion to believe that we need only live through the war, as a rabbit hides under the bush to await the end of a thunderstorm to trot merrily off in his old accustomed gait when all is over. The world war has changed the condition of our struggle, and has changed *us* most of all. Not that the laws of capitalist development or the life and death conflict between capital and labor have been changed or minimized. Even now, in the midst of the war, the masks are falling, and the old well-known faces grinning at us. But evolution has received a mighty forward impetus through the outbreak of the imperialist volcano. The enormity of the tasks that tower before the socialist proletariat in the immediate future make the past struggles of the labor movement seem but a delightful idyll in comparison.

Historically the war is ordained to give to the cause of labor a mighty impetus. Marx, whose prophetic eyes foresaw so many historic events as they lay in the womb of the future, writes in *The Class Struggles in France* the following significant passage: "In France the middle class does what should normally be done by the industrial bourgeoisie [i.e., to fight for the democratic republic]; but who shall solve the problems of labor? They will not be solved in France. They will be proclaimed in France. They will nowhere be solved within national boundaries. Class war in France will revert into a world war. The solution will begin only when the world war has driven the proletariat into the leadership of that nation which controls the world market, to the leadership of England. The revolution that will here find, not its end, but its organizatory beginning, is no short-lived one. The present generation is like the Jews who were led by Moses through the wilderness. Not only must it conquer a new world, it must go down to make way for those who will be better able to cope with its problems."

This was written in 1850, at a time when England was the only capitalistically developed nation, when the English proletariat was the best organized and seemed destined through the industrial growth of its nation to take the leadership in the international labor movement. Read Germany instead of England, and the words of Karl Marx become an inspired prophecy of the present world war. It is ordained to drive the German proletariat "to the leadership of the people, and thus to create the organizatory beginning of the great international conflict between labor and capital for the political supremacy of the world."

Have we ever had a different conception of the role to be played by the working class in the great world war? Have we forgotten how we were wont to describe the coming event, only a few short years ago? "Then will come the catastrophe. All Europe will be called to arms, and sixteen to eighteen million men, the flower of the nations, armed with the best instruments of murder will make war upon each other. But I believe that behind this march there looms the final crash. Not we, but they themselves will bring it. They are driving things to the extreme, they are leading us straight into a catastrophe. They will harvest what they have sown. The *Götterdämmerung*[11] of the bourgeois world is at hand. Be sure of that. It is coming." Thus spoke Bebel, the speaker of our group in the Reichstag in the Morocco debate.

An official leaflet published by the Party, *Imperialism and Socialism*, that was distributed in hundreds of thousands of copies only a few years ago, closes with the words: "Thus the struggle against militarism daily becomes more and more clearly a decisive struggle between capital and labor. War, high prices and capitalism—peace, happiness for all, Socialism! Yours is the choice. History is hastening onward toward a decision. The proletariat must work unceasingly at its world mission, must strengthen the power of its organization and the clearness of its understanding. Then, come what will, whether it will succeed, by its power, in saving humanity from the horrible cruelties of the world war, or whether capitalism shall sink back into history, as it was born, in blood and violence, the historic moment will find the working class prepared, and preparedness is everything."

---

11. **Götterdämmerung**: (German). Literally: "The Twilight of the Gods." The word has literary overtones since its use by Wagner as title for his opera based on an episode from the *Nibelungenlied*.

The official handbook for socialist voters in 1911, the date of the last Reichstag elections, contains on page 42 the following comments on the expected world war: "Do our rulers and our ruling classes dare to demand this awful thing of the people? Will not a cry of horror, of fury and of indignation fill the country and lead the people to put an end to this murder? Will they not ask: 'For whom and for what? Are we insane that we should be treated thus or should tolerate such treatment?' He who dispassionately considers the possibility of a great European world war can come to no other conclusion.

"The next European war will be a game of *va-banque*,[12] whose equal the world has never seen before. It will be, in all probability, the last war."

With such words the Reichstag representatives won their 110 seats in the Reichstag.

When in the summer of 1911, the *Panther* made its spring to Agadir, and the noisy clamour of German imperialists brought Europe to the precipice of war,[13] an international meeting in London, on the 4th of August, adopted the following resolution:

"The German, Spanish, English, Dutch and French delegates of labor organizations hereby declare their readiness to oppose every declaration of war with every means in their power. Every nationality here represented pledges itself, in accordance with the decisions of its national and international congresses to oppose all criminal machinations on the part of the ruling classes."

But when in November 1912, the International Peace Congress met at Basel,[14] when the long train of labor representatives en-

12. **Va-banque:** (French). Literally. To go bank. A sheer gamble, staking one's all.

13. In July 1911, the German gunboat *Panther* sailed to Agadir, Morocco, "to protect German interests," i.e., to secure sources of iron ore for Mannesmann Steel. War almost broke out between France and Germany, but on Lloyd-George's threat of British intervention, Germany withdrew. At the Treaty of Berlin, November 1911, Germany was given a slice of the Cameroons and gave up her claims to Morocco. (See Chapter 4, Note 6.)

14. **The Peace Congress at Basel** (Switzerland) was held at the Basel Minster on November 24 and 25th, 1912. The immediate occasion was the fear of general European war, as Montenegro had declared war on Turkey in October, embroiling the Balkans. It was the last pre-war general meeting of the Second International, and its significance is that for the first time a socialist peace conference had recognized that the period of national wars in Europe was over and that all future wars would be imperialist wars.

tered the Minster, a presentiment of the coming hour of fate made them shudder and the heroic resolve took shape in every breast.

The cool, sceptical Victor Adler cried out: "Comrades, it is most important that we here, at the common source of our strength, that we, each and every one of us take from hence the strength to do in his country what he can, through the forms and means that are at his disposal, to oppose this crime of war, and if it should be accomplished, if we should really be able to prevent war, let this be the cornerstone of our coming victory. That is the spirit that animates the whole International.

"And when murder and arson and pestilence sweep over civilized Europe—we can think of it only with horror and indignation, and protests ring from our hearts. And we ask, are the proletarians of today really nothing but sheep to be led mutely to the slaughter?"

Troelstra spoke in the name of the small nations, in the name of the Belgians as well:

"With their blood and with all that they possess the proletariat of the small nations swear their allegiance to the International in everything that it may decide to prevent war. Again we repeat that we expect, when the ruling classes of the large nations call the sons of the proletariat to arms to satiate the lust for power and the greed of their rulers, in the blood and on the lands of the small peoples, we expect that then the sons of the proletariat, under the powerful influence of their proletarian parents and of the proletarian press, will think thrice before they harm us, their friends, in the service of the enemies of culture."

And Jaurès closed his speech, after the anti-war manifesto of the International Bureau had been read:

"The International represents the moral forces of the world! And when the tragic hour strikes, when we must sacrifice ourselves, this knowledge will support and strengthen us. Not lightly, but from the bottom of our hearts we declare that we are ready for all sacrifices!"

It was like a Ruetli pledge.[15] The whole world looked toward

15. c. 1291, at Ruetli Wood, west of Lake Uri, Switzerland, representatives of the three "Forest Cantons"—Schwyz, Uri and Unterwalden—met by night and took an oath and conspired to oust Austrian overlords from Switzerland.

the Minster of Basel, where the bells, slowly and solemnly, rang to the approaching great fight between the armies of labor and capital.

On the 3rd of September 1912, the Social Democratic deputy, David, spoke in the German Reichstag:

"That was the most beautiful hour of my life. That I here avow. When the chimes of the Minster rang in the long train of international Social Democrats, when the red flags were planted in the nave of the church about the altar, when the emissaries of the people were greeted by the peals of the organ that resounded the message of peace, that was an impression that I can never forget. . . .

"You must realize what it was that happened here. The masses have ceased to be will-less, thoughtless herds. That is new in the history of the world. Hitherto the masses have always blindly followed the lead of those who were interested in war, who drove the peoples at each other's throats to mass murder. That will stop. The masses have ceased to be the instruments, the yeomen of war profiteers."

A week before the war broke out, on the 26th of July 1914, the German party papers wrote:

"We are no marionettes; we are fighting with all our might against a system that makes men the powerless tools of blind circumstances, against this capitalism that is preparing to change Europe, thirsty for peace, into a smoking battlefield. If destruction takes its course, if the determined will for peace of the German, of the international proletariat, that will find expression in the next few days in mighty demonstrations, should not be able to prevent the world war, then it must be at least, the last war, it must be the *Götterdämmerung* of capitalism."

On the 30th of July 1914, the central organ of the German Social Democracy cried out:

"The socialist proletariat rejects all responsibility for the events that are being precipitated by a ruling class that is blinded, and

---

On November 14, 1315, Swiss footmen routed the cavalry of the Habsburg Leopold and one and a half centuries of war began. The medieval legend has lent a certain sacredness to the wood. In 1940, Swiss officers were made to take an oath of resistance to the Nazis at Ruetli.

on the verge of madness. We know that for us new life will spring from the ruins. But the responsibility falls upon the rulers of today.

"For them it is a question of existence!

"Die Weltgeschichte ist das Weltgericht!"[16]

And then came the awful, the incredible 4th of August 1914.

Did it *have* to come? An event of such importance cannot be a mere accident. It must have its deep, significant, objective causes. But perhaps these causes may be found in the errors of the leader of the proletariat, the Social Democracy itself, in the fact that our readiness to fight has flagged, that our courage and our convictions have forsaken us. Scientific socialism has taught us to recognize the objective laws of historical development. Man does not make history of his own volition, but he makes history nevertheless. The proletariat is dependent in its actions upon the degree of righteousness to which social evolution has advanced. But again, social evolution is not a thing apart from the proletariat; it is in the same measure its driving force and its cause as well as its product and its effect. And though we can no more skip a period in our historical development than a man can jump over his shadow, it lies within our power to accelerate or to retard it.

Socialism is the first popular movement in the world that has set itself a goal and has established in the social life of a man a conscious thought, a definite plan, the free will of mankind. For this reason Friedrich Engels calls the final victory of the socialist proletariat a stride by humankind from the animal kingdom into the kingdom of liberty. This step, too, is bound by unalterable historical laws to the thousands of rungs of the ladder of the past with its tortuous sluggish growth. But it will never be accomplished, if the burning spark of the conscious will of the masses does not spring from the material conditions that have been built up by past development. Socialism will not fall as manna from heaven. It can only be won by a long chain of powerful struggles, in which the proletariat, under the leadership of the Social Democracy, will learn to take hold of the rudder of

16. **"Die Weltgeschichte is das Weltgericht":** "World History is the Last Judgement."

society to become instead of the powerless victim of history, its conscious guide.

Friedrich Engels once said, "Capitalist society faces a dilemma, either an advance to socialism or a reversion to barbarism." What does a "reversion to barbarism" mean at the present stage of European civilization? We have read and repeated these words thoughtlessly without a conception of their terrible import. At this moment one glance about us will show us what a reversion to barbarism in capitalist society means. *This world war* means a reversion to barbarism. The triumph of imperialism leads to the destruction of culture, sporadically during a modern war, and forever, if the period of world wars that has just begun is allowed to take its damnable course to the last ultimate consequence. Thus we stand today, as Friedrich Engels prophesied more than a generation ago, before the awful proposition: Either the triumph of imperialism and the destruction of all culture, and, as in ancient Rome, depopulation, desolation, degeneration, a vast cemetery; or, the victory of socialism, that is, the conscious struggle of the international proletariat against imperialism, Against its methods, against war. This is the dilemma of world history, its inevitable choice, whose scales are trembling in the balance awaiting the decision of the proletariat. Upon it depends the future of culture and humanity. In this war imperialism has been victorious. Its brutal sword of murder has dashed the scales, with overbearing brutality, down into the abyss of shame and misery. If the proletariat learns *from* this war and *in* this war to exert itself, to cast off its serfdom to the ruling classes, to become the lord of its own destiny, the shame and misery will not have been in vain.

The modern working class must pay dearly for each realization of its historic mission. The road to the Golgotha[17] of its class liberation is strewn with awful sacrifices. The June combatants,[18]

17. **Golgotha:** Site of Christ's Sepulchre.
18. **June Combattants:** When the French Republic, established after the overthrow of Louis Phillippe on 24th February 1848, attempted to compel young workers 18–25 years of age to join the army or to compulsory labor, the workers met on 23rd June 1848, on the Place de la Bastille, and decided to oppose the government. The workers were crushed at the barricades by the army, and within a few days, in addition to the thousands dead, there were 15,000 working-class prisoners.

the victims of the Commune, the martyrs of the Russian Revolution—an endless line of bloody shadows. They have fallen on the field of honor, as Marx wrote of the heroes of the Commune, to be enshrined forever in the great heart of the working class. Now millions of proletarians are falling on the field of dishonor, of fratricide, of self-destruction, the slave-song on their lips. And that too has not been spared us. We are like the Jews whom Moses led through the desert. But we are not lost, and we will be victorious if we have not forgotten how to learn. And if the modern leaders of the proletariat do not know how to learn, they will go down "to make room for those who will be more able to cope with the problems of a new world."

Chapter II

"We are now facing the irrevocable fact of war. We are threatened by the horrors of invasion. The decision, today, is not for or against war; for us there can be but one question: By what means is this war to be conducted? Much, aye everything, is at stake for our people and its future, if Russian despotism, stained with the blood of its own people, should be the victor. This danger must be averted, the civilization and the independence of our people must be safeguarded. Therefore we will carry out what we have always promised: In the hour of danger we will not desert our fatherland. In this we feel that we stand in harmony with the International, which has always recognized the right of every people to its national independence, as we stand in agreement with the International in emphatically denouncing every war of conquest. Actuated by these motives, we vote in favour of the war credits demanded by the Government."

With these words[1] the Reichstag group issued the countersign that determined and controlled the position of the German working class during the war. Fatherland in danger, national defense, people's war for existence, "Kultur,"[2] liberty—these were the slo-

---

1. The words quoted are those of the statement of the Social Democratic members of the Reichstag, read out by Haase. Rosa Luxemburg's suspicion proved to be correct; the statement was drafted in consultation with and approved by the Government.

2. "Kultur"—a national, German culture. Part of the struggle for this culture—the Kulturkampf—were Bismarck's May laws of 1873, aimed against the Catholic Church, aimed at reducing the Church to a State department. 1500 priests were expelled, the Archbishops of Cologne and Posen were jailed. This led to an alliance, at trade union level, between the Catholics and the Social Democrats. In 1877 the laws were repealed with the exception of state supervision of schools and compulsory civil marriage. Jesuits, however, were excluded from German soil till 1904.

gans proclaimed by the parliamentary representatives of the Social Democracy. What followed was but the logical sequence. The position of the Party and the labor union press, the patriotic frenzy of the masses, the civil peace,[3] the disintegration of the International, all these things were the inevitable consequence of that momentous orientation in the Reichstag.

If it is true that this war is really a fight for national existence, for freedom, if it is true that these priceless possessions can be defended only by the iron tools of murder, if this war is the holy cause of the people, then everything else follows as a matter of course, we must take everything that the war may bring as a part of the bargain. He who desires the purpose must be satisfied with the means. War is methodical, organized, gigantic murder. But in normal human beings this systematic murder is possible only when a state of intoxication has been previously created. This has always been the tried and proven method of those who make war. Bestiality of action must find a commensurate bestiality of thought and senses; the latter must prepare and accompany the former. Thus the *Wahre Jacob*[4] of August 28, 1914, with its brutal picture of the German thresher, the Party papers of Chemnitz, Hamburg, Kiel, Frankfurt A.M., Koburg and others, with their patriotic drive in poetry and prose, were the necessary narcotic for a proletariat that could rescue its existence and its liberty only by plunging the deadly steel into its French and English brothers. These chauvinistic papers are after all a great deal more logical and consistent than those others who attempted to unite hill and valley, war with humanity, murder with brotherly love, the voting for war credits with socialist internationalism.

---

3. The concept of **"Burgfriede"** or civil peace was based on an old medieval custom, that private quarrels should cease when the castle was besieged. In Germany 1914, it meant the complete cessation of opposition and the class struggle. On August 3rd, the Kaiser declared: "I no longer know parties, I know only Germans. . ." The truce between classes was shortlived and on May 1st 1916, with the arrest of Karl Liebknecht, civil peace broke down completely.

In France, they had the "Union Sacree": M. Deschanel, in eulogizing Jaures, said: "There are no more adversaries here, there are only Frenchmen. . . ."

4. **Wahre Jacob** was a comic paper published by the German Social Democracy, selling about 371,000 copies.

If the stand taken by the German Reichstag group on the 4th of August was correct, then the death sentence of the proletarian International has been spoken, not only for this war, but for ever. For the first time since the modern labor movement exists there yawns an abyss between the commandments of international solidarity of the proletariat of the world and the interests of freedom and nationalist existence of the people; for the first time we discover that the independence and liberty of the nations command that working men kill and destroy each other. Up to this time we have cherished the belief that the interests of the people of all nations, that the class interests of the proletariat are a harmonious unit, that they are identical, that they cannot possibly come into conflict with one another. That was the basis of our theory and practice, the soul of our agitation. Were we mistaken in the cardinal point of our whole world philosophy? We are holding an inquest over international Socialism.

This world war is not the first crisis through which our international principles have passed. Our Party was first tried 45 years ago. At that time, on the 21st of July 1870, Wilhelm Liebknecht and August Bebel made the following historical declaration before the Reichstag:

"The present war is a dynastic war in the interest of the Bonaparte dynasty as the war of 1866 was conducted in the interest of the Hohenzollern dynasty.[5]

"We cannot vote for the funds which are demanded from the Reichstag to conduct this war because this would be, in effect, a vote of confidence in the Prussian Government. And we know that the Prussian Government by its action in 1866, prepared this war. At the same time we cannot vote against the budget, lest this be construed to mean that we support the conscienceless and criminal policies of Bonaparte.

"As opponents, on principle, of every dynastic war, as Socialist Republicans and members of the 'International Workingmen's

5. **The War of 1866.** In the words of Moltke, Chief of Staff, it "was a fight for hegemony . . . long contemplated and calmly prepared. . . ." Prussia, having secured the neutrality of Russia, France and Italy turned against its ally of 1884, and with lightning victories ending at Sadowa, defeated Austria, annexing new territories and establishing the domination of the Hohenzollerns over the North German Confederation, and ending the German Confederation.

Association'[6] which without regard to nationality has fought all oppressors, has tried to unite all the oppressed into a great band of brothers, we cannot directly or indirectly lend support to the present war. We therefore refuse to vote, while expressing the earnest hope that the peoples of Europe, taught by the present unholy events, will strive to win the right to control their own destinies, to do away with the present rule of might and class as the cause of all social and national evil."

With this declaration the representatives of the German proletariat put their cause clearly and unreservedly under the banner of the International and definitely repudiated the war against France as a national war of independence. It is well known that Bebel, many years later, in his memoirs, stated that he would have voted against the war loan had he known, when the vote was taken, the things that were revealed in the years that followed.

Thus, in a war that was considered by the whole bourgeois public and by a powerful majority of the people under the influence of Bismarckian strategy, as a war in the national life interest of Germany, the leaders of the German Social Democracy held firmly to the conviction that the life interest of a nation and the class interest of the proletariat are one, that both are opposed to war. It was left to the present world war and to the Social Democratic Reichstag group to uncover, for the first time, the terrible dilemma—either you are for national liberty—or for international socialism.

Now the fundamental fact in the declaration of our Reichstag group was, in all probability, a sudden inspiration. It was simply an echo of the Crown speech and of the Chancellor's speech of August 4th. "We are not driven by the desire for conquest," we hear in the Crown speech, "we are inspired by the unalterable determination to preserve the land upon which God has placed us for ourselves, and for all coming generations. From the documents that have been presented to you, you will have seen how

6. **The International Workingmen's Association:** The First International founded by Karl Marx and Friedrich Engels in 1864. In its "first phase" it served as the rallying point of various European national sections. After the Paris Commune, in 1872, the center was moved to New York. It was later dissolved.

My Government, and above all My Chancellor strove, to the last, to avert the utmost. We grasp the sword in self-defence, with a clear conscience and a clean hand." And Bethmann-Hollweg declared: "Gentlemen, we are acting in self-defence, and necessity knows no law. He who is threatened as we are threatened, he who is fighting for the highest aims can be guided by but one consideration, how best to beat his way out of the struggle. We are fighting for the fruits of our peaceful labour, for the heritage of our great past, for the future of our nation." Wherein does this differ from the Social Democratic declaration? 1. We have done everything to preserve peace, the war was forced upon us by others; 2. Now that the war is here we must act in self-defense; 3. In this war the German people is in danger of losing everything. This declaration of our Reichstag group is an obvious rehashing of the government declaration. As the latter based their claims upon diplomatic negotiations and imperial telegrams, so the socialist group points to peace demonstrations of the Social Democracy before the war. Where the Crown speech denies all aims of conquest, the Reichstag group repudiates a war of conquest by standing upon its Socialism. And when the Emperor and Chancellor cry out, "We are fighting for the highest principles. We know no parties, we know only Germans," the Social Democratic declaration echoes: "Our people risks everything. In this hour of danger we will not desert our Fatherland." Only in one point does the Social Democratic declaration differ from its government model, it placed the danger of Russian despotism in the foreground of its orientation, as a danger to German freedom. The Crown speech says, regarding Russia: "With a heavy heart I have been forced to mobilize against a neighbour with whom I have fought upon so many battlefields. With honest sorrow I have seen a friendship faithfully kept by Germany, fall to pieces." The Social Democratic group changed this sorrowful rupture of a true friendship with the Russian Czar into a fanfare for liberty against despotism, used the revolutionary heritage of socialism to give to the war a democratic mantle, a popular halo. Here alone the Social Democratic declaration gives evidence of independent thought on the part of our Social Democrats.

As we have said, all these things came to the Social Democracy as a sudden inspiration on the 4th of August. All that they had said up to this day, every declaration that they had made, down to the very eve of the war, was in diametrical opposition to the declaration of the Reichstag group. The *Vorwaerts*[7] wrote on July 25, when the Austrian ultimatum to Serbia was published:

"They want the war, the unscrupulous elements that influence and determine the Wiener Hofburg.[8] They want the war—it has been ringing out of the wild cries of the black-yellow press for weeks. They want the war—the Austrian ultimatum to Serbia makes it plain and clear to the world.

"Because the blood of Franz Ferdinand and his wife flowed under the shots of an insane fanatic, shall the blood of thousands of workers and farmers be shed? Shall one insane crime be purged by another even more insane? . . . The Austrian ultimatum may be the torch that will set Europe in flames at all four corners.

"For this ultimatum, in its form and in its demands, is so shameless, that a Serbian Government that should humbly retreat before this note, would have to reckon with the possibility of being driven out by the masses of the people between dinner and dessert. . . .

"It was a crime of the chauvinistic press of Germany to egg on our dear Ally to the utmost in its desire for war. And beyond a doubt, Herr von Bethmann-Hollweg promised Herr Berchtold our support. But Berlin is playing a game as dangerous as that being played by Vienna."

The *Leipziger Volkszeitung* wrote on July 24:

"The Austrian military party has staked everything on one card, for in no country in the world has national and military chauvinism anything to lose. In Austria chauvinistic circles are particularly bankrupt; their nationalistic howls are a frantic attempt to cover up Austria's economic ruin, the robbery and murder of war to fill its coffers. . . ."

7. **Voerwaerts:** (Forward). Central Organ of the German Social Democracy, published in Berlin 1891–1933, daily. Till October 1916, it was controlled by Left and Center groups.

The German Social Democracy, in addition, published a large number of other local dailies, which Rosa Luxemburg quotes in this pamphlet.

8. The **Wiener Hofburg** was the imperial palace in Vienna where the Emperor held Court.

The *Dresden Volkszeitung* said, on the same day:

"Thus far the war maniacs of the Wiener Ballplatz[9] have failed to furnish proof that would justify Austria in the demands it has made upon Serbia. So long as the Austrian Government is not in a position to do this, it places itself, by its provocative and insulting attacks upon Serbia, in a false position before all Europe. And even if Serbia's guilt was proven, even if the assassination in Sarajevo had actually been prepared under the eyes of the Serbian Government, the demands made in the note are far in excess of normal bounds. Only the most unscrupulous war lust can explain such demands upon another state. . . ."

The *Muenchener Post,* on July 25, wrote:

"This Austrian note is a document unequalled in the history of the last two centuries. Upon the findings of an investigation whose contents have, till now, been kept from the European public, without court proceedings against the murderer of the heir presumptive and his spouse, it makes demands on Serbia, the acceptance of which would mean national suicide to Serbia. . . ."

The *Schleswig-Holstein Volkszeitung* declared, on the 24th of July:

"Austria is provoking Serbia. Austria-Hungary wants war, and is committing a crime that may drown all Europe in blood. . . . Austria is playing *va banque.* It dares a provocation of the Serbian state that the latter, if it is not entirely defenceless, will certainly refuse to tolerate. . . .

"Every civilized person must protest emphatically against the criminal behaviour of the Austrian rulers. It is the duty of the workers above all, and of all other human beings who honour peace and civilization, to try their utmost to prevent the consequences of the bloody insanity that has broken out in Vienna."

The *Magdeburger Volksstimme* of July 25 said:

"Any Serbian Government that even pretended to consider these demands seriously would be swept out in the same hour by the Parliament and by the people.

---

9. The **Ballplatz** was the Foreign Office completely dominated by titled militarists.

"The action of Austria is the more despicable because Berchtold is standing before the Serbian Government and before Europe with empty hands.

"To precipitate a war such as this at the present time, means to invite a world war. To act thus shows a desire to disturb the peace of an entire hemisphere. One cannot thus make moral conquests, or convince non-participants of one's own righteousness. It can be safely assumed that the press of Europe, and with it the European governments, will call the vainglorious and senseless Viennese statesmen energetically and unmistakeably to order."

On July 24 the *Frankfurter Volksstimme* wrote:
"Upheld by the agitation of the clerical press, which mourns in Franz Ferdinand its best friend and demands that his death be avenged upon the Serbian people, upheld by German war patriots whose language becomes daily more contemptible and more threatening, the Austrian Government has allowed itself to be driven to send an ultimatum to Serbia couched in language that, for presumptiousness, leaves little to be desired; containing demands whose fulfilment by the Serbian Government is manifestly impossible."

On the same day the *Elberfelder Freie Presse* wrote:
"A telegram of the semi-official Wolff Bureau reports the terms of the demands made on Serbia by Austria. From these it may be gathered that the rulers in Vienna are pushing toward war with all their might. For the conditions imposed by the note that was presented in Belgrade last night are nothing short of a protectorate of Austria over Serbia. It is eminently necessary that the diplomats of Berlin make the war agitators of Vienna understand that Germany will not move a finger to support such outrageous demands, that a withdrawal of the threats would be advisable."

The *Bergische Arbeiterstimme* of Solingen writes:
"Austria demands a conflict with Serbia, and uses the assassination at Sarajevo as a pretext for putting Serbia morally in the wrong. But the whole matter has been approached too clumsily to influence European public opinion.

"But if the war agitators of the Wiener Ballplatz believe that their allies of the Triple Alliance,[10] Germany and Italy, will come to their assistance in a conflict in which Russia too will be involved, they are suffering from a dangerous illusion. Italy would welcome the weakening of Austria-Hungary, its rival on the Adriatic and in the Balkans, and would certainly decline to burn its fingers to help Austria. In Germany, on the other hand, the powers that be—even should they be so foolish as to wish it—would not dare to risk the life of a single soldier to satisfy the criminal lust for power of the Habsburgers without arousing the fury of the entire people."

Thus the entire working class press, without exception, judged the war's causes a week before its outbreak. Obviously the question was one of neither the existence nor the freedom of Germany, but a shameful adventure of the Austrian war party; not a question of self-defense, national protection and a holy war forced upon us in the name of freedom, but a bold provocation, an abominable threat against foreign, Serbian independence and liberty.

What was it that happened on August 4 to turn this clearly defined and so unanimously accepted attitude of the Social Democracy upside down? Only one new factor had appeared— the *White Book* that was presented to the Reichstag by the German Government on that day. And this contained, on page four the following:

"Under these circumstances Austria must say to itself that it is incompatible with the dignity and the safety of the monarchy to remain inactive any longer in the face of the occurrences across the border. The Austrian Imperial Government has notified us of this, their attitude, and has begged us to state our views. Out of a full heart we could but assure our Ally of our agreement with this interpretation of conditions and assure him that any action that would seem necessary to put an end to Serbian attempts against the existence of the Austrian monarchy would meet with

10. **The Triple Alliance:** Following the Dual Alliance of 1879 (Germany and Austria-Hungary) the Triple Alliance was formed in 1882 between Germany, Austria-Hungary and Italy. Rumania joined in 1883. It was repudiated by Italy in 1906 at the Algeciras Conference, and Italy finally joined the "Entente" nations (Britain, France, Russia) in 1915.

our approval. We fully realized that eventual war measures undertaken by Austria must bring Russia into the situation and that we, in order to carry out our duty as ally, might be driven into war. But we could not, realizing as we did that the most vital interests of Austria-Hungary were threatened, advise our Ally to adopt a policy of acquiescence, that could not possibly be brought into accord with its dignity, nor could we refuse to lend our aid in this attitude.

"And we were particularly prevented from taking this stand by the fact that the persistent subversive Serbian agitation seriously jeopardized us. If the Serbians had been permitted, with the aid of Russia and France, to continue to threaten the existence of the neighbouring monarchy, there would have ensued a gradual collapse of Austria and a subjection of all the Slavic races under the Russian sceptre, which would have rendered untenable the situation of the Germanic race in Central Europe. A morally weakened Austria, succumbing before the advance of Russian Pan-Slavism, would no longer be an ally on which we could count and depend, as we are obliged to do in view of the increasingly menacing attitude of our neighbours to the East and to the West. We therefore gave Austria a free hand in her proceedings against Serbia. We have had no share in the preparations."

These were the words that lay before the Social Democratic Reichstag group on August 4, the only important and determining phrases in the entire *White Book,* a concise declaration of the German Government beside which all other yellow, grey, blue, orange books on the diplomatic passages that preceded the war and its most immediate causes become absolutely irrelevant and insignificant. Here the Reichstag group had the key to a correct judgement of the situation in hand. The entire Social Democratic press, a week before, had cried out that the Austrian ultimatum was a criminal provocation of the world war and demanded preventative and pacific action on the part of the German Government. The entire socialist press assumed that the Austrian ultimatum had descended upon the German government like a bolt from the blue as it had upon the German public. But now the White Book declared, briefly and clearly: (1) that the Austrian Government had requested German sanction before taking a final step against Serbia, (2) that the German Government clearly understood that the action undertaken by Austria would lead to war with Serbia, and ultimately to European war, (3) that the German Government did not advise Austria to give in, but on the contrary declared that an acquiescent, weakened Austria could not be regarded as a worthy ally of Germany, (4) that the German Government assured Austria, before it advanced against Serbia, of its assistance under all circumstances, in case of war, and finally, (5) that the German Government, withal, had not reserved for itself control over the decisive ultimatum from Austria to Serbia, upon which the whole world war depended, but had left to Austria "an absolutely free hand."

All of this our Reichstag group learned on August 4. And still another fact it learned from the Government—that German forces already had invaded Belgium. And from all this the Social Democratic group concluded that this is a war of defense against foreign invasion, for the existence of the fatherland, for "Kultur," a war for liberty against Russian despotism.

Was the obvious background of the war, and the scenery that so scantily concealed it, was the whole diplomatic performance that was acted out at the outbreak of the war, with its clamor about a world of enemies, all threatening the life of Germany, all moved by the one desire to weaken, to humiliate, to subjugate the German people and nation—were all these things such a complete surprise? Did these factors actually call for more judgment, more critical sagacity than they possessed? Nowhere was this less true than of our Party. It had already gone through two great German wars, and in both of them had received memorable lessons.

Even a poorly informed student of history knows that the war of 1866 against Austria was systematically prepared by Bismarck long before it broke out, and that his policies from the very beginning led inevitably to a rupture and to war with Austria. The Crown Prince himself, the later Emperor Frederick, in his memoirs under the date of November 14 of that year, speaks of this purpose of the Chancellor:

"He (Bismarck), when he went into office, was firmly resolved to bring Prussia to a war with Austria, but was very careful not to betray this purpose, either at that time or on any other premature occasion to His Majesty, until the time seemed favourable."

"Compare with this confession," says Auer in his brochure *Die Sedanfeier und die Sozialdemokratie* "the proclamation that King William sent out '*to my people*':

'The Fatherland is in danger! Austria and a large part of Germany have risen in arms against us.

'It is only a few years ago since I, of my own free will, without thinking of former misunderstandings, held out a fraternal hand to Austria in order to save a German nation from foreign domination. But my hopes have been blasted. Austria cannot forget that its lords once ruled Germany; it refuses to see in the younger, more virile Prussia an ally, but persists in regarding it as a dangerous rival. Prussia—so it believes—must be opposed in all its aims, because whatever favours Prussia harms Austria. The old unholy jealousy has again broken out; Prussia is to be weakened, destroyed, dishonoured. All treaties with Prussia are void, German lords are not only called upon, but persuaded, to sever their alliance with Prussia. Wherever we look, in Germany, we are surrounded by enemies whose war cry is—Down with Prussia!' "

Praying for the blessings of heaven, King William ordered a general day of prayer and penance for the 18th of July, saying:

"It has not pleased God to crown with success my attempts to preserve the blessings of peace for my people."

Should not the official accompaniment to the outbreak of the war on August 4th have awakened in the minds of our group vivid memories of long remembered words and melodies? Had they completely forgotten their party history?

But not enough! In the year 1870 there came the war with France, and history has united its outbreak with an unforgettable occurrence: the Ems dispatch,[11] a document that has become a classic byword for capitalist-government art in war making, and which marks a memorable episode in our party history. Was it not old Liebknecht, was it not the German Social Democracy who felt in duty bound, at that time, to disclose these facts and to show to the masses "how wars are made?"

Making war simply and solely for the protection of the Father-

11. **Ems Despatch:** See Note 8, chapter I.

land was, by the way, not Bismarck's invention. He only carried out, with characteristic unscrupulousness, an old, well-known and truly international recipe of capitalist statesmanship. When and where has there been a war since so-called public opinion has played a role in governmental calculations, in which each and every belligerent party did not, with a heavy heart, draw the sword from its sheath for the single and sole purpose of defending its Fatherland and its own righteous cause from the shameful attacks of the enemy? This legend is as inextricably a part of the game of war as powder and lead. The game is old. Only the Social Democratic Party's playing it is new.

Chapter III

Our Party should have been prepared to recognize the real aims of this war, to meet it without surprise, to judge it by its deeper relationship according to their wide political experience. The events and forces that led to August 4, 1914 were no secrets. The world had been preparing for decades, in broad daylight, in the widest publicity, step by step and hour by hour, for the world war. And if today a number of socialists threaten with horrible destruction the "secret diplomacy" that has brewed this deviltry behind the scenes, they are ascribing to these poor wretches a magic power that they little deserve, just as the Botokude[1] whips his fetish for the outbreak of a storm. The so-called captains of nations are, in this war, as at all times, merely chessmen moved by all-powerful historic events and forces on the surface of capitalist society. If ever there were persons capable of understanding these events and occurrences, it was the members of the German Social Democracy.

Two lines of development in recent history lead straight to the present war. One has its origin in the period when the so-called national states, i.e., the modern states, were first constituted from the time of the Bismarckian war against France. The war of 1870, which, by the annexation of Alsace-Lorraine, threw the French Republic into the arms of Russia, split Europe into two opposing camps and opened up a period of insane competitive armament, first piled up the fire-brands for the present world conflagration. Bismarck's troops were still stationed in France when Marx wrote to the *Braunschweiger Ausschuss*:

"He who is not deafened by the momentary clamour and is

---

1. **Botokudes:** South American natives of the Amazon Basin, Brazil.

not interested in deafening the German people, must see that the war of 1870 carries with it, of necessity, a war between Germany and Russia, just as the war of 1866 bore the war of 1870. I say of necessity, unless the unlikely should happen, unless a revolution breaks out in Russia before that time. If this does not occur, a war between Germany and Russia may even now be regarded as 'un fait accompli.' It depends entirely upon the attitude of the German victor to determine whether this war has been useful or dangerous. If they take Alsace-Lorraine, then France with Russia will arm against Germany. It is superfluous to point out the disastrous consequences."

At that time this prophecy was laughed down. The bonds which united Russia and Prussia seemed so strong that it was considered madness to believe in a union of autocratic Russia with Republican France. Those who supported this conception were laughed at as madmen. And yet everything that Marx has prophesied has happened, to the last letter. "For that is," says Auer in his *Sedanfeier,* "Social Democratic politics, seeing things clearly as they are, and differing therein from the day-by-day politics of the others, bowing blindly down before every momentary success."

This must not be misunderstood to mean that the desire for revenge for the robbery accomplished by Bismarck has driven the French into a war with Germany, that the kernel of the present war is to be found in the much discussed "revenge for Alsace-Lorraine." This is the convenient nationalist legend of the German war agitator, who creates fables of a darkly-brooding France that "cannot forget" its defeat, just as the Bismarckian press-servants ranted of the dethroned Princess Austria who could not forget her erstwhile superiority over the charming Cinderella Prussia. As a matter of fact revenge for Alsace-Lorraine has become the theatrical property of a couple of patriotic clowns, the "Lion de Belfort"[2] nothing more than an ancient survival.

The annexation of Alsace-Lorraine long ago ceased to play a role in French politics, being superseded by new, more pressing

2. **Lion de Belfort:** A 36-foot high sculpture by F. A. Bartholdi commemorating the seige of Belfort (November 3, 1870–February 15, 1871) during the Franco-Prussian war. The town was completely cut off from the main French forces, was shelled and lost 4750 men.

cares; and neither the government nor any serious party in France thought of a war with Germany because of these territories. If nevertheless, the Bismarck heritage has become the firebrand that started this world conflagration, it is rather in the sense of having driven Germany on the one hand, and France, and with it all of Europe, on the other, along the downward path of military competition, of having brought about the Franco-Russian alliance, of having united Austria with Germany as an inevitable consequence. This gave to Russian Czarism a tremendous prestige as a factor in European politics. Germany and France have systematically fawned before Russia for her favor. At that time the links were forged that united Germany with Austria-Hungary, whose strength, as the words quoted from the *White Book* show, lie in their "brotherhood in arms" in the present war.

Thus the war of 1870 brought in its wake the outward political grouping of Europe about the axes of the Franco-German antagonisı , and established the rule of militarism in the lives of the European peoples. Historical development has given to this rule and to this grouping an entirely new content. The second line that leads to the present world war, and which again brilliantly justifies Marx's prophesy, has its origin in international occurrences that Marx did not live to see, in the imperialist development of the last twenty-five years.

The growth of capitalism, spreading out rapidly over a reconstituted Europe after the war period of the 1860's and 1870's, particularly after the long period of depression that followed the inflation and the panic of the year 1873, reaching an unnatural zenith in the prosperity of the 1890's opened up a new period of storm and danger among the nations of Europe. They were competing in their expansion toward the noncapitalist countries and zones of the world. As early as the 1880's a strong tendency toward colonial expansion became apparent. England secured control of Egypt and created for itself, in South Africa, a powerful colonial empire. France took possession of Tunis in North Africa and Tonkin in East Asia; Italy gained a foothold in Abyssinia; Russia accomplished its conquests in Central Asia and pushed forward into Manchuria; Germany won its first colonies in Africa and in the South Sea, and the United States joined the circle when it procured the Phillipines with "interests" in Eastern

Asia. This period of feverish conquests has brought on, beginning with the Chinese-Japanese War in 1895, a practically uninterrupted chain of bloody wars, reaching its height in the Great Chinese invasion, and closing with the Russo-Japanese War of 1904.[3]

All these occurrences, coming blow upon blow, created new, extra-European antagonisms on all sides: between Italy and France in Northern Africa, between France and England in Egypt, between England and Russia in Central Asia, between Russia and Japan in Eastern Asia, between Japan and England in China, between the United States and Japan in the Pacific Ocean—a very restless ocean, full of sharp conflicts and temporary alliances, of tension and relaxation, threatening every few years to break out into a war between European powers. It was clear to everybody, therefore, that the secret underhand war of each capitalist nation against every other, on the backs of Asiatic and African peoples must sooner or later lead to a

3. England took Egypt from Turkey in 1881, and consolidated its hold on South Africa after the Boer War of October 1899–May 1902. France, having been given a free hand in Tunisia by Britain in return for having been permitted to annex Cyprus, established a "protectorate" over Tunisia by the Treaty of Kassar, May 11, 1881. Tunisia achieved independence only in 1956. The French invasion of Tonkin (presently in North Vietnam) dated from 1873. Russia expanded into Central Asia following the Treaty of Berlin 1878 which forced her to cede the conquests of the Russo-Turkish war. Italy's fortunes in Abyssinia fluctuated from 1869 to the 1889 Treaty; in 1896 Italy was defeated, and the war ended for the time with the Treaty of Addis Ababa, October 1896. After the Spanish American War and Peace of 1898, the United States of America annexed Guam, Puerto Rico and the Philippines. Germany annexed the Cameroons and Togoland in 1884; exchanged Zanzibar for the Heligoland with Britain in 1890. In 1897 it compelled China to "lease" Tsingtau in the Kiachow Bay for 99 years, and the German flag finally flew in the Far East.

The Sino-Japanese War of 1895 came to a quick end when Germany, Russia and France stopped Japan. Hostilities began in Korea and at sea in July-August 1894. By the peace treaty at Shimoneseki on April 17, 1895 Japan got Formosa, Liaotung Peninsula and the Pescadores, while Korea gained its independence.

The Russo-Japanese War began on February 8, 1904 when Japan attacked Port Arthur without warning. After a long siege, Port Arthur surrendered on January 2, 1905. In March, Mukden fell. May 27–28, the entire Russian fleet was sunk at Tsushima. On the intervention of Theodore Roosevelt, the Peace Treaty of Portsmouth was signed. Russia lost Port Arthur, its lease of Kwantung and was forced to evacuate Manchuria and the half of Sakhalin Island she had occupied since 1875.

general reckoning, that the wind that was sown in Africa and Asia, would return to Europe as a terrific storm, the more certainly since increased armament of the European States was the constant associate of these Asiatic and African occurrences; and that the European world war would have to come to an outbreak as soon as the partial and changing conflicts between the imperialist states found a centralized axis, a conflict of sufficient magnitude to group them for the time being into large, opposing factions. This situation was created by the appearance of German imperialism.

In Germany one may study the development of imperialism, crowded as it was into the shortest possible space of time, in concrete form. The unprecedented rapidity of German industrial and commercial development since the foundation of the Empire, brought out during the 1880's two characteristically peculiar forms of capitalist accumulation: the most pronounced growth of monopoly in Europe and the best developed and most concentrated banking system in the whole world. The monopolies have organized the steel and iron industry, i.e., the branch of capitalist endeavor most interested in government orders, in militaristic equipment and in imperialistic undertakings (railroad building, the exploitation of mines, etc.) into the most influential factor in the nation. The latter has cemented the money interests into a firmly organized whole with the greatest, most virile energy, creating a power that autocratically rules the industry, commerce and credit of the nation, dominating in private as well as public affairs, boundless in its powers of expansion, ever hungry for profit and activity, impersonal, and therefore, liberal-minded, reckless and unscrupulous, international by its very nature, ordained by its capacities to use the world as its stage.

Germany is under a personal regime with strong initiative and spasmodic activity, with the weakest kind of parliamentarism, incapable of opposition, uniting all capitalist strata in the sharpest opposition to the working class. It is obvious that this live, unhampered imperialism, coming upon the world stage at a time when the world was practically divided up, with gigantic appetites, soon became an irresponsible factor of general unrest.

This was already foreshadowed by the radical upheaval that

took place in the military polices of the Empire at the end of the 1890's. At that time two naval budgets were introduced which doubled the naval power of Germany and provided for a naval program covering almost two decades. This meant a sweeping change in the financial and trade policy of the nation. In the first place, it involved a striking change in the foreign policy of the Empire. The policy of Bismarck was founded upon the principle that the Empire is and must remain a land power, that the German fleet, at best, is but a very dispensable requisite for coastal defense. Even the secretary of state, Hollmann declared in March 1897, in the Budget Commission of the Reichstag: "We need no navy for coastal defence. Our coasts protect themselves." With the two naval bills an entirely new program was promulgated: on land and sea, Germany first! This marks the change from Bismarckian continental policies to "Welt-Politik,"[4] from the defensive to the offensive as the end and aim of Germany's military program. The language of these facts was so unmistakable that the Reichstag itself furnished the necessary commentary. Lieber, the leader of the Centrum[5] at that time, spoke on March 11, 1896, after a famous speech of the Emperor on the occasion of the twenty-fifth anniversary of the founding of the German Empire, which had developed the new program as a forerunner to the naval bills in which he mentioned "shoreless naval plans" against which Germany must be prepared to enter into active opposition. Another Centrum leader, Schadler, cried out in the Reichstag on March 23, 1898 when the first naval bill was under discussion, "The nation believes that we cannot be first on land and first on sea. You answer, gentlemen, that is

4. **Welt-Politik:** (German)—World politics (as opposed to European politics) Bismarck's ambition to have Germany recognized as a world power was realized in 1878 when he presided at the Treaty of Berlin, during the Anglo-Russian crisis.

5. **Centrum**—The Center, the Roman Catholic Party of Germany, founded 1870, so named because they sat in the Center of the Reichstag Chamber. The party also maneuverd between the Government and the Left during and after the "Kulturkampf."

The National Liberals were the industrialists and shipowners.

Conservatives were the Junkers who held safe seats East of the Elbe, semi-feudal, anti-semitic militarists.

Progressives or Radicals were a middle class organization opposed to the Junkers and Bismarck, free-traders, led by Eugene Richter (1838–1906).

not what we want! Nevertheless, gentlemen, you are at the beginning of such a conception, at a very strong beginning!" When the second bill came, the same Schadler declared in the Reichstag on February 5, 1900 referring to previous promises that there would be no further naval bills, "and today comes this bill, which means nothing more and nothing less than the inauguration of a world fleet, as a basis of support for world policies, by doubling our navy and binding the next two decades by our demands." As a matter of fact the government openly defended the political program of its new course of action. On December 11, 1899 von Bulow, at that time State Secretary of the Foreign Office, in a defense of the second naval bill stated, "when the English speak of 'a greater Britain,' when the French talk of 'la nouvelle France',[6] when the Russians open up Asia for themselves, we too have a right to aspire to a greater Germany. If we do not create a navy sufficient to protect our trade, our natives in foreign lands, our missions and the safety of our shores, we are threatening the most vital interests of our nation. In the coming century the German people will be either the hammer or the anvil." Strip this of its coastal defense ornamentation, and there remains the colossal program: greater Germany, as the hammer upon other nations.

It is not difficult to determine the direction toward which these provocations, in the main, were directed. Germany was to become the rival of the world's great naval force—England. And England did not fail to understand. The naval reform bills, and the speeches that ushered them in, created a lively unrest in England, an unrest that has never again subsided. In March, 1910 Lord Robert Cecil said in the House of Commons, during a naval debate: "I challenge any man to give me a plausible reason for the tremendous navy that Germany is building up, other than to take up the fight against England." The fight for supremacy on the ocean that lasted for one and a half decades on both sides and culminated in the feverish building of dreadnoughts and super-dreadnoughts, was, in effect, the war between Germany and England. The naval bill of December 11,

6. **La Nouvelle France**—"The New France"

1899 was a declaration of war by Germany, which England answered on August 4, 1914.

It should be noted that this fight for naval supremacy had nothing in common with the economic rivalry for the world market. The English "monopoly of the world market" which ostensibly hampered German industrial development, so much discussed at the present time, really belongs to the sphere of those war legends of which the ever green French "Revanche"[7] is the most useful. This "monopoly" had become an old time fairy tale to the lasting regret of the English capitalists. The industrial development of France, Belgium, Italy, Russia, India and Japan, and above all, of Germany and America, had put an end to this monopoly of the first half of the nineteenth century. Side by side with England, one nation after another stepped into the world market, capitalism developed automatically, and with gigantic strides, into world economy.

English supremacy on the sea, which has robbed so many Social Democrats of their peaceful sleep, and which, it seems to these gentlemen, must be destroyed to preserve international socialism, had, up to this time, disturbed German capitalism so little that the latter was able to grow up into a lusty youth, with bursting cheeks, under its "yoke." Yes, England itself, and its colonies, were the cornerstones for German industrial growth. And similarly, Germany became, for the English nation, its most important and most necessary customer. Far from standing in each other's way, British and German capitalist development were mutually highly interdependent, and united by a far-reaching system of division of labor, strongly augmented by England's free trade policy. German trade and its interests in the world market, therefore, had nothing whatever to do with a change of front in German politics and with the building of its fleet.

Nor did German colonial possessions at that time come into conflict with the English control of the seas. German colonies were not in need of protection by a first-class sea power. No

7. **Revanche**—(French) Revenge. In this case, revenge for the defeat of Sedan and the loss of Alsace-Lorraine.

one, certainly not England, envied Germany her possessions. That they were taken during the war by England and Japan, that the booty had changed owners, is but a generally accepted war measure, just as German imperialist appetites clamor for Belgium, a desire that no man outside of an insane asylum would have dared to express in time of peace. Southeast and Southwest Africa, Wilhelmsland or Tsingtau would never have caused any war, by land or by sea, between Germany and England. In fact, just before the war broke out, a treaty regulating a peaceable division of the Portuguese colonies in Africa between these two nations had been practically completed.[8]

When Germany unfolded its banner of naval power and world policies it announced the desire for new and far reaching conquest in the world by German imperialism. By means of a first class aggressive navy, and by military forces that increased in a parallel ratio, the apparatus for a future policy was established, opening wide the doors for unprecedented possibilities. Naval building and military armaments became the glorious business of German industry, opening up a boundless prospect for further operations by trust and bank capital in the whole wide world. Thus, the acquiescence of all capitalist parties and their rallying under the flag of imperialism was assured. The Centrum followed the example of the National Liberals, the staunchest defenders of the steel and iron industry, and, by adopting the naval bill it had loudly denounced in 1900, became the party of the government. The Progressives trotted after the Centrum when the successor to the naval bill—the high-tariff party—came up; while the Junkers, the staunchest opponents of the "horrid navy" and of the Canal brought up the rear as the most enthusiastic porkers and parasites of the very policy of sea-militarism and colonial robbery they had so vehemently opposed. The Reichstag election of 1907, the so-called Hottentot

8. Following an original agreement of August 30, 1898, Britain and Germany agreed, on August 13, 1913, upon spheres of influence in Portugal's African Colonies in the event of Portugal applying for a state loan backed by its colonial revenue. The agreement was finalized on October 20, 1913. At the same time discussions took place on the Berlin-Baghdad railway, but there was no final agreement as the war broke out.

Elections,[9] found the whole of Germany in a paroxysm of imperialistic enthusiasm, firmly united under one flag, that of the Germany of von Bulow, the Germany that felt itself ordained to play the role of the hammer in the world. These elections, with their spiritual pogrom atmosphere, were a prelude to the Germany of August 4, a challenge not only to the German working class, but to other capitalist nations as well, a challenge directed to no one in particular, a mailed fist shaken in the face of the entire world.

9. In 1906, in German West Africa, some 80,000 Herreros and 10,000 Hottentots rose in rebellion. General Trotha's troops killed them all, taking no prisoners. Some 10,000 men, women and children were forced into the Kalahari desert to die of thirst and starvation. In 1907 at the elections, known as the Hottentot elections, the Social Democracy which had refused to vote for war credits in 1906, dropped its representation from its 81 seats (since 1903 elections) to 43, although it increased its vote by 8 per cent. In 1912, however the Social Democracy gained 110 seats with 34.9 per cent of the total vote.

Chapter IV

Turkey became the most important field of operations of German imperialism; the Deutsche Bank, with its enormous Asiatic business interests, about which all German oriental policies centre, became its peacemaker. In the 1850's and 1860's Asiatic Turkey worked chiefly with English capital which built the railroad from Smyrna, and leased the first stretch of the Anatolian railroad up to Ismit. In 1888 German capital appeared upon the scene and produced from Abdul Hamid the control of the railroad that English capital had built and the franchise for the new stretch from Ismit to Angora and branch lines to Scutari, Bursa, Konya and Kaizarili. In 1899 the Deutsche Bank secured concessions for the building and operation of a harbor and improvements in Hardar Pasha, and the sole control over trade and tariff collections in the harbor. In 1901 the Turkish Government turned over to the Deutsche Bank the concession for the Great Baghdad railroad[1] to the Persian Gulf, and in 1907 a concession for the drainage of the Sea of Karaviran and the irrigation of the Koma plain.

The reverse of this wonderful work of "peaceful culture" is the "peaceful" and wholesale ruin of the farming population of Asia Minor. The cost of this tremendous undertaking was advanced, of course, by the Deutsche Bank on the security of a widely diversified system of public indebtedness. Turkey will be, to all eternity, the debtor of Messrs. Siemens, Gwinner, Helfferich,

---

1. **The Berlin-Baghdad railroad,** as a Eurasian axis with oil on both sides of it (Rumania and Iraq) and a short route to the Indian Ocean, was mooted in 1871 by Wilhelm I and the Deutsche Bank. Abdul Hamid granted the concession in 1899. Britain supported the idea as against the Czar and opposed it for its own fears. Britain had her plans for a railroad from Cape to Cairo, while the Russians planned one from St. Petersburg to the Persian Gulf.

etc., as it was formerly that of English, French and Austrian capital. This debtor was forced not only to squeeze enormous sums out of the state to pay the interest on these loans, but, in addition, to guarantee a net income upon the railway thus built. The most modern methods of transportation were grafted upon a primitive, in many cases purely agricultural, population. From the unfruitful soil of farming sections that had been exploited unscrupulously for years by an oriental despotism, producing scarcely enough to feed the population after the huge state debts had been paid, it is practically impossible to secure the profits demanded by the railroads. Freight and travelling are exceedingly undeveloped, since the industrial and cultural character of the region is most primitive, and can improve only at a slow rate. The deficit that must be paid to raise the required profit is, therefore, paid by the Turkish Government in the form of a so-called kilometer guarantee. European Turkey was built up according to this system by Austrian and French capital, and the same system has been adopted by the Deutsche Bank in its operations in Asiatic Turkey. As bond and surety that the subsidy will be paid, the Turkish Government has handed over to the representatives of European capital, the so-called Executive Board in control of public debt, the main source of Turkish national income, which has given to the Deutsche Bank the right to collect the tithe from a number of provinces. In this way, for instance, the Turkish Government paid, from 1893 to 1910, for the railroad to Angora and for the line from Eskishehir to Konya, a subsidy of about 9,000,000 francs. The tithes thus leased by the Turkish Government to its European creditors are ancient payments rendered in produce such as corn, sheep, silk, etc. They are not collected directly but through sub-lessees, somewhat similar to the famous tax-collectors so notorious in pre-revolutionary France, the state selling the right to raise the amount required from each vilayet (province) by auction, against cash payment. When the speculator or company has thus procured the right to collect the tithe of a vilayet, it, in turn, sells the tithe of each individual sanjak (district) to other speculators, who again divide their portion among a veritable band of smaller agents. Since each one of these collectors must not only cover his own expenses but secure as large a profit as possible besides, the tithe grows like a landslide as it approaches the farmer. If the lessee has been mistaken in his calculation, he seeks to recompense himself at the expense of the farmer. The latter, practically always in debt, waits impatiently for the time when he can sell his crop. But after his grain is cut he must frequently wait for weeks before the tithe collector comes to take his portion. The collector, who is usually a graindealer as well, exploits this need of the farmer whose crop threatens to rot in the field, and persuades him to sell at a reduced price, knowing full well that it will be easy to secure the assistance of public officials and particularly of the muktar (town mayor) against the dissatisfied. When no tax collector can be found the government itself collects the tithe in produce, puts it into storage houses and turns it over as part payment to the capitalists. This is the inner mechanism of the "industrial regeneration of Turkey" by European capital.

Thus a twofold purpose is accomplished. The farming population of Asia Minor becomes the object of a well organized process of exploitation in the interest of European, in this case German, financial and industrial capital. This again promotes the growth of the German sphere of interest in Turkey and lays the foundation for Turkey's "political protection." At the same time the instrument that carries out the exploitation of the farming population, the Turkish Government, becomes the willing tool and vassal of Germany's foreign policies. For many years Turkish finance, tariff policies, taxation and state expenditures have been under European control. German influence has made itself particularly felt in the Turkish military organization.

It is obvious from the foregoing, that the interests of German imperialism demand the protection of the Turkish State, to the extent at least of preventing its complete disintegration. The liquidation of Turkey would mean its division between England, Russia, Italy, and Greece among others and the basis for a large-scale operation by German capital would vanish. Moreover, an extraordinary increase in the power of Russia, England and the Mediterranean States would result. For German imperialism, therefore, the preservation of this accommodating apparatus of the "independent Turkish State," the "integrity" of Turkey is a matter of necessity. And this necessity will exist until such time as this state will fall, having been consumed from within by German capital, as was Egypt by England and more recently Morocco by France, into the lap of Germany. The well-known spokesman of German imperialism, Paul Rohrbach, expressed this candidly and honestly in his book *The War and German Policy:*

"In the very nature of things Turkey, surrounded on all sides by envious neighbours, must seek the support of a power that has practically no teritorial interests in the Orient. That power is Germany. We, on the other hand, would be at a disadvantage if Turkey should disappear. If Russia and England fall heir to the Turkish state, obviously it will mean to both of these states a considerable increase in power. But even if Turkey should be so divided that we should also secure an extensive portion, it would mean for us endless difficulties. Russia, England, and in a certain sense France and Italy as well, are neighbours of present Turkish possessions and are in a position to hold and defend their portion by land and by sea. But we have no direct connection with the Orient. A German Asia Minor or Mesopotamia can become a reality only if Russia, and in consequence France as well, should be forced to relinquish their present political aims and ideals, i.e., if the world war should take a decisive turn in favour of German interests."[2]

Germany swore solemnly on November 8, 1898 in Damascus, by the shade of the great Saladin, to protect and to preserve the Mohammedan world and the green flag of the Prophet, and in so doing strengthened the regime of the bloody Sultan Abdul Hamid for over a decade. It has been able, after a short period of enstrangment, to exert the same influence upon the Young Turk regime.[2] Aside from conducting the profitable business of

2. **The Young Turks:** Or the Committee of Union and Progress were an essentially military organization. On July 23, 1908 they compelled Sultan Abdul Hamid II to proclaim a constitution. On the Sultan's attempt early in 1909 to stage a counterrevolution with the help of the counterrevolutionary Moslem Brotherhood (Istanbul was held by them for three days), he was deposed on April 23. In May-June 1912, "Saviour Officers," another counterrevolutionary group was formed, and on July 17 they compelled the Government to resign. The Committee of Union and Progress was ousted. On January 23, 1913, a coup d'etat took place and Turkey was from then till 1922 under the dictatorship of a triumvirate of Pashas.

the Deutsche Bank, the German mission busied itself chiefly
with the reorganization and training of Turkish militarism,
under German instructors with von der Goltz Pasha at the head.
The modernization of the army, of course, piled new burdens
upon the Turkish farmers, but it was a splendid business arrangement for Krupp and the Deutsche Bank. At the same time
Turkish militarism became entirely dependent upon Prussian
militarism, and became the center of German ambitions in the
Mediterranean and in Asia Minor.

That this "regeneration" of Turkey is a purely artificial attempt to galvanize a corpse, the fate of the Turkish revolutions
best shows. In the first stage, while ideal considerations still
predominated in the Young Turkish movement, when it was still
fired with ambitious plans and illusions of a real springtime of
life and of a rejuvenation for Turkey, its political sympathies
were decidedly in favor of England. This country seemed to
them to represent the ideal state of modern liberal rule, while
Germany, which has so long played the role of protector of the
holy regime of the old Sultan was felt to be its natural opponent. For a while it seemed as if the revolution of 1908 would
mean the bankruptcy of German oriental policies. It seemed
certain that the overthrow of Abdul Hamid would go hand in
hand with the downfall of German influence. As the Young
Turks assumed power, however, and showed their complete in-
ability to carry out any modern industrial, social or national
reform on a large scale, as the counterrevolutionary hoof became
more and more apparent, they turned of necessity to the tried
and proven methods of Abdul Hamid, which meant periodic
bloody massacres of oppressed peoples, goaded on until they
flew at each other's throats. Boundless, truly oriental exploitation
of the farming population became the foundation of the nation.
The artificial restoration of rule by force again became the most
important consideration for "Young Turkey" and the traditional
alliance of Abdul Hamid with Germany was re-established
as the deciding factor in the foreign policy of Turkey.

The multiplicity of national problems that threaten to dis-
rupt the Turkish nation make its regeneration a hopeless undertaking. The Armenian, Kurdian, Syrian, Arabian, Greek, and
(up to the most recent times) the Albanian and Macedonian

questions, the manifold economic and social problems that exist in the different parts of the realm are a serious menace. The growth of a strong, hopeful capitalism in the neighboring Balkan states and the long years of destructive activity of international capital and international diplomacy stamp every attempt to hold together this rotting pile of timber as nothing but a reactionary undertaking. This has long been apparent, particularly to the German Social Democracy. As early as 1896, at the time of the Cretan uprising,[3] the German Party press was filled with long discussions on the Oriental problem, that led to a revision of the attitude taken by Marx at the time of the Crimean War[4] and to definite repudiation of the "integrity of Turkey" as a heritage of European reaction. Nowhere was the Young Turkish regime, its inner sterility and its counterrevolutionary character, so quickly and so thoroughly recognized as in the German Social Democratic press. It was a real Prussian idea, this building of strategic railroads for rapid mobilization, this sending of capable military instructors to prop up the crumbling edifice of the Turkish state.

In 1912 the Young Turkish regiment was forced to abdicate to the counterrevolution. Characteristically, the first act of "Turkish regeneration" in this war was a coup d'etat, the annihilation of the constitution. In this respect too there was a formal return to the rule of Abdul Hamid.

The first Balkan war[5] brought bankruptcy to Turkish milita-

3. **Cretan Uprising:** In 1897, the Christian peoples of Crete, which had been conquered by Turkey 1645–1669, rose against their rulers with the help of Greece, and the Turks, though victorious in the war, were forced to withdraw in November 1898. Crete was placed under European trusteeship. In March 1905, another insurrection took place under the leadership of Venizelos. This lasted till 1906, and in 1907, a new constitution was proclaimed, and the island annexed to Greece.

4. **Crimean War:** Britain, France and Turkey fought Russia in 1854-56 for the control of Crimea. Piedmont (Italy) joined them in 1855. On September 8, 1855 Sevastopol was taken from the Russians and they were soon defeated.

5. **Balkan Wars:** The first, broke out in October 1912. The Turks were pushed back to Constantinople. It ended with the Treaty of London, May 30, 1913. Turkey was forced to give up all claims to its former European possessions. Albania was created as a new state. In June 1913, the Second Balkan War began: Bulgaria attacked Serbia and Greece, and Rumania and Turkey opposed Bulgaria. It ended with the Treaty of Bucharest, July 30, 1913. Italy invaded Albania in 1914.

rism, in spite of German training. And the present war, into which Turkey was precipitated as Germany's "charge," will lead, with inevitable fatality, to the further or to the final liquidation of the Turkish Empire.

The position of German militarism—and its essence, the interests of the Deutsche Bank—has brought the German Empire in the Orient into opposition to all other nations. Above all to England. The latter had not only rival business relations and fat profits in Mesopotamia and Anatolia which were forced to retreat before their German rivals. This was a situation that English capitalism grudgingly accepted. But the building of strategic railroad, and the strengthening of Turkish militarism under German influence was felt by England to be a sore point, in a strategic question of its world political relations; lying as it did at the cross roads between Central Asia, Persia and India, on the one side, and Egypt on the other.

"England," writes Rohrbach in his *Baghdadbahn*, "can be attacked and mortally wounded on land in Egypt. The loss of Egypt will mean to England not only the loss of control over the Suez Canal and its connections with India and Asia, but probably the sacrifice of its possessions in Central and Eastern Africa as well. A Mohamedan power like Turkey, moreover could exercise a dangerous influence over the sixty millions of Mohammedan subjects of England in India, in Afghanistan and Persia, should Turkey conquer Egypt. But Turkey can subjugate Egypt only if it possesses an extended system of railroads in Asia Minor and Syria, if by an extension of the Anatolian Railway it is able to ward off an English attack upon Mesopotamia, if it increases and improves its army, if its general economic and financial conditions are improved."

And in his *The War and German Policy*, which was published after the outbreak of the war, he says:

"The Baghdad Railroad was destined from the start to bring Constantinople and the military strongholds of the Turkish Empire in Asia Minor into direct connection with Syria and the provinces on the Euphrates and on the Tigris. Of course it was to be foreseen that this railway, together with the projected and, partly or wholly, completed railroads in Syria and Arabia, would make it possible to use Turkish troops in the direction of Egypt.

No one will deny that, should the Turkish-German alliance remain in force, and under a number of other important conditions whose realization will be even more difficult than this alliance, the Baghdad railway is a political life insurance policy for Germany."

Thus the semi-official spokesman of German imperialism openly revealed its plan and its aims in the Orient. Here German policies were clearly marked out, and an aggressive fundamental tendency most dangerous for the existing balance of world power, with a clearly defined point against England, was disclosed. German oriental policies became the concrete commentary to the naval policy inaugurated in 1899.

With its program for Turkish integrity, Germany came into conflict with the Balkan states, whose historic completion and inner growth are dependent upon the liquidation of European Turkey. It came into conflict with Italy, finally, whose imperialistic appetite was likewise longing for Turkish possessions. At the Morocco Conference at Algeciras[6] in 1905, Italy already sided with England and France. Six years later the Italian expedition to Tripoli,[7] which followed the Austrian annexation of Bosnia and gave the signal for the Balkan War, already indicated a withdrawal of Italy, foreshadowed the disruption of the Triple Alliance[8] and the isolation of German policies on this side as well. The other tendency of German expansionist desires in the West became evident in the Morocco affair.[9] Nowhere was the negation of the Bismarck policy in Germany more clearly shown. Bismarck, as is well known, supported the colonial aspirations of France in order to distract its attention from Alsace-

6. **Algeciras Conference:** When a crisis between France and Britain (who had entered into an "Entente Cordiale" in 1904) on the one hand, and Germany and Austria Hungary on the other threatened with the Kaiser's personal attempt to lead an expedition to Tangier Morocco in March 1905, Theodore Roosevelt organized a conference in Algeciras, Spain on 16 January 1906. An agreement was signed on April 7, 1906, but the Morocco crisis was to brew again.

7. **Tripoli** which had been under Turkish rule from 1551, was attacked by Italy in September 1911. Turkey was defeated, but the local population put up a courageous resistance. Under the Treaty of Lausanne, October 1912, Tripoli and Cyrenaica became Italian colonies and remained so till 1943.

8. **Triple Alliance:** See Note 10, chapter II.

9. See Notes 13 and 14, chapter I.

Lorraine. The new course of Germany, on the other hand, ran exactly counter to French colonial expansion. Conditions in Morocco were quite different from those that prevailed in Asiatic Turkey. Germany had few legitimate interests in Morocco. To be sure, German imperialists puffed up the claims of the German firm of Mannesmann, which had made a loan to the Moroccan Sultan and demanded mining concessions in return, into a national issue. But the well known fact that both of these rival groups in Morocco, the Mannesmann as well as the Krupp-Schneider Company are a thoroughly international mixture of German, French and Spanish capitalists, prevents anyone from seriously speaking of a German sphere of interest. The more symptomatic was the determination and the decisiveness with which the German Empire in 1905 suddenly announced its claim to participation in the regulation of Moroccan affairs, and protested against French rule in Morocco. This was the first world-political clash with France. In 1895 Germany, together with France and Russia, assumed a threatening attitude toward victorious Japan to prevent it from exploiting its victory over China at Shimonoseki.[10] Five years later it went arm in arm with France all along the line on a plundering expedition against China. Morocco caused a radical reorientation in Germany's relations with France. The Moroccan crisis which in seven years of its duration twice brought Europe to the verge of war between France and Germany, was not a question of "revenge" for continental conflicts between the two nations. An entirely new conflict had arisen. German imperialism had come into competition with that of France. In the end, Germany was satisfied with the French Congo region, and in accepting this admitted that it had no special interests to protect in Morocco itself. This very fact gave to the German attack in Morocco a far reaching political significance. The very indefinitiveness of its tangible aims and demands betrayed its insatiable appetite, the seeking and feeling for prey—it was a general imperialistic declaration of war against France. The contrast between the two nations here was brought into the limelight. On the one

10. **The Treaty of Shimonoseki** ended the Sino-Japanese war of 1895 and foreigners were granted the right to invest in China.

hand, a slow industrial development, a stagnant population, a nation living on its investments, concerned chiefly with foreign financial business, burdened with a large number of colonial possessions that it could hold together only with the utmost difficulty. On the other hand, a mighty young giant, a capitalism forging toward the first place among nations, going out into the world to hunt for colonies. English colonies were out of the question. So the hunger of German imperialism, besides feeding on Asiatic Turkey, turned at once to the French heritage. The French colonies moreover were a convenient bait with which Italy might eventually be attracted and repaid for Austrian desires of expansion on the Balkan peninsula, and be thus more firmly welded into the Triple Alliance by mutual business inter-ests. The demands Germany made upon French imperialism were exceedingly disturbing, especially when it is remembered that Germany, once it had taken a foothold in any part of Morocco, could at any time set fire to the entire French North-African possessions, whose inhabitants were in a chronic state of incipient warfare with the French conquerors, by supplying them with ammunition. Germany's final withdrawal for suitable compensation did away with this immediate danger. But they could not allay the general disturbance in France and the world-political conflict that had been created.

Its Morocco policy not only brought Germany into conflict with France but with England as well. Here in Morocco, in the immediate neighborhood of Gibraltar, the second important center of world-political interests of the British Government, the sudden appearance of German imperialism with its demands, and the drastic impressiveness with which these demands were supported, were regarded as a demonstration against England as well. Furthermore the first formal protest of 1911 was directed specifically against the agreement of 1904 between England and France concerning Egypt and Morocco.[11] Germany in-sisted briefly and definitely that England be disregarded in all further regulations of Moroccan affairs. The effect that such a

11. Under the terms of the Entente Cordiale between Britain and France in 1904, France was given a free hand in Morocco in exchange for a free hand for Britain in Egypt.

demand was certain to have on German-English relations is obvious. The situation was commented upon in the *Frankfurter Zeitung* of November 8, 1911, by a London correspondent:

"This is the outcome: a million negroes in Congo, a great Katzenjammer[14] and a furious resentment against *perfides Albion*.[13] The Katzenjammer Germany will live down. But what is to become of our relations with England? As they stand today matters are untenable. According to every historic probability they will either lead to something worse, that is war, or they will have to be speedily patched up. . . . The trip of the *Panther* was, as a Berlin correspondent said so well in the *Frankfurter Zeitung* the other day, a dig into the ribs of France to show that Germany is still here. . . . Concerning the effect that this event would create here, Berlin cannot possibly entertain the slightest doubt. Certainly no correspondent in London was for a moment in doubt that England would stand energetically on the side of France. How can the *Norddeutsche Allgemeine Zeitung* still insist that Germany must treat with France alone? For several hundred years Europe has been the scene of a steadily increasing interweaving of political interests. The misfortune of one, according to the laws of politics, fills some with joy, others with apprehension. When two years ago Austria had its difficulties with Russia, Germany appeared upon the scene with shimmering armour, although Vienna, as was afterwards stated, would have preferred to settle matters without German intervention. It is very unlikely that England, having just emerged from a period of anti-German feeling, should consider that our dealings with France are none of its business. In the last analysis, it was a question of might; for a dig in the ribs, be it ever so friendly, it is a very tangible matter. For no one can be quite sure when a blow on the teeth may follow. Since then the situation has become less critical. At the moment when Lloyd George spoke, the danger of a war between Germany and England was acute. Are we justified in expecting a different attitude from Sir Edward Grey after the policies that he and his followers have been

12. **Katzenjammer:** A caterwaul.
13. **Perfides Albion:** *La perfide Angleterre,* perfidious England, had become by the French Revolution to Albion perfide.

pursuing? If Berlin entertained such ideas then it seems to me that the German foreign policies have been weighed and found wanting."

Thus did our imperialistic policies create sharp conflicts in Asia Minor and Morocco, between England and Germany, between Germany and France. But what of German relations with Russia? In the murderous spirit that took possession of the German public during the first weeks of the war everything seemed credible. The German populace believed that Belgian women had gouged out the eyes of the German wounded, that Cossacks ate tallow candles, that they had taken infants by the legs and torn them to pieces; they believed that Russia aspired to the annexation of the German Empire, to the destruction of German "Kultur," to the introduction of absolutism from Kiel to Munich, from the Warthe to the Rhine. The Social Democratic *Chemnitzer Volksstimme* wrote on August 2:

"At this moment we all feel it our duty to fight first against the Russian knout. German women and children shall not become the victims of Russian bestiality, German territory must not fall into the hands of the Cossacks. For if the Entente is victorious, not the French Republicans, but the Russian Czar will rule over Germany. In this moment we defend everything that we possess of German culture and German freedom against a pitiless and barbarous foe."

On the same day the *Fraenkische Tagespost* cried out:

"Shall the Cossacks, who have already taken possession of our border towns, in their onrush on our country, bring destruction to our cities? Shall the Russian Czar, whose love of peace the Social Democrats refused to trust even on the day when his peace manifesto was published, who is the worst enemy of the Russian people themselves, rule over one man of German blood?"

And the *Koenigsberger Volkzeitung* wrote on August 3:

"Not one of us can doubt, whether he is liable for military service or not, that he must do everything to keep these worthless vandals from our borders so long as the war may last. For if they should be victorious, thousands of our comrades will be condemned to horrible prison sentences. Under the Russian sceptre there is no such thing as self-expression of the people, no Social Democratic press is allowed to exist, Social Democratic meetings and organizations are prohibited. We cannot conceive for a moment the possibility of a Russian victory. While still upholding our opposition to war, we will all work together to protect ourselves against these vandals that rule the Russian nation."

We shall later enter a little more fully into the relations that exist between German culture and Russian Czarism. They form a chapter by itself in the position of the German Social Democracy on the war. This much may be said now, one might with as much justification assume that the Czar desires to annex Europe or the moon, as to speak of his desire to annex Germany. In the present war only two nations are threatened in their national existence, Belgium and Serbia. While we howled about safeguarding the national existence of Germany, our cannon were directed against these two states. It is impossible to discuss with people who still believe in the possibility of ritual murder. But to those who do not act from mob instinct, who do not think in terms of clumsy slogans that are invented to catch the rabble, who guide their thoughts by historic facts, it must be obvious that Russian Czarism cannot have such intentions. Russia is ruled by desperate criminals, but not by maniacs. And after all, the policies of absolutism, in spite of all their characteristic differences, have this similarity in all nations, that they live not on thin air but upon very real possibilities in a realm where concrete things come into the closest contact with each other. We need have no fear of the arrest of our German comrades and their banishment to Siberia, nor of the introduction of Russian absolutism into Germany. For the statesmen of the bloody Czar, with all their mental inferiority, have a clearer materialistic conception of the situation than some of our party editors. These statesmen know very well that political forms of government cannot be "introduced" anywhere and everywhere according to the desire of the rulers; they know full well that every form of government is the outcome of certain economic and social foundations, they know from bitter experience that even in Russia itself conditions are almost beyond their power to control; they know, finally, that reaction in every country can use only the forms that are in accord with the nature of the country, and that the absolutism that is in accord with our class and party conditions is the Hohenzollern police state and the Prussian three-class electoral system. A dispassionate consideration of the whole situation will show that we need not fear that Russian Czarism, even if it should win a complete victory over Germany, would feel called upon to do away with these products of German culture.

In reality the conflicts that exist between Germany and Russia are of an entirely different nature. These differences are not to be found in the field of inner politics. Quite the contrary, their mutual tendencies and internal relationships have established a century-old traditional friendship. But in spite of and notwithstanding their solidarity on questions of inner policy, they have come to blows in the field of foreign, world-political hunting grounds.

Russian imperialism, like that of western nations, consists of widely diversified elements. Its strongest strain is not, however, as in Germany or England, the economic expansion of capital hungry for territorial accumulation, but the political interests of the nation. To be sure, Russian industry can show a considerable export to the Orient, to China, Persia and Central Asia, and the Czarist Government seeks to encourage this export trade because it furnishes a desirable foundation for its sphere of interest. But national policies here play an active, not a passive, role. On the one hand, the traditional tendencies of a conquest-loving Czardom, ruling over a mighty nation whose population today consists of 172 million human beings, demand free access to the ocean, to the Pacific Ocean on the East, to the Mediterranean on the South, for industrial as well as for strategic reasons. On the other hand, the very existence of absolutism, and the necessity of holding a respected place in the world-political field, and finally the need of financial credit in foreign countries without which Czarism cannot exist, all play their important part. We must add to these, as in every other monarchy, the dynastic interest. Foreign prestige and temporary forgetfulness of inner problems and difficulties are well known family remedies in the art of ruling, when a conflict arises between the government and the great mass of the people.

But modern capitalist interests are becoming more and more

a factor in the imperialist aims of the Czarist nation. Russian capitalism, still in its earliest youth, cannot hope to perfect its development under an absolutist regime. On the whole it has advanced little beyond the primitive stage of home industry. But it sees a gigantic future before its eyes in the exploitation of the nation's natural resources. As soon as Russia's absolutism is swept away, of this there can be no doubt, Russia will develop rapidly into the foremost capitalist nation, provided always that the international situation will give it the time necessary for such development. It is this hope, and the appetite for foreign markets that will mean increased capitalistic development even at the present time, that has filled the Russian bourgeoisie with imperialistic desires and led them to eagerly voice their demands in the coming division of the world's resources. This historic desire is actively supported by very tangible immediate interests. There are, in the first place, the armament industry and its purveyors. In the second place the conflicts with the "enemy within," the revolutionary proletariat, have given to the Russian bourgeoisie an increased appreciation of the powers of militarism and the distracting efforts of a world-political evangel. It has bound together the various capitalist groups and the nobility under one counterrevolutionary regime. The imperialism of bourgeois Russia, particularly among the liberals, has grown enormously in the stormy atmosphere of the revolutionary period, and has given to the traditional foreign policies of the Romanovs a modern stamp. Chief among the aims of the traditional policies of monarchic Russia, as well as of the more modern appetites of the Russian bourgeoisie, are the Dardanelles. They are, according to the famous remark made by Bismarck, the latchkey to the Russian possessions on the Black Sea. Since the eighteenth century, Russia has waged a number of bloody wars against Turkey, has undertaken its mission as the liberator of the Balkans, for the realization of this goal. For this ideal, Russia has piled up mountains of dead in Ismail, in Navarin, in Sinope, Silistria and Sevastopol, in Plevna and Shipka. To the Russian muzhik, the defense of his Slavic and Christian brothers from the horrors of Turkish oppression has become as potent a war legend as the defense of German culture and freedom against the horrors of Russia has become to the German Social Democracy.

But the Russian bourgeoisie also was much more enthusiastic over the Mediterranean prospect than for its Manchurian and Mongolian "mission." The liberal bourgeoisie of Russia criticized the Japanese war so severely as a senseless adventure, because it distracted the attention of Russian politics from the problem that was to them more important, the Balkans. And in another way, the unfortunate war with Japan had the same effect. The extension of Russian power into Eastern and Central Asia, to Tibet and down into Persia necessarily aroused a feeling of discomfort in the minds of English imperialists. England, fearing for its enormous Indian Empire, viewed the Asiatic movements of Russia with growing suspicion. In fact, at the beginning of the present century the English-Russian conflict in Asia was the strongest world-conflict in the international situation. Moreover this will be, in all probability, the most critical issue in future world-political developments when the present war is over. The crushing defeat of Russia in 1904 and the subsequent outbreak of the Russian revolution only temporarily changed the situation. The apparent weakening of the Czar's empire brought about a relaxation of the tension between England and Russia. In 1907 a treaty was signed between the two nations providing for a mutual control of Persia[14] that established, for the time being, friendly relations in Central Asia. This kept Russia from undertaking great projects in the East, and her energies reverted all the more vigorously to their old occupation, Balkan politics. Here the Russia of the Czar came for the first time into sharp conflict with German culture, after a century of faithful and well-founded friendship. The road to the Dardanelles leads over the corpse of Turkey. But for more than a decade Germany has regarded the "integrity" of this corpse as its most important world-political task. Russian methods in the Balkans had changed at various times. Embittered by the ingratitude of the liberated

14. By the **Anglo-Russian Treaty** of August 31, 1907, which discussed Tibet, Afghanistan and Persia, Persia was divided into three zones for development. Britain lost in the deal, as oil was soon discovered in the area which she had abandoned. However the Anglo-Persian Oil Company was soon formed.

Balkan Slavs who tried to escape from their position as vassals to the Czarist Government, Russia for a time supported the program of Turkish integrity with the silent understanding that the division of that country should be postponed to some more auspicious time. But today the final liquidation of Turkey coincides with the plans of both Russian and English politics. The latter aims to unite Arabia and Mesopotamia and the Russian territories that lie between Egypt and India, under British rule, into a great Mohammedan empire, thus conserving its own position in India and Egypt. In this way Russian imperialism, as in earlier times English imperialism, came into opposition with that of Germany. For this privileged exploiter of Turkish disintegration had taken up her position as sentinel on the Bosphorus.

Russian interests came to a clash in the Balkans not only directly with Germany but with Austria as well. Austrian imperialism is the political complement of German imperialism, at the same time is its Siamese twin brother and its fate.

Germany having isolated herself on all sides by her world policy, has in Austria her only ally. The alliance with Austria is old, having been founded by Bismarck in 1879. But since that time it has completely changed its character. Like the enmity toward France, the alliance with Austria received an entirely new content through the development of the last decades. In 1879 its chief purpose was the mutual defense of the possessions gained in the wars of 1864–1870.[15] The Bismarck Triple Alliance was conservative in character, especially since it signified Austria's final renunciation of admission to the German federation of states, its acceptance of the state of affairs created by Bismarck, and the military hegemony of Greater Prussia. The Balkan aspirations of Austria were as distasteful to Bismarck as the South African conquests of Germany. In his *Gedanken und Erinerungen*[16] he says:

"It is natural that the inhabitants of the Danube region should have needs and aspirations that extend beyond the present

15. **The Wars of 1864–1870:** Were Bismarck's successful efforts to establish Prussian domination over Germany. With Austria, Prussia fought Denmark in January 1864. Prussia annexed Schleswig, Austria took Holstein.

16. **Gedanken und Erinerungen:** (German) Bismarck's *Reflections and Reminiscences,* written 1896–98.

boundaries of their monarchy. The German national constitution points out the way along which Austria can form a union of the political and material interests that exist between the most eastern Rumanian tribe and the Bay of Cattaro. But the duty of the German Empire does not demand that it satisfy the desires of its neighbours for increased territory with the blood and wealth of its subjects."

He expressed the same thought still more drastically when he uttered the well known sentiment that, to him, the whole of Bosnia was not worth the bone of a Pomeranian grenadier. Indeed, a treaty drawn up with Russia in 1884 proves conclusively that Bismarck never desired to place the Triple Alliance at the service of Austrian annexationist desires. By this treaty, the German Empire promised, in the event of a war between Austria and Russia, not to support the former, but rather to observe a "benevolent neutrality."

But since imperialism has taken hold of German politics, its relations to Austria have changed as well. Austria-Hungary lies between Germany and the Balkans, in other words, on the road over the critical point in German Oriental politics. To make Austria its enemy at this time would mean complete isolation, and complete abdication by Germany of its world-political plan. But the weakening of Austria, which would signify the final liquidation of Turkey, with a consequent strengthening of Russia, the Balkan states, and England, would probably accomplish the national unification of Germany, but would, at the same time, wipe out, forever, its imperialistic aspirations. The safety of the Hapsburg monarchy has therefore logically become a necessary complement to German imperialism, the preservation of Turkey its chief problem.

But Austria means a constantly latent state of war in the Balkans. For Turkish disintegration has promoted the existence and growth of the Balkan States in the immediate neighborhood of the Hapsburg monarchy, and the resulting state of chronic incipient warfare. Obviously the existence of virile and independent national states on the border of a monarchy that is made up of fragments of these same nationalities, which it can rule only by the whip-lash of dictatorship must hasten its downfall. Austrian Balkan politics and particularly its Serbian relations have plainly revealed its inner decay. Although its imperialistic appetites wavered between Salonika and Durazzo, Austria was not in a position to annex Serbia, even before the latter had grown in strength and size through the two Balkan wars. For the forcible annexation of Serbia would have dangerously strengthened in its interior one of the most refractory southern Slavic nationalities, a people that even now, because of Austria's stupid regime of reaction, can scarcely be held in check. But neither can Austria tolerate the normal independent development of Serbia or profit from it by normal commercial relations. For the Hapsburg monarchy is not the political expression of a capitalist state, but a loose syndicate of a few parasitic cliques, striving to grasp everything within reach, utilizing the political powers of the nation so long as this weak edifice still stands. For the benefit of Hungarian agrarians, and for the purpose of increasing the prices of agricultural products, Austria has forbidden Serbia to send cattle and fruits into Austria, thus depriving this nation of farmers of its most important market.[17] In the interest of Austrian monopolies it has forced Serbia to import industrial products exclusively from Austria, and at the highest prices. To keep Serbia in a state of economic and political dependence, it prevented Serbia from uniting on the East with Bulgaria, to secure access to the Black Sea, and from securing access to the Adriatic on the West, by prohibiting the acquisition of a harbor in Albania. In short, the Balkan policy of Austria was nothing more than a barefaced attempt to choke off Serbia. Also it was directed against the establishment of mutual relations between and against the inner growth of the Balkan states, and was, therefore, a constant menace for them.

Austrian imperialism constantly threatened the existence and development of the Balkan States, now by the annexation of Bosnia, now by its demands upon the Sanjak of Novibazar and on Saloniki, now by its encroachments upon the Albanian coast. To satisfy these tendencies on the part of Austria, and to meet the competition of Italy as well, the caricature of an independent

17. Beginning 1906, Austria applied economic sanctions against Serbia which found its market for livestock in Austria-Hungary. This led to the "Pig War" of 1906 and later political friction.

Albania under the rule of a German nobleman was created after the second Balkan war, a country which was, from the first hour, little more than the plaything in the intrigues of imperialistic rivals.

Thus the imperialistic policies of Austria during the last decade were a constant hindrance to the normal progressive development of the Balkans, and led to the inevitable alternative: either the Hapsburg monarchy or the capitalist development of the Balkan States.

Emancipated from Turkish rule, the Balkans now faced their new hindrance, Austria, and the necessity of removing it from its path. Historically the liquidation of Austria-Hungary is the logical sequence of Turkish disintegration, and both are in direct line with the process of historical development.[18]

There was but one solution: war—a world war. For behind Serbia stood Russia, unable to sacrifice its influence in the Balkans and its role of "protector" without giving up its whole imperialistic program in the Orient as well. In direct conflict with Austrian politics, Russia aimed to unite the Balkan States under a Russian protectorate, to be sure. The Balkan union that had almost completely annihilated European Turkey in the victorious war of 1912 was the work of Russia, and was directly and intentionally aimed against Austria. In spite of Russian efforts, the Balkan union was smashed in the second Balkan war. But Serbia, emerging the victor, became dependent upon the friendship of Russia in the same degree as Austria had become Russia's bitter enemy. Germany, whose fate was firmly linked to that of the Hapsburg monarchy, was obliged to back up the stupid Balkan policy of the latter, step by step, and was thus brought into a doubly aggravated opposition to Russia.

But the Balkan policies of Austria, furthermore, brought Austria into conflict with Italy, which was actively interested in the dissolution of the Turkish and Austrian Empires. The imperialism of Italy has found in the Italian possessions of Austria a most popular cloak for its own annexationist desires. Its eyes

---

18. Luxemburg's prediction proved correct. At Versailles the Austro-Hungarian Empire was carved up, and Austria was left with almost the same territory as she now occupies.

are directed especially toward the Albanian coast of the Adriatic, should a new regulation of Balkan affairs take place. The Triple Alliance, having already sustained a severe blow in the Tripolitan war, was destroyed by the acute crisis in the Balkans during the two Balkan wars. The Central Powers were thus brought into conflict with the entire outside world. German imperialism, chained to two decaying corpses, was steering its course directly toward a world war.

Moreover, Germany embarked upon this course with a full realization of its consequences. Austria, as the motive power, was rushing blindly into destruction. Its clique of clerical-militarist rulers with the Archduke Franz Ferdinand and his right hand man Baron von Chlumezki at the head, fairly jumped at every excuse to strike the first blow. In 1909 Austria framed up the famous documents by Professor Friedmann, exposing what purported to be a widespread, criminal conspiracy of the Serbs against the Hapsburg Monarchy, for the sole purpose of infusing the German nations with the necessary war enthusiasm. These papers had only one slight drawback—they were forged from beginning to end. A year later the rumor of the horrible martyrdom of the Austrian consul Prohaska in Ueskub was busily spread for days to serve as the spark that would ignite the keg of powder, while Prohaska roamed unmolested and happy through the streets of Ueskub. Then came the assassination at Sarajevo, a long desired, truly shameful crime.[19] "If ever a blood sacrifice has had a liberating, releasing effect, it was the case here," rejoiced the spokesman of German imperialism. Among Austrian imperialists the rejoicing was still greater, and they

19. On June 28, 1914—the anniversary of the defeat of Serbia by Turkey in 1389 and the defeat of the Turks in the first Balkan War—Archduke Franz Ferdinand, Crown Prince of Austria, and his wife, who were visiting Sarajevo, then part of Austro-Hungary, were fired at and killed by a Serbian patriot, Gavrilo Princip.

This provided the excuse for Austria's ultimatum to Serbia July 23, 1914 and the declaration of war on July 27.

Germany, whose General Staff, had had the army ready for war since the first of June, declared war on Russia, August 1, and on the same day the German armies rolled into Belgium and Luxemburg against France.

Today Sarajevo is the capital of the Yugoslav Republic of Bosnia, and the spot where Princip fired the historic shots is marked by a commemorative plaque, and a bridge nearby is named after him.

decided to use the noble corpses while they were still warm. After a hurried conference with Berlin, war was virtually decided and the ultimatum sent out as a flaming torch that was to set fire to the capitalist world at all four corners.

But the occurrence at Sarajevo only furnished the immediate pretext. Causes and conflicts for the war had been overripe for a long time. The conjuncture that we witness today was ready a decade ago. Every year, every political occurrence of recent years has but served to bring war a step nearer: the Turkish revolution, the annexation of Bosnia, the Morocco crisis, the Tripoli expedition, the two Balkan wars. All military bills of the last years were drawn up in direct preparation for this war; the countries of Europe were preparing, with open eyes, for the inevitable final contest. Five times during recent years this war was on the verge of an outbreak: in the summer of 1905, when Germany for the first time made her decisive demands in the Morocco crisis; in the summer of 1908, when England, Russia and France threatened with war after the conference of the monarchs in Reval over the Macedonian question, and war was prevented only by the sudden outbreak of the Turkish revolution; in the beginning of 1909 when Russia replied to the Bosnian annexation with a mobilization, when Germany in Petersburg formally declared its readiness to go to war on the side of Austria; in the summer of 1911 when the *Panther* was sent to Agadir, an act that would certainly have brought on war if Germany had not finally acquiesced in the Morocco question and allowed itself to be compensated with the Congo concession; and finally, in the beginning of 1913, when Germany, in view of the proposed Russian invasion of Albania, a second time threatened Petersburg with its readiness for warlike measures.

Thus the world war has been hanging fire for eight years. It was postponed again and again only because always one of the two sides in question was not yet ready with its military preparations.

So, for instance, the present world war was imminent at the time of the *Panther* adventure in 1911—without a murdered Grand Duke, without French fliers over Nuremberg, without a Russian invasion into East Prussia. Germany simply put it off for a more favorable moment—one need only read the frank explanation of a German imperialist: "The German government has been accused by the so-called pan-Germans of weakness in the Morocco crisis in 1911. Let them disabuse their minds of this false impression. It is a fact that, at the time when we sent the *Panther* to Agadir, the reconstruction of the North-East Sea Canal was still in progress, that building operations on Helgoland for the construction of a great fort were nowhere near completion, that our fleet of dreadnoughts and accessories, in comparison with the English sea power, was in a far more unfavourable position than was the case three years later.

"Compared to the present time, 1914, the canal as well as Helgoland were in a deplorable state of unreadiness, were almost absolutely useless for war purposes. Under such circumstances, where one knows that one's chances will be far more favourable in a few years, it would be worse than foolish to provoke a war. First the German fleet had to be put in order; the great military bill had to be pushed through the Reichstag. In the summer of 1914 Germany was prepared for war, while France was still labouring over its three years military service programme, while in Russia neither the army nor the naval programme were ready. It was up to Germany to utilize the auspicious moment."

The same Rohrbach, who is not only the most serious representative of imperialism in Germany, but is also in intimate touch with the leading circles in German politics and is their semi-official mouthpiece, comments upon the situation in July, 1914, as follows: "At this time there was only one danger, that we might be morally forced, by an apparent acquiescence on the part of Russia, to wait until Russia and France were really prepared." In other words, Germany feared nothing so much as that Russia might give in. "With deep pain we saw our untiring efforts to preserve world peace shipwrecked. . . ."[20]

The invasion of Belgium, therefore, and the accomplished fact of war was not a bolt from the blue. It did not create a new, unheard of situation. Nor was it an event that came, in its political associations, as a complete surprise to the Social Democratic group. The world war that began officially on August 4, 1914, was the same world war toward which German imperial-

20. The words quoted are those of Kaiser Wilhelm II.

ism had been driving for decades, the same war whose coming the Social Democracy had prophesied year after year. This same war has been denounced by Social Democratic parliamentarians, newspapers and leaflets a thousand times as a frivolous imperialistic crime, as a war that is against every interest of culture and against every interest of the nation.

And, indeed, not the "existence and the independent development of Germany in this war" are at stake, in spite of the reiterations of the Social Democratic press, but the immediate profits of the Deutsche Bank in Asiatic Turkey and the future profits of the Mannesmann and Krupp interests in Morocco, the existence and the reactionary character of Austria, "this heap of organized decay, that calls itself the Hapsburg monarchy," as the *Vorwaerts* wrote on July 25, 1914; Hungarian pigs and prunes, paragraph fourteen, the "Kultur" of Friedmann-Prohaska, the existence of Turkish rule in Asia Minor and of counterrevolution in the Balkans.

Our party press was filled with moral indignation over the fact that Germany's foes should drive black men and barbarians, Negroes, Sikhs and Maoris into the war. Yet these peoples play a role in this war that is approximately identical with that played by the socialist proletariat in the European states. If the Maoris of New Zealand were eager to risk their skulls for the English king, they showed only as much understanding of their own interests as the German Social Democratic group that traded the existence, the freedom and the civilization of the German people for the existence of the Hapsburg monarchy, for Turkey and for the vaults of the Deutsche Bank.

There is one difference between the two. A generation ago, Maori negroes were still cannibals and not students of Marxist philosophy.

Chapter V

But Czarism! In the first moments of the war this was undoubt-edly the factor that decided the position of our party. In its declaration, the Social Democratic group had given the slogan: "Against Czarism!" And out of this the socialist press has made a fight for European culture.

The *Frankfurter Volksstimme* wrote on July 31:
"The German Social Democracy has always hated Czardom as the bloody guardian of European reaction: From the time that Marx and Engels followed, with far-seeing eyes, every movement of this barbarian government, down to the present day, where its prisons are filled with political prisoners, and yet it trembles before every labour movement. The time has come when we must square accounts with these terrible scoundrels, under the German flag of war."

The *Pfaelzische Post* of Ludwighafen wrote on the same day:
"This is a principle that was first established by our August Bebel. This is the struggle of civilization against barbarism, and in this struggle the proletariat will do its share."

The *Muenchener Post* of August 1:
"When it comes to defending our country against the bloody Czardom we will not be made citizens of the second class."

The *Halle Volksblatt* wrote on August 5:
"If this is so, if we have been attacked by Russia, and every-thing seems to corroborate this statement—then the Social De-mocracy, as a matter of course, must vote in favour of all means of defence. With all our strength we must fight to drive Czarism from our country!"

And on August 18:

"Now that the die is cast in favour of the sword, it is not only the duty of national defence and national existence that puts the weapon into our hands as into the hands of every German, but also the realization that in the enemy whom we are fighting in the east we are striking a blow at the foe of all culture and all progress. . . . The overthrow of Russia is synonymous with the victory of freedom in Europe"

On August 5, the *Braunschweiger Volksfreund* wrote:

"The irresistible force of military preparation drives everything before it. But the class-conscious labour movement obeys, not an outside force, but its own conviction, when it defends the ground upon which it stands, from attack in the east."

The *Essener Arbeiterzeitung* cried out on August 3:

"If this country is threatened by Russia's determination then the Social Democrats, since the fight is against Russian Blood-Czarism, against the perpetrator of a million crimes against freedom and culture, will allow none to excel them in the fulfilment of their duty, in their willingness to sacrifice. Down with Czarism! Down with the home of Barbarism! Let that be our slogan!"

Similarly the *Bielefelder Volkswacht* writes on August 4:

"Everywhere the same cry: against Russian despotism and faithlessness."

The Elberfeld party organ on August 5:

"All Western Europe is vitally interested in the extermination of rotten murderous Czarism. But this human interest is crushed by the greed of England and France to check the profits that have been made possible by German capital."

The *Rheinische Zeitung* in Cologne:

"Do your duty, friends, wherever fate may place you. You are fighting for the civilization of Europe, for the independence of your fatherland, for your own welfare."

The *Schleswig-Holstein Volkszeitung* of August 7 writes:

"Of course we are living in an age of capitalism. Of course we will continue to have class struggles after the great war is over. But these class struggles will be fought out in a freer state, they will be far more confined to the economic field than before. In the future the treatment of Socialists as outcasts, as citizens of the second class, as politically rightless will be impossible, once the Czardom of Russia has vanished."

On August 11, the *Hamburger Echo* cried:

"We are fighting to defend ourselves not so much against England and France as against Czarism. But this war we carry on with the greatest enthusiasm, for it is the war for civilization."

And the Luebeck party organ declared, as late as September 4:

"If European liberty is saved, then Europe will have German arms to thank for it. Our fight is a fight against the worst enemy of all liberty and all democracy."

Thus the chorus of the German party press sounded and resounded.

In the beginning of the war the German government accepted the profferred assistance. Nonchalantly it fastened the laurels of the liberator of European culture to its helmet. Yes, it endeavored to carry through the role of the "liberator of nations," though often with visible discomfort and rather awkward grace. It flattered the Poles and the Jews in Russia, and egged one nation on against the other, using the policies that had proven so successful in their colonial warfare where again and again they played up one chief against the other. And the Social Democrats followed each leap and bound of German imperialism with remarkable agility. While the Reichstag group covered up every shameful outrage with a discrete silence the Social Democratic press filled the air with jubilant melodies, rejoicing in the liberty that "German riflebutts" had brought to the poor victims of Czarism.

Even the theoretical organ of the Party, the *Neue Zeit*, wrote on the 28th of August:

"The border population of the 'Little Father's'[1] realm greeted the coming of the German troops with cries of joy. For these Poles and Jews have but one conception of their fatherland, that of corruption and rule by the knout. Poor devils, really fatherlandless creatures, these downtrodden subjects of bloody Nicholas. Even should they desire to do so, they could find nothing to

1. The Czar of Russia was known to his subjects as the "Little Father."

defend but their chains. And so they live and toil, hoping and longing that German rifles, carried by German men, will crush the whole Czarist system. . . . A clear and definite purpose still lives in the German working class, though the thunder of a world war is crashing over its head. It will defend itself from the allies of Russian barbarism in the west to bring about an honourable peace. It will give to the task of destroying Czarism the last breath of man and beast."

After the Social Democratic group had stamped the war as a war of defense for the German nation and European culture, the Social Democratic press proceeded to hail it as the "saviour of the oppressed nations." Hindenburg became the executor of Marx and Engels.

The memory of our party has played it a shabby trick. It forgot all its principles, its pledges, the decision of international congresses just at the moment when they should have found their application. And to its great misfortune, it remembered the heritage of Karl Marx and dug it out of the dust of passing years at the very moment when it could serve only to decorate Prussian militarism, for whose destruction Karl Marx was willing to sacrifice "the last breath of man and beast." Long forgotten chords that were sounded by Marx in the *Neue Rheinische Zeitung* against the vassal state of Nicholas I during the German March Revolution of 1848, suddenly reawakened in the ears of the German Social Democracy in the year of Our Lord 1914, and called them to arms, arm in arm with Prussian junkerdom against the Russia of the Great Revolution of 1905.

This is where a revision should have been made; the slogans of the March Revolution should have been brought into accord with the historical experiences of the last seventy years.

In 1848 Russian Czarism was, in truth, "the guardian of European reaction." The product of Russian social conditions, firmly rooted in its medieval, agricultural state, absolutism was the protector and at the same time the mighty director of monarchical reaction. This was weakened, particularly in Germany where a system of small states still obtained. As late as 1851 it was possible for Nicholas I to assure Berlin through the Prussian consul von Rochow "that he would, indeed, have been pleased to see the revolution destroyed by the roots when General von Wrangel advanced upon Berlin in November, 1848." At another time, in a warning to Manteuffel, the Czar stated, "that he relied upon the Imperial Ministry, under the leadership of His Highness, to defend the rights of the crown against the chambers, and give to the principles of conservatism their due." It was possible for the same Nicholas I to bestow the Order of Alexander Nevski on a Prussian Ministerial President in recognition of his "constant efforts . . . to preserve legal order in Prussia."

The Crimean War worked a noticeable change in this respect. It ended with the military and therefore with the political bankruptcy of the old system. Russian absolutism was forced to grant reforms, to modernize its rule, to adjust itself to capitalist conditions. In so doing, it gave its little finger to the devil who already holds it firmly by the arm, and will eventually get it altogether. The Crimean War was, by the way, an instructive example of the kind of liberation that can be brought to a downtrodden people "at the point of a gun." The military overthrow at Sedan brought France its republic. But this republic was not the gift of the Bismarck soldiery. Prussia, at that time as today, can give to other peoples nothing but its own junker rule. Republican France was the ripe fruit of inner social struggles and of the three revolutions that had preceded it. The crash at Sevastopol was in effect similar to that of Jena.[2] But because there was no revolutionary movement in Russia, it led to the outward renovation and reaffirmation of the old regime.

But the reforms that opened the road for capitalist development in Russia during the 1860's were possible only with the money of a capitalist system. This money was furnished by Western European capital. It came from Germany and France, and has created a new relationship that has lasted down to the present day. Russian absolutism is now subsidized by the western European bourgeoisie. No longer does the Russian ruble "roll in diplomatic chambers" as Prince William of Prussia bitterly complained in 1854, "into the very chambers of the King." On the contrary, German and French money is rolling to Petersburg to feed a regime that would long ago have breathed its last without this life-giving juice. Russian Czarism is today no longer the product

2. At Jena, in Saxony, on October 14, 1806, Napoleon I routed the Prussian forces, and by November 7, destroyed the Prussian war machine. By the Peace of Tilsit, Prussia was hopelessly mutilated.

of Russian conditions; its root lies in the capitalist conditions of Western Europe. And the relationship is shifting from decade to decade. In the same measure as the old root of Russian absolutism in Russia itself is being destroyed, the new, western European root is growing stronger and stronger. Besides lending their financial support, Germany and France, since 1870, have been vying with each other to lend Russia their political support as well. As revolutionary forces arise from the womb of the Russian people itself to fight against Russian absolutism, they meet with an ever growing resistance in western Europe, which stands ready to lend to threatened Czarism its moral and political support. So when, in the beginning of the 1880's the older Russian socialist movement severely shook the Czarist government and partly destroyed its authority within and without, Bismarck made his treaty with Russia and strengthened its position in international politics.[3]

Capitalist development, tenderly nurtured by Czarism with its own hands, finally bore fruit: in the 1890's the revolutionary movement of the Russian proletariat began. The erstwhile "guardian of reaction" was forced to grant a meaningless constitution, to seek a new protector from the rising flood in its own country.[4] And it found this protector—in Germany. The Germany of Bulow must pay the debt of gratitude that the Prussia of Wrangel and Manteuffel had incurred. Relations were completely reversed. Russian support against the revolution in Germany is superseded by German aid against the revolution in Russia. Spies, outrages, betrayals—a demagogic agitation, like that which blessed the times of the Holy Alliance,[5] was unleashed in Germany against

3. In continuation of the politics of the "Drei-Kaiser-Bund" (Union of Three Kings) of June 18, 1881, Bismarck entered into a reinsurance treaty with Russia on June 18, 1887, promising her aid in Bulgaria and the Straits.

4. By Act of March 13, 1881, Czar Alexander II proclaimed an embryonic constitution. However, he was assassinated the same year and the very word "constitution" was outlawed in Russia.

5. **The Holy Alliance** of the post-Napoleonic era, was proposed by Czar Alexander I in 1814, and agreed to by Francis I of Austria and Frederick Wilhelm III of Prussia. It was to be an alliance of Christian nations irrespective of victory or guilt. Great Britain joined but without enthusiasm. It was signed in Paris on September 26, 1915. In effect it was an alliance between Russia, Austria and Prussia and lasted until 1922.

the fighters for the cause of Russian freedom, and followed to the very doorsteps of the Russian Revolution. In the Koenigsberg trial of 1904 this wave of persecution was at its height. This trial threw a scathing light upon a whole historical development since 1848 and showed the complete change of relations between Russian absolutism and European reaction. *"Tua res agitur!"*[6] cried a Prussian Minister of Justice to the ruling classes of Germany, pointing to the tottering foundation of the Czarist regime. "The establishment of a democratic republic in Russia would strongly influence Germany," declared First District Attorney Schulze in Koenigsberg. "When my neighbour's home burns my own is also in danger." And his assistant Casper also emphasized: "It is naturally not indifferent to Germany's public interests whether this bulwark of absolutism stands or falls. Certainly the flames of a revolutionary movement may easily spring over into Germany. . . ."

The Revolution was overthrown, but the very causes that led to its temporary downfall are valuable in a discussion of the position taken by the German Social Democracy in this war. That the Russian uprising in 1905–1906 was unsuccessful in spite of its unequalled expenditure of revolutionary force, its clearness of purpose and tenacity, can be ascribed to two distinct causes. The one lies in the inner character of the Revolution itself, in its enormous historical program, in the mass of economic and political problems that it was forced to face. Some of them, for instance, the agrarian problem, cannot possibly be solved within capitalist society. There was the difficulty furthermore, of creating a class state for the supremacy of the modern bourgeoisie against the counterrevolutionary opposition of the bourgeoisie as a whole. To the onlooker it would seem that the Russian revolution was doomed to failure because it was a proletarian revolution with bourgeois duties and problems, or if you wish, a bourgeois revolution waged by socialist proletarian methods, a crash of two generations amid lightning and thunder, the fruit of the delayed industrial development of class conditions in Russia and their overripeness in western Europe. From this point of view its downfall in 1906 signifies not its bankruptcy, but the natural

6. **Tua Res Agitur:** (Latin) Your problem is being attended to.

closing of the first chapter, upon which the second must follow with the inevitability of a natural law. The second cause of external nature lay in Western Europe: European reaction once more hastened to help its endangered protegé. Not with lead and bullets, although "German guns" were in German fists even in 1905 and only waited for a signal from Petersburg to attack the neighboring Poles. Europe rendered an assistance that was equally valuable: financial subsidy and political alliances were arranged to help Czarism in Russia. French money paid for the armed forces that broke down the Russian Revolution; from Germany came the moral and political support that helped the Russian government to clamber out from the depths of shame into which Japanese torpedoes and Russian proletarian fists had thrust it. In 1910, in Potsdam official Germany received Russian Czarism with open arms. The reception of the blood-stained monarch at the gates of the German capital was not only the German blessing for the throttling of Persia,[7] but above all for the hangman's work of the Russian counterrevolution. It was the official banquet of German and European "Kultur" over what they believed to be the grave of the Russian Revolution.

And strange! At that time, when this challenging feast upon the grave of the Russian Revolution was held in its own home, the German Social Democracy remained silent, and had completely forgotten "the heritage of our masters" from 1848. At that time, when the hangman was received in Potsdam, not a sound, not a protest, not an article vetoed this expression of solidarity with the Russian counterrevolution. Only since this war has begun, since the police permit it, the smallest party organ intoxicates itself with bloodthirsty attacks upon the hangman of

---

7. At the end of 1905, following the first Russian revolution, the Persians rose against the Shah, compelling him to grant a constitution in August 1906 and convene the Majlis in October. After the Anglo-Russian Treaty on Persia, in June 1908, the Russian government, under the pretext of protecting Persia against Turkey, sent a Cossack brigade under Colonel Liakhov. The Majlis was dissolved, several deputies executed, and Liakhov was made Military Governor of Teheran. The peasant movement and the revolutionary unrest in the country did not cease, and in July 1909, revolutionary detachments defeated the Cossacks, captured Teheran and deposed the Shah Mohamed Ali. In 1911, Russia captured parts of Northern Persia, the British landed in the South and restored the Shah and feudal rule.

Russian liberty. Yet nothing could have disclosed more clearly than did this triumphal tour of the Czar in 1910, that the oppressed Russian proletariat was the victim not only of domestic reaction but of western European reaction as well. Their fight, like that of the March revolutionists of 1848, was against reaction, not only in their own country, but against its guardians in all other European countries.

After the inhuman crusades of the counterrevolution had somewhat subsided, the revolutionary ferment in the Russian proletariat once more became active. The flood began to rise and to boil. Economic strikes in Russia, according to the official reports, involved 46,623 workers and 256,386 days in 1910; 96,730 workers and 768,556 days in 1911; and 89,771 workers and 1,214,881 days in the first five months of 1912. Political mass strikes, protests and demonstrations comprised 1,005,000 workers in 1912; 1,272,000 in 1913. In 1914 the flood rose higher and higher. On January 22, the anniversary of the beginning of the Revolution there was a demonstration mass strike of 200,000 workers. As in the days before the revolution of 1905, the flame broke out in June, in the Caucasus. In Baku, 40,000 workers were on a general strike. The flames leaped over to Petersburg. On the 17th of June 80,000 workers in Petersburg laid down their tools, on the 20th of July, 200,000 were out; on July 23, the general strike movement was spreading out all over Russia, barricades were being built, the revolution was on its way. A few more months and it would have come, its flags fluttering in the wind. A few more years, and perhaps the whole world-political constellation would have been changed, imperialism, perhaps would have received a firm check on its mad impulse.

But German reaction checked the revolutionary movement. From Berlin and Vienna came declarations of war, and the Russian revolution was buried beneath its wreckage. "German guns" are shattering, not Czarism, but its most dangerous enemy. The hopefully fluttering flag of the revolution sank down amid a wild whirlpool of war. But it sank honorably, and it will rise again out of the horrible massacre, in spite of "German guns," in spite of victory or defeat for Russia on the battlefields.

The national revolts in Russia which the Germans tried to foster were also unsuccessful. The Russian provinces were evidently less inclined to fall for the bait of Hindenburg's cohorts than the German Social Democracy. The Jews, practical people that they are, were able to count on their fingers that "German fists" which have been unable to overthrow their own Prussian reaction, can hardly be expected to smash Russian absolutism. The Poles, exposed to the triple headed war, were not in a position to answer their "liberators" in audible language. But they will have remembered that Polish children were taught to say the Lord's prayer in the German language with bloody welts on their backs, will not have forgotten the liberality of Prussian anti-Polish laws. All of them, Poles, Jews and Russians had no difficulty in understanding that the "German gun," when it descends upon their heads, brings not liberty, but death.

To couple the legend of Russian liberation with its Marxian heritage is worse than a poor joke on the part of the German Social Democracy. It is a crime. To Marx, the Russian Revolution was a turning point in the history of the world. Every political and historical perspective was made dependent upon the one consideration, "provided the Russian revolution has not already broken out." Marx believed in the Russian revolution and expected it even at a time when Russia was only a state of vassals. When the war broke out the Russian revolution had occured. Its first attempt had not been victorious; but it could not be ignored; it is on the order of the day. And yet our German Social Democrats came with "German guns," declaring the Russian revolution null and void; struck it from the pages of history. In 1848 Marx spoke from the German barricades; in Russia there was a hopeless reaction. In 1914 Russia was in the throes of a revolution, while its German "liberators" were cowed by the fists of Prussian junkerdom.

But the liberating mission of the German armies was only an episode. German imperialism soon raised its uncomfortable mask and turned openly against France and England. Here, too, it was supported valiantly by a large number of the party papers. They ceased railing against the bloody Czar, and held up "perfidious Albion" and its merchant soul to the public disdain. They set out to free Europe, no longer from Russian absolutism, but from English naval supremacy. The hopeless confusion in which the party had become entangled found a drastic illustration in the desperate attempt made by the more thoughtful portion of our party press to meet this new change of front. In vain they tried to force the war back into its original channels, to nail it down to the "heritage of our masters"—that is, to the myth that they, the Social Democracy—had themselves created. "With heavy heart I have been forced to mobilize the army against a neighbour at whose side I have fought on so many battlefields. With honest sorrow I saw a friendship, truly served by Germany, break." That was simple, open, honest. But when the rhetoric of the first weeks of war backed down before the lapidary language of imperialism, the German Social Democracy lost its only plausible excuse.

Chapter VI

Of equal importance in the attitude of the Social Democracy was the official adoption of a progam of civil peace, i.e., the cessation of the class struggle for the duration of the war. The declaration that was read by the Social Democratic group in the Reichstag on the 4th of August had been agreed upon in advance with representatives of the government and the capitalist parties. It was little more than a patriotic grandstand play, prepared behind the scenes and delivered for the benefit of the people at home and in other nations.

To the leading elements in the labor movement, the vote in favor of the war credits by the Reichstag group was a cue for the immediate settlement of all labor controversies. Nay more, they announced this to the manufacturers as a patriotic duty incurred by labor when it agreed to observe a civil peace. These same labor leaders undertook to supply city labor to farmers in order to assure a prompt harvest. The leaders of the Social Democratic Women's Movement united with capitalist women for "National Service" and placed the most important elements that remained after the mobilization at the disposal of national Samaritan work. Socialist women worked in soup kitchens and on advisory commissions instead of carrying on agitation work for the party. Under the Socialist exception laws[1] the party had utilized parliamentary elections to spread its agitation and to keep a firm hold upon the population in spite of the state of siege that had been declared against the party and the persecution of the social-

---

1. **Socialist Exception Laws:** Prepared by Bismarck since 1862, were put into operation even before they were passed by the Reichstag, in October 1878. All extra-parliamentary activity of the Socialists was banned. The laws were repealed in 1890, the year Bismarck was dropped.

ist press. In this crisis the Social Democratic movement has voluntarily relinquished all propaganda and education in the interest of the proletarian class struggle, during Reichstag and Landtag elections. Parliamentary elections have everywhere been reduced to the simple bourgeois formula; the catching of votes for the candidates of the party on the basis of an amicable and peaceful settlement with its capitalist opponents. When the Social Democratic representatives in the Landtag and in the municipal commissions—with the laudable exceptions of the Prussian and Alsatian Landtag—with high sounding references to the existing state of civil peace, voted their approval of the war credits that had been demanded, it only emphasized how completely the party had broken with things as they were before the war. The Social Democratic press, with a few exceptions, proclaimed the principle of national unity as the highest duty of the German people. It warned the people not to withdraw their funds from the savings banks lest by so doing they unbalance the economic life of the nation, and hinder the savings banks in liberally buying war-loan bonds. It pleaded with proletarian women that they should spare their husbands at the front the tales of suffering that they and their children were being forced to undergo, to bear in silence the neglect of the government, to cheer the fighting warriors with happy stories of family life and favorable reports of prompt assistance through government agencies. They rejoiced that the educational work that had been conducted for so many years in and through the labor movement had become a conspicuous asset in conducting the war. Something of this spirit the following example taken from the *Frankfurter Volksstimme*, August 18, 1914 will show:

"A friend in need is a friend indeed. This old adage has once more proven its soundness. The Social Democratic proletariat that has been prosecuted and clubbed for its opinions went, like one man, to protect our homes. German labour unions that had so often suffered both in Germany and in Prussia report unanimously that the best of their members have joined the colours. Even capitalist papers like the *General-Anzeiger* note the fact and express the conviction that 'these people' will do their duty as well as any man, that blows will rain most heavily where they stand.

"As for us, we are convinced that our labour unionists can do more than deal out blows. Modern mass armies have by no means simplified the work of their generals. It is practically impossible to move forward large troop divisions in close marching order under the deadly fire of modern artillery. Ranks must be carefully widened, must be more accurately controlled. Modern warfare requires discipline and clearness of vision not only in the divisions but in every individual soldier. The war will show how vastly human material has been improved by the educational work of the labour unions, how well their activity will serve the nation in these times of awful stress. The Russian and the French soldier may be capable of marvellous deeds of bravery. But in cool, collected consideration none will surpass the German labour unionists. Then too, many of our organized workers know the ways and by-ways of the borderland as well as they know their own pockets, and not a few of them are accomplished linguists. The Prussian advance in 1866 has been termed a schoolmasters' victory. This will be a victory of labour union leaders."

In the same strain the *Neue Zeit*, the theoretical organ of the party declared (No. 23, September 25, 1914):

"Until the question of victory or defeat has been decided, all doubts must dissappear, even as to the causes of the war. Today there can be no difference of party, class and nationality within the army or the population."

And in No. 8, November 27, 1914, the same *Neue Zeit* declared in a chapter on *"The Limitations of the International"*:

"The world war divides the socialists of the world into different camps and especially into different national camps. The International cannot prevent this. In other words, the International ceases to be an effective instrument in times of war. It is, on the whole, a peace instrument. Its great historic problem is the struggle for peace and the class struggle in times of peace."

Briefly, therefore, beginning with the 4th of August until the day when peace shall be declared, the Social Democracy has declared the class struggle extinct. The first thunder of Krupp cannons in Belgium welded Germany into a wonderland of class solidarity and social harmony.

How is this miracle to be understood? The class struggle is not known to be a Social Democratic invention that can be arbitrarily set aside for a period of time whenever it may seem convenient to do so. The proletarian class struggle is older than the Social Democracy, is an elementary product of class society. It flamed up all over Europe when capitalism first came into power. The modern proletariat was not led by the Social Democracy into the class struggle. On the contrary the international Social Democratic movement was called into being by the class struggle to bring a conscious aim and unity into the various local and scattered fragments of the class struggle. What then has changed in this respect when the war broke out? Have private property, capitalist exploitation, and class rule ceased to exist? Or have the propertied classes in a spell of patriotic fervor declared: "In view of the needs of the war we hereby turn over the means of production, the earth, the factories and the mills therein, into the possession of the people"? Have they relinquished the right to make profits out of these possessions? Have they set aside all political privileges, will they sacrifice them upon the altar of the fatherland, now that it is in danger? It is, to say the least, a rather naive hypothesis, and sounds almost like a story from a kindergarten primer. And yet the declaration of our official leaders that the class struggle has been suspended, permits no other interpretation. Of course nothing of the sort has occurred. Property rights, exploitation and class rule, even political oppression in all its Prussian thoroughness have remained intact. The cannon in Belgium and in Eastern Prussia have not had the slightest influence upon the fundamental social and political structure of Germany.

The cessation of the class struggle was, therefore, a deplorably one-sided affair. While capitalist oppression and exploitation, the worst enemies of the working class remain, socialist and labor union leaders have generously delivered the working class, without a struggle, into the hands of the enemy for the duration of the war. While the ruling classes are fully armed with the property and supremacy rights, the working class at the advice of the Social Democracy has laid down its arms.

Once before, in 1848 in France, the proletariat experienced this miracle of class harmony, this fraternity of all classes of a modern capitalist state of society. In his *Class Struggles in France*, Karl Marx writes: "In the eyes of the proletariat, who confused the moneyed aristocracy with the bourgeoisie, in the imagination of republican idealists, who denied the very existence of classes, or attributed them to a monarchical form of government, in the deceitful phrases of those bourgeois who had hitherto been excluded from power, the rule of the bourgeoisie was ended when the republic was proclaimed. At that time all royalists became republican, all millionaires in Paris became laborers. In the word *Fraternite*, the brotherhood of man, this imaginary destruction of classes found official expression. This comfortable abstraction from class differences, this sentimental balancing of class interests, this utopian disregard of the class struggle, this *Fraternite* was the real slogan of the February revolution. . . . The Parisian proletariat rejoiced in an orgy of brotherhood. . . . The Parisian proletariat, looking upon the republic as its own creation, naturally acclaimed every act of the provisional bourgeois government. Willingly it permitted Caussidiere to use its members as policemen to protect the property of Paris. With unquestioning faith it allowed Louis Blanc to regulate wage differences between workers and masters. In their eyes it was a matter of honour to preserve the fair name of the Republic before the peoples of Europe."

Thus in February, 1848 a naive Parisian proletariat set aside the class struggle. But let us not forget that even they committed this mistake only after the July monarchy[2] had been crushed by their revolutionary action, after a Republic had been established. The 4th of August 1914 is an inverted February Revolution. It is the setting aside of class differences, not under a republic, but under a military monarchy; not after a victory of the people over reaction, but after a victory of reaction over the people; not with the proclamation of *Liberte, Egalite, Fraternite*, but with the proclamation of a state of siege, after the press had been choked and the constitution annihilated.

Impressively the government of Germany proclaimed a civil peace. Solemnly the parties promised to abide by it. But as experienced politicians these gentlemen know full well that it is

2. By the July Revolution of 1830, Bourbon Charles X was deposed and replaced by Louis Philippe, of the younger Orleans branch of the same House. He styled himself "King of the French," and reigned till the February Revolution, 1848.

fatal to trust too much to promises. They secured civil peace for themselves by the very real measure of a military dictatorship. This too the Social Democratic group accepted without protest or opposition. In the declarations of August 4 and December 2 there is not a syllable of indignation over the affront contained in the proclamation of military rule. When it voted for civil peace and war credits, the Social Democracy silently gave its consent to military rule as well, and laid itself, bound and gagged, at the feet of the ruling classes. The declaration of military rule was purely an anti-socialist measure. From no other side were resistance, protest, action, and difficulties to be expected. As a reward for its capitulation the Social Democracy merely received what it would have received under any circumstances, even after an unsuccessful resistance, namely, military rule. The impressive declaration of the Reichstag group emphasizes the old socialist principle of the right of nations to self-determination, as an explanation of their vote in favor of war credits. Self-determination for the German proletariat was the straight jacket of a state of siege. Never in the history of the world has a party made itself more ridiculous.

But, more! In refuting the existence of the class struggle, the Social Democracy has denied the very basis of its own existence. What is the very breath of its body, if not the class struggle? What role could it expect to play in the war, once having sacrificed the class struggle, the fundamental principle of its existence? The Social Democracy has destroyed its mission for the period of the war as an active political party, as a representative of working class politics. It has thrown aside the most important weapon it possessed, the power of criticism of the war from the peculiar point of view of the working class. Its only mission now is to play the role of the gendarme over the working class under a state of military rule.

German freedom, that same German freedom for which, according to the declaration of the Reichstag group, Krupp cannons are now fighting, has been endangered by this attitude of the Social Democracy far beyond the period of the present war. The leaders of the Social Democracy are convinced that democratic liberties for the working class will come as a reward for its allegiance to the fatherland. But never in the history of the world has an oppressed class received political rights as a reward for service rendered to the ruling classes. History is full of examples of shameful deceit on the part of the ruling classes, even when solemn promises were made before the war broke out. The Social Democracy has not assured the extension of liberty in Germany. It has sacrificed those liberties that the working class possessed before the war broke out. The indifference with which the German people have allowed themselves to be deprived of the freedom of the press, of the right of assembly and of public life. The fact that they not only calmly bore, but even applauded the state of siege, is unexampled in the history of modern society. In England the freedom of the press has nowhere been violated, in France there is incomparably more freedom of public opinion than in Germany. In no country has public opinion so completely vanished, nowhere has it been so completely superseded by official opinion, by the order of the government, as in Germany. Even in Russia there is only the destructive work of a public censor who effectively wipes out opposition of opinion. But not even there have they descended to the custom of providing articles ready for the press to the opposition papers. In no other country has the government forced the opposition press to express in its columns the politics that have been dictated and ordered by the government in "Confidential Conferences." Such measures were unknown even in Germany during the war of 1870. At that time the press enjoyed unlimited freedom, and accompanied the events of the war, to Bismarck's active resentment, with criticism that was often exceedingly sharp. The newspapers were full of active discussion on war aims, on questions of annexation, and constitutionality. When Johann Jacobi was arrested, a storm of indignation swept over Germany, so that even Bismarck felt obliged to disavow all responsibility for this "mistake" of the powers of reaction. Such was the situation in Germany at a time when Bebel and Liebknecht, in the name of the German working class, had declined all community of interests with the ruling jingoes.[3]

3. **Jingo:** A rabid nationalist. The word was used originally in a popular song written during the Anglo-Russian crisis of 1878 (when Russia defeated Turkey): "We don't want to fight, but by jingo if we do. . . ."

It took a Social Democracy with four and a half million votes to conceive of the touching "Burgfrieden,"[4] to assent to war credits, to bring upon us the worst military dictatorship that was ever suffered to exist. That such a thing is possible in Germany today, that not only the bourgeois press, but the highly developed and influential socialist press as well permits these things without even the pretence of opposition bears a fatal significance for the future of German liberty. It proves that society in Germany today has within itself no foundation for political freedom, since it allows itself to be thus lightly deprived of its most sacred rights. Let us not forget that the political rights that existed in Germany before the war were not won, as were those of France and England in great and repeated revolutionary struggles; are not firmly anchored in the lives of the people by the power of revolutionary tradition. They are the gift of a Bismarckian policy granted after a period of victorious counterrevolution that lasted over twenty years. German liberties did not ripen on the field of revolution, they are the product of diplomatic gambling by Prussian military monarchy, they are the cement with which this military monarchy has united the present German Empire. Danger threatens the free development of German freedom not, as the German Reichstag group believe, from Russia, but in Germany itself. It lies in the peculiar counterrevolutionary origin of the German constitution, and looms dark in the reactionary powers that have controlled the German state since the empire was founded, conducting a silent but relentless war against these pitiful "German liberties." The Junkers of East of the Elbe, the business jingoes, the archreactionaries of the Center, the degraded "German liberals," the personal rulership, the sway of the sword, the Zabern policy[5] that triumphed all over Germany be-

4. **Burgfriede:** See note 5, chapter II.
5. **Zabern:** Or, Saverne, is in Alsace which had not been completely Germanized since the annexation in 1870–1, was the scene of friction between the army and the people in 1913. Lt. Baron Von Forstner had insulted the French flag while drilling recruits. The story leaked out, and the recruits were arrested on a charge of betraying military secrets. On November 10, 1913 crowds were fired upon by German troops and Forstner called upon them to give the miners a hot time. On November 28, Forstner said he was insulted in the streets and armed troops were sent out against a crowd of women, children and cripples.

fore the war broke out, these are the real enemies of culture and liberty, and the war, the state of seige and the attitude of the Social Democracy are strengthening the powers of darkness all over the land. The Liberal, to be sure, can explain away this graveyard quiet in Germany with a characteristically liberal explanation; to him it is only a temporary sacrifice for the duration of the war. But to a people that is politically ripe, a sacrifice of its rights and its public life, even temporarily, is as impossible as for a human being to give up, for a time, his right to breathe. A people that gives silent consent to military government in times of war thereby admits that political independence at any time is superfluous. The passive submission of the Social Democracy to the present state of siege and its vote for war credits without attaching the slightest condition thereto, its acceptance of a civil peace, has demoralized the masses, the only existing pillar of German constitutional government, has strengthened the reaction of its rulers, the enemies of constitutional government.

By sacrificing the class struggle, our Party has moreover, once and for all, given up the possibility of making its influence effectively felt in determining the extent of the war and the terms of peace. To its own official declaration, its acts have been a stinging blow. While protesting against all annexations, which are, after all, the logical consequences of an imperialist war that is successful from the military point of view, it has handed over every weapon that the working class possessed that might have empowered the masses to mobilize public opinion in their own direction, to exert an effective pressure upon the terms of war and of peace. By assuring militarism of peace and quiet at home, the Social Democracy has given its military rulers permission to follow their own course without even con-

---

Martial law was proclaimed, houses searched and the town judge and public prosecutor locked up for the night with twenty-eight others. On December 3, the matter was taken up by the Reichstag, War Minister Falkenheyn refused to disclose the punishment meted out to Forstner. The Reichstag passed a vote of no-confidence on the Chancellor Bethmann-Hollweg, 293 to 54. On December 19, the Alsatian recruits were sentenced three to six weeks for complaining, Forstner to forty-three days. On January 4, Commanding Officer Reuter and Forstner were acquitted by Court Martial, and the Crown Prince congratulated Reuter.

sidering the interests of the masses, has unleashed in the hearts of the ruling classes the most unbridled imperialistic tendencies. In other words, when the Social Democracy adopted its platform of civil peace and the political disarmament of the working class, it condemned its own demand of no annexations to impotency.

Thus the Social Democracy has added another crime to the heavy burden it already has to bear, namely the lengthening of the war. The commonly accepted dogma that we can oppose the war only so long as it is threatened has become a dangerous trap. As an inevitable consequence, once the war has come, Social Democratic political action is at an end. There can be, then, but one question: victory or defeat, i.e., the class struggle must stop for the period of the war. But actually the greatest problem for the political movement of the Social Democracy begins only after the war has broken out. At the International Congresses held in Stuttgart in 1907 and in Basel in 1912, the German party and labor union leaders unanimously voted in favor of a resolution which says:

"Should war nevertheless break out, it shall be the duty of the Social Democracy to work for a speedy peace, and to strive with every means in its power to utilize the industrial and political crisis to accomplish the awakening of the people, thus hastening the overthrow of capitalist class rule."

What has the Social Democracy done in this war? Exactly the contrary. By voting in favor of war credits and entering upon a civil peace, it has striven, by all the means in its power, to prevent the industrial and political crisis, to prevent an awakening of the masses by the war. It strives "with all the means in its power" to save the capitalist state from its own anarchy to reduce the number of its victims. It is claimed—we have often heard this argument used by Reichstag deputies—that not one man less would have fallen upon the battlefields if the Social Democratic group had voted against the war credits. Our party press has steadfastly maintained that we must support and join in the defense of our country in order to reduce the number of bloody victims that this war shall cost. But the policy that we have followed out has had exactly the opposite effect. In the first place, thanks to the civil peace and the patriotic attitude of the Social Democracy, the imperialist war unleashed its furies without fear. Hitherto, fear of restiveness at home, fear of the fury of the hungry populace, have been a load upon the minds of the ruling classes that effectively checked them in their bellicose desires. In the well-known words of Bulow: "They are trying to put off the war chiefly because they fear the Social Democracy." Rohrbach says in his *Krieg und die Deutsche Politik*,[6] "Unless elemental catastrophies intervene, the only power that can force Germany to make peace is the hunger of the breadless." Obviously he meant a hunger that attracts attention, that forces itself unpleasantly upon the ruling classes in order to force them to pay heed to its demands. Let us see finally what a prominent military theoretician, General Bernhardi, says in his great work *Vom Heutigen Kriege*[7]: "Thus modern mass armies make war difficult for a variety of reasons. Moreover they constitute, in and of themselves, a danger that must never be underestimated.

"The mechanism of such an army is so huge and so complicated, that it can remain efficient and flexible only so long as its cogs and wheels work, in the main, dependably, and obvious moral confusion is carefully prevented. These are things that cannot be completely avoided, as little as we can conduct a war exclusively with victorious battles. They can be overcome if they appear only within certain restricted limits. But when great, compact masses once shake off their leaders, when a spirit of panic becomes widespread, when a lack of sustenance becomes extensively felt, when the spirit of revolt spreads out among the masses of the army, then the army becomes not only ineffectual against the enemy, it becomes a menace to itself and to its leaders. When the army bursts the bands of discipline, when it voluntarily interrupts the course of military operation, it creates problems that its leaders are unable to solve.

"War, with its modern mass armies is, under all circumstances, a dangerous game, a game that demands the greatest possible sacrifice, personal and financial sacrifice the state can offer. Under such circumstances it is clear that provision must be

6. *The War & German Policy*, p. 7.
7. *On the Present War*.

made everywhere that the war, once it has broken out, be brought to an end as quickly as possible, to release the extreme tension that must accompany this supreme effort on the part of whole nations."

Thus capitalist politicians and military authorities alike believe war, with its modern mass armies, to be a dangerous game. And therein lay for the Social Democracy the most effectual opportunity to prevent the rulers of the present day from precipitating war and to force them to end it as rapidly as possible. But the position of the Social Democracy in this war cleared away all doubts, has torn down the dams that held back the storm-flood of militarism. In fact it has created a power for which neither Bernhadi nor any other capitalist statesman dared hope in his wildest dreams. From the camp of the Social Democrats came the cry: "Durchhalten",[8] i.e., a continuation of this human slaughter. And so the thousands of victims that have fallen for months on the battlefields lie upon our conscience.

8. Halt

Chapter VII

"But since we have been unable to prevent the war, since it has come in spite of us, and our country is facing invasion, shall we leave our country defenceless! Shall we deliver it into the hands of the enemy? Does not Socialism demand the right of nations to determine their own destinies? Does it not mean that every people is justified, nay more, is in duty bound, to protect its liberties, its independence? 'When the house is on fire, shall we not first try to put out the blaze before stopping to ascertain the incendiary?'"

These arguments have been repeated, again and again in defense of the attitude of the Social Democracy in Germany and in France.

Even in the neutral countries this argument has been used. Translated into Dutch we read for instance: "When the ship leaks must we not seek, first of all, to stop the hole?"

To be sure. Fie upon a people that capitulates before invasion and fie upon a party that capitulates before the enemy within.

But there is one thing that the fireman in the burning house has forgotten: that in the mouth of a Socialist, the phrase "defending one's fatherland" cannot mean playing the role of cannon fodder under the command of an imperialistic bourgeoisie.

Is an invasion really the horror of all horrors, before which all class conflict within the country must subside as though spellbound by some supernatural witchcraft? According to the police theory of bourgeois patriotism and military rule, every evidence of the class struggle is a crime against the interests of the country because they maintain that it constitutes a weakening of the stamina of the nation. The Social Democracy has allowed itself to be perverted into this same distorted point of view. Has not the history of modern capitalist society shown that in the eyes of capitalist society, foreign invasion is by no means the unmitigated terror as it is generally painted; that on the contrary, it is a measure to which the bourgeoisie has frequently and gladly resorted as an effective weapon against the enemy within? Did not the Bourbons and the aristocrats of France invite foreign invasion against the Jacobins? Did not the Austrian counterrevolution in 1849 call out the French invaders against Rome, the Russian against Budapest? Did not the "Party of Law and Order"[1] in France in 1850 openly threaten an invasion of the Cossacks in order to bring the National Assembly to terms? And was not the Bonaparte army released, and the support of the Prussian army against the Paris Commune assured, by the famous contract between Jules Favre, Thiers and Co., and Bismarck? This historical evidence led Karl Marx, forty-five years ago, to expose the "national wars" of modern capitalist society as miserable frauds. In his famous address to the General Council of the International on the downfall of the Paris Commune, he said:

"That, after the greatest war of modern times the belligerent armies, the victor and the vanquished, should unite for the mutual butchery of the proletariat—this incredible event proves, not as Bismarck would have us believe, the final overthrow of the new social power—but the complete disintegration of the old bourgeois society. The highest heroic accomplishment of which the old order is capable, is the national war. And this has now proved to be a fraud perpetrated by government for no other purpose than to put off the class struggle, a fraud that is bared as soon as the class struggle flares up in a civil war. Class rule can no longer hide behind a national uniform. The national governments are united against the proletariat."

In capitalist history, invasion and class struggle are not oposites, as the official legend would have us believe, but one is the means and the expression of the other. Just as invasion is the true and tried weapon in the hands of capital against the

---

1. **Party of Law and Order:** The royalist coalition of landowners and industrialists formed in 1848 in France.

class struggle, so on the other hand the fearless pursuit of the class struggle has always proven the most effective preventative of foreign invasions. On the brink of modern times are the examples of the Italian cities, Florence and Milan, with their century of bitter struggle against the Hohenstauffen. The stormy history of these cities, torn by inner conflicts, proves that the force and the fury of inner class struggles not only does not weaken the defensive powers of the community, but that on the contrary, from their fires shoot the only flames that are strong enough to withstand every attack from a foreign foe.

But the classic example of our own times is the great French Revolution. In Paris in 1793, the heart of France was surrounded by enemies. And yet Paris and France at that time did not succumb to the invasion of a stormy flood of European coalition; on the contrary, it welded its force in the face of the growing danger, to a more gigantic opposition. If France, at that critical time, was able to meet each new coalition of the enemy with a new miraculous and undiminished fighting spirit, it was only because of the impetuous loosening of the inmost forces of society in the great struggle of the classes of France. Today, in the perspective of a century, it is clearly discernible that only this intensification of the class struggle, that only the dictatorship of the French people and their fearless radicalism, could produce means and forces out of the soil of France, sufficient to defend and to sustain a new-born society against a world of enemies, against the intrigues of a dynasty, against the traitorous machinations of the aristocrats, against the attempts of the clergy, against the treachery of their generals, against the opposition of sixty departments and provincial capitals, and against the united armies and navies of monarchical Europe. The centuries have proven that not the state of siege, but relentless class struggle is the power that awakens the spirit of self-sacrifice, the moral strength of the masses, that the class struggle is the best protection and the best defense against a foreign enemy.

This same tragic *quid pro quo* victimized Social Democracy when it based its attitude in this war upon the doctrine of the right of national self-determination.

It is true that Socialism gives to every people the right of independence and the freedom of independent control of its own destinies. But it is a veritable perversion of Socialism to regard present day capitalist society as the expression of this self-determination of nations. Where is there a nation in which the people have had the right to determine the form and conditions of their national, political and social existence? In Germany the determination of the people found concrete expression in the demands formulated by the German revolutionary democrats of 1848; the first fighters of the German proletariat, Marx, Engels, Lassalle, Bebel and Liebknecht, proclaimed and fought for a united German Republic. For this ideal the revolutionary forces in Berlin and in Vienna, in those tragic days of March, shed their heart's blood upon the barricades. To carry out this program, Marx and Engels demanded that Prussia take up arms against Czarism. The foremost demand made in the national program was for the liquidation of "the heap of organized decay, the Habsburg monarchy," as well as of two dozen other dwarf monarchies within Germany itself. The overthrow of the German revolution, the treachery of the German bourgeoisie to its own democratic ideals, led to the Bismarck regime and to its creature, present day Greater Prussia, twenty-five fatherlands under one helm, the German Empire. Modern Germany is built upon the grave of the March Revolution[2] upon the wreckage of the right of self-determination of the German people. The present war, supporting Turkey and the Hapsburg monarchy, and strengthening German military autocracy is a second burial of the March revolutionists, and of the national program of the German people. It is a fiendish jest of history that the Social Democrats, the heirs of the German patriots of 1848, should go forth in this war with the banner of "self-determination of nations" held aloft in their hands. But, perhaps the third French Republic, with its colonial possessions in four continents and its colonial horrors in two, is the expression of the self-deter-

---

2. **March Revolution** in Germany, 1848: Began March 18 when troops attacked demonstrators in Berlin. On the 18th, the Palace was surrounded and there were many casualties. On the 29th, a new ministry was formed; on April 8, general, secret but indirect suffrage was promised. Later the National Assembly met at Frankfurt. Though the Prussian monarchy escaped in a number of lesser states throughout Germany, governments were overthrown.

mination of the French nation? Or the British nation, with its India, with its South African rule of a million whites over a population of five million colored people? Or perhaps Turkey, or the Empire of the Czar?

Capitalist politicians, in whose eyes the rulers of the people and the ruling classes are the nation, can honestly speak of the "right of national self-determination" in connection with such colonial empires. To the Socialist, no nation is free whose national existence is based upon the enslavement of another people, for to him colonial peoples, too, are human beings, and, as such, parts of the national state. International Socialism recognizes the right of free independent nations with equal rights. But Socialism alone can create such nations, can bring self-determination of their peoples. This slogan of Socialism is like all its others, not an apology for existing conditions, but a guide-post, a spur for the revolutionary, regenerative, active policy of the proletariat. So long as capitalist states exist, i.e., so long as imperialistic world policies determine and regulate the inner and the outer life of a nation, there can be no "national self-determination" either in war or in peace.

In the present imperialistic milieu there can be no wars of national self-defense. Every socialist policy that depends upon this determining historic milieu, that is willing to fix its policies in the world whirlpool from the point of view of a single nation is built upon a foundation of sand.

We have already attempted to show the background for the present conflict between Germany and her opponents. It was necessary to show up more clearly the actual forces and relations that constitute the motive power behind the present war, because this legend of the defense of the existence, the freedom and civilization of Germany plays an important part in the attitude of our group in the Reichstag and our Socialist press. Against this legend historical truth must be emphasized to show that this is a war that has been prepared by German militarism and its world-political ideas for years, that it was brought about in the Summer of 1914 by Austrian and German diplomacy, with a full realization of its import.

In a discussion of the general causes of the war, and of its significance, the question of the "guilty party" is completely

beside the issue. Germany certainly has not the right to speak
of a war of defense, but France and England have little more
justification. They too, are protecting, not their national, but
their world-political existence, their old imperialistic possessions,
from the attacks of the German upstart. Doubtless the raids of
German and Austrian imperialism in the Orient started the
conflagration, but French imperialism, by devouring Morocco,
and English imperialism, in its attempts to rape Mesopotamia,
and all the other measures that were calculated to secure its
rule of force in India, Russia's Baltic policies, aiming toward
Constantinople, all of these factors have carried together and
piled up, brand for brand, the firewood that feeds the conflagration. If capitalist armaments have played an important
role as the mainspring that times the outbreak of the catastrophe,
it was a competition of armaments in all nations. And if Germany laid the cornerstone for European competitive armaments
by Bismarck's policy of 1870, this policy was furthered by that
of the second Empire and by the military-colonial policies of
the third Empire, by its expansions in East Asia and in Africa.

The French Socialists have some slight foundation for their
illusion of "national defense," because neither the French government nor the French people entertained the slightest warlike
desires in July 1914. "Today everyone in France is honestly, up-
rightly and without reservation for peace," insisted Jaures in
the last speech of his life, on the eve of the war when he ad-
dressed a meeting in the People's House in Brussels. This was
absolutely true, and gives the psychological explanation for
the indignation of the French Socialists when this criminal war
was forced upon their country. But this fact was not sufficient
to determine the Socialist attitude on the world war as an
historic occurrence.

The events that bore the present war did not begin in July
1914 but reach back for decades. Thread by thread they have
been woven together on the loom of an inexorable natural
development until the firm net of imperialist world politics has
encircled five continents. It is a huge historical complex of
events, whose roots reach deep down into the Plutonic deeps
of economic creation, whose outermost branches spread out
and point away into a dimly dawning new world, events before

whose all-embracing immensity, the conception of guilt and retribution, of defense and offense, sink into pale nothingness.

Imperialism is not the creation of any one or of any group of states. It is the product of a particular stage of ripeness in the world development of capital, an innately international condition, an indivisible whole, that is recognizable only in all its relations, and from which no nation can hold aloof at will. From this point of view only is it possible to understand correctly the question of "national defense" in the present war.

The national state, national unity and independence were the ideological shield under which the capitalist nations of central Europe constituted themselves in the past century. Capitalism is incompatible with economic and political divisions, with the accompanying splitting up into small states. It needs for its development large, united territories, and a state of mental and intellectual development in the nation that will lift the demands and needs of society to a plane corresponding to the prevailing stage of capitalist production, and to the mechanism of modern capitalist class rule. Before capitalism could develop, it sought to create for itself a territory sharply defined by national limitations. This program was carried out only in France at the time of the great revolution, for in the national and political heritage left to Europe by the feudal middle ages, this could be accomplished only by revolutionary measures. In the rest of Europe this nationalization, like the revolutionary movement as a whole, remained the patchwork of half-kept promises. The German empire, modern Italy, Austria-Hungary, and Turkey, the Russian Empire and the British world-empire, are all living proofs of this fact. The national program could play a historic role only so long as it represented the ideological expression of a growing bourgeoisie, lusting for power, until it had fastened its class rule, in some way or other, upon the great nations of central Europe and had created within them the necessary tools and conditions of its growth. Since then, imperialism has buried the old bourgeois democratic program completely by substituting expansionist activity irrespective of national relationships for the original program of the bourgeoisie in all nations. The national phrase, to be sure, has been preserved, but its real content, its function has been perverted into its very opposite. Today the nation is but a cloak that covers imperialistic desires, a battle cry for imperialistic rivalries, the last ideological measure with which the masses can be persuaded to play the role of cannon fodder in imperialistic wars.

This general tendency of present day capitalist policies determines the policies of the individual states as their supreme blindly operating law, just as the laws of economic competition determine the conditions under which the individual manufacturer shall produce.

Let us assume for a moment, for the sake of argument, for the purpose of investigating this phantom of "national wars" that controls Social Democratic politics at the present time, that in one of the belligerent states, the war at its outbreak was purely one of national defense. Military success would immediately demand the occupation of foreign territory. But the existence of influential capitalist groups interested in imperialistic annexations will awaken expansionist appetites as the war goes on. The imperialistic tendency that, at the beginning of hostilities, may have been existent only in embryo, will shoot up and expand in the hot-house atmosphere of war until they will in a short time determine its character, its aims and its results. Furthermore, the system of alliance between military states that has ruled the political relations of these nations for decades in the past, makes it inevitable that each of the belligerent parties in the course of war, should try to bring its allies to its assistance, again purely from motives of self-defense. Thus one country after another is drawn into the war, inevitably new imperialistic circles are touched and others are created. Thus England drew in Japan, and, spreading the war into Asia, has brought China into the circle of political problems and has influenced the existing rivalry between Japan and the United States, between England and Japan, thus heaping up new material for future conflicts. Thus Germany has dragged Turkey into the war, bringing the question of Constantinople, of the Balkans and of Western Asia directly into the foreground of affairs. Even he who did not realize at the outset that the world war, in its causes, was purely imperialistic, cannot fail to see after a dispassionate view of its effects that war, under the present conditions, automatically and inevitably develops into a process of world division. This was apparent from the very first. The wavering balance of power between the two belligerent parties forces each, if only for military reasons, in order to strengthen its own position, or in order to frustrate possible attacks, to hold the neutral nations in check by intensive deals in peoples and nations, such as the German-Austrian offers to Italy, Rumania, Bulgaria and Greece on the one hand, and the English-Russian bids on the other. The "national war of defense" has the surprising effect of creating, even in the neutral nations, a general transformation of ownership and relative power, always in direct line with expansionist tendencies. Finally the fact that all modern capitalist states have colonial possessions that will, even though the war may have begun as a war of national defense, be drawn into the conflict from purely military considerations, the fact that each country will strive to occupy the colonial possessions of its opponent or at least to create disturbances therein, automatically turns every war into an imperialistic world conflagration.

Thus the conception of even that modest, devout fatherland-loving war of defense that has become the ideal of our parliamentarians and editors is pure fiction, and shows, on their part, a complete lack of understanding of the whole war and its world relations. The character of the war is determined, not by solemn declaration, not even by the honest intentions of leading politicians, but by the momentary configuration of society and its military organizations. At the first glance the term "national war of defense" might seem applicable in the case of a country like Switzerland. But Switzerland is no national state, and, therefore, no object of comparison with other modern states. Its very "neutral" existence, its luxury of a militia, are after all only the negative fruits of a latent state of war in the surrounding great military states. It will hold this neutrality only so long as it is willing to oppose this condition. How quickly such a neutral state is crushed by the military heel of imperialism in a world war the fate of Belgium shows. This brings us to the peculiar position of the "small nation." A classic example of such "national wars" is Serbia. If ever a state, according to formal considerations, had the right of national defense on its side, that state is Serbia. Deprived through Austrian annexations of its national unity, threatened by Austria in its very existence as a nation, forced by Austria into war, it is fighting, according to all human conceptions, for existence, for freedom, and for the civilization of its people. But if the Social Democratic group is right in its position, then the Serbian Social Democrats who protested against the war in the parliament at Belgrade and refused to vote war credits are actually traitors to the most vital interests of their own nation. In reality the Serbian Socialists Laptchevic and Kaclerovic have not only enrolled their names in letters of gold in the annals of the international socialist movement, but have shown a clear historical conception of the real causes of the war.[3] In voting against war credits they therefore have done their country the best possible service. Serbia is formally engaged in a national war of defense. But its monarchy and its ruling classes are filled with expansionist desires as are the ruling classes in all modern states. They are indifferent to ethnic lines, and thus their warfare assumes an aggressive character. Thus Serbia is today reaching out toward the Adriatic coast where it is fighting out a real imperialistic conflict with Italy on the backs of the Albanians, a conflict whose final outcome will be decided not by either of the powers directly interested, but by the great powers that will speak the last word on terms of peace. But above all this we must not forget: behind Serbian nationalism stands Russian imperialism. Serbia itself is only a pawn in the great game of world politics. A judgement of the war in Serbia from a point of view that fails to take these great relations and the general world-political background into account, is necessarily without foundation. The same is true of the recent Balkan war. Regarded as an isolated occurrence, the young Balkan states were historically justified in defending the old democratic program of the national state. In their historical connection, however, which makes the Balkans the burning point and the center of imperialistic world policies, these Balkan wars were also objectively only a fragment of

3. Laptchevic and Kaclerovic, Socialist Deputies to the Serbian Parliament, opposed war credits, despite the fact that Austria was the aggressor.

the general conflict, a link in the chain of events that led with fatal necessity to the present world war. After the Balkan war the international Social Democracy tendered to the Balkan Socialists, for their determined refusal to offer moral or political support to the war, a most enthusiastic ovation at the peace Congress at Basel. In this act alone the International condemned in advance the position taken by the German and French Socialists in the present war.

All small states, as for instance Holland, are today in a position like that of the Balkan states. "When the ship leaks, the hole must be stopped"; and what, forsooth, could little Holland fight for but for its national existence and for the independence of its people? If we consider here merely the determination of the Dutch people, even of its ruling classes, the question is doubtlessly one purely of national defense. But again proletarian politics cannot judge according to the subjective purposes of a single country. Here again it must take its position as a part of the International, according to the whole complexity of the world's political situation. Holland, too, whether it wishes to be or not, is only a small wheel in the great machine of modern world politics and diplomacy. This would become clear at once, if Holland were actually torn into the maelstrom of the world war. Its opponents would direct their attacks against its colonies. Automatically Dutch warfare would turn to the defense of its present possessions. The defense of the national independence of the Dutch people on the North Sea would expand concretely to the defense of its rule and right of exploitation over the Malays in the East Indian Archipalego. But that is not enough. Dutch militarism if forced to rely upon itself, would be crushed like a nutshell in the whirlpool of the world war. Whether it wished to or not it would become a member of one of the great national alliances. On one side or the other it must be the bearer and the tool of purely imperialistic tendencies.

Thus it is always the historic milieu of modern imperialism that determines the character of the war in the individual countries, and this milieu makes a war of national self-defense impossible.

Kautsky also expressed this, only a few years ago, in his pamphlet *Patriotism and Social Democracy:*

"Though the patriotism of the bourgeoisie and of the proletariat are two entirely different, actually opposite, phenomena there are situations in which both kinds of patriotism may join forces for united action, even in times of war. The bourgeoisie and the proletariat of a nation are equally interested in their national independence and self-determination, in the removal of all kinds of oppression and exploitation at the hands of a foreign nation. In the national conflicts that have sprung from such attempts, the patriotism of the proletariat has always united with that of the bourgeoisie. But the proletariat has become a power that may become dangerous to the ruling classes at every great national upheaval; revolution looms dark at the end of every war, as the Paris Commune of 1871 and Russian terrorism after the Russo-Japanese war have proven. In view of this the bourgeoisie of those nations which are not sufficiently united have actually sacrificed their national aims where these can be maintained only at the expense of their government, for they hate and fear the revolution even more than they love national independence and greatness. For this reason, the bourgeoisie sacrifices the independence of Poland and permits ancient constellations like Austria and Turkey to remain in existence, though they have been doomed to destruction for more than a generation. National struggles as the bringers of revolution have ceased in civilized Europe. National problems that today can be solved only by war or revolution, will be solved in the future only by the victory of the proletariat. But then, thanks to international solidarity, they will at once assume a form entirely different from that which prevails today in a social state of exploitation and oppression. In capitalistic states this problem needs no longer to trouble the proletariat in its practical struggles. It must divert its whole strength to other problems. . . .

"Meanwhile the likelihood that proletarian and bourgeois patriotism will unite to protect the liberty of the people is becoming more and more rare." Kautsky then goes on to say that the French bourgeoisie has united with Czarism, that Russia has ceased to be a danger for western Europe because it has been weakened by the Revolution. "Under these circumstances a war in defence of national liberty in which bourgeois and proletarian may unite, is nowhere to be expected. . . .

"We have already seen that conflicts which, in the nineteenth century, might still have led some liberty loving peoples to oppose their neighbors, by warfare, have ceased to exist. We have seen that modern militarism nowhere aims to defend important popular rights, but everywhere strives to support profits. Its activities are dedicated not to assure the independence and invulnerability of its own nationality, that is nowhere threatened, but to the assurance and the extension of over-sea conquests that again only serve the aggrandizement of capitalist profits. At the present time the conflicts between states can bring no war that proletarian interests would not, as a matter of duty, energetically oppose."[3]

In view of all these considerations, what shall be the practical attitude of the Social Democracy in the present war? Shall it declare: since this is an imperialist war, since we do not enjoy in our country, any Socialist self-determination, its existence or nonexistence is of no consequence to us, and we will surrender it to the enemy? Passive fatalism can never be the role of a revolutionary party like the Social Democracy. It must neither place itself at the disposal of the existing class state, under the command of the ruling classes, nor can it stand silently by to wait until the storm is past. It must adopt a policy of active class politics, a policy that will whip the ruling classes forward in every great social crisis and that will drive the crisis itself far beyond ts original extent. That is the role that the Social Democracy must play as the leader of the fighting proletariat. Instead of covering this imperialist war with a lying mantle of national self-defense, the Social Democracy should have demanded the right of national self-determination seriously, should have used it as a lever against the imperialist war.

The most elementary demand of national defense is that the nation takes its defense into its own hands. The first step in this

3. Kautsky, *Patriotism and Social Democracy* (Leipzig, 1907), pp. 12–14, 16, 23.

direction is the militia; not only the immediate armament of the entire adult male populace, but above all, popular decision in all questions of peace and war. It must demand, furthermore, the immediate removal of every form of political oppression, since the greatest political freedom is the best basis for national defense. To proclaim these fundamental measures of national defence, to demand their realization, that was the first duty of the Social Democracy.

For forty years we have tried to prove to the ruling classes as well as to the masses of the people that only the militia is really able to defend the fatherland and to make it invincible. And yet, when the first test came, we turned over the defense of our country, as a matter of course, into the hands of the standing army to be the cannon fodder under the club of the ruling classes. Our parliamentarians apparently did not even notice that the fervent wishes with which they sped these defenders of the fatherland to the front were, to all intents and purposes, an open admission that the imperial Prussian standing army is the real defender of the fatherland. They evidently did not realize that by this admission they sacrificed the fulcrum of our political program, that they gave up the militia and dissolved the practical significance of forty years of agitation against the standing army into thin air. By the act of the Social Democratic group our military program became a utopian doctrine, a doctrinaire obsession, that none could possibly take seriously.

The masters of the international proletariat saw the idea of the defense of the fatherland in a different light. When the proletariat of Paris, surrounded by Prussians in 1871, took the reins of the government into its own hands, Marx wrote enthusiastically:

"Paris, the centre and seat of the old government powers, and simultaneously the social centre of gravity of the French working class, Paris has risen in arms against the attempt of Monsieur Thiers and his Junkers to reinstate and perpetuate the government of the old powers of imperial rule. Paris was in a position to resist only, because through a state of seige, it was rid of its army, because in its place there had been put a national guard composed chiefly of working men. It was necessary that this innovation be made a permanent institution. The first act of the Commune was, therefore, the suppression of the standing army and the substitution of an armed people. . . . If now, the Commune was the true representative of all healthy elements of French society and, therefore, a true national government, it was likewise, as a proletarian government, as the daring fighter for the liberation of labour, international in the truest sense of that word. Under the eyes of the Prussian army, which has annexed two French Provinces to Germany, the Commune has annexed the workers of a whole world to France." (*Address to the General Council of the International.*)

But what did our masters say concerning the role to be played by the Social Democracy in the present war? In 1892 Friedrich Engels expressed the following opinion concerning the fundamental lines along which the attitude of proletarian parties in a great war should follow:

"A war in the course of which Russians and Frenchmen should invade Germany would mean for the latter a life and death struggle. Under such circumstances it could assure its national existence only by using the most revolutionary methods. The present government, should it not be forced to do so, will certainly not bring on the revolution, but we have a strong party that may force its hand, or that, should it be necessary, can replace it, the Social Democratic party.

"We have not forgotten the glorious example of France in 1793. The one hundredth anniversary of 1793 is approaching. Should Russia's desire for conquest, or the chauvinistic impatience of the French bourgeoisie, check the victorious but peaceable march of the German Socialists, the latter are prepared—be assured of that—to prove to the world that the German proletarians of today are not unworthy of the French Sansculottes, that 1893 will be worthy of 1793. And should the soldiers of Monsieur Constans set foot upon German territory we will meet them with the words of the Marsellaise:

> Shall hateful tyrants, mischief breeding,
> With hireling host, a ruffian band,
> Affright and desolate the land?

"In short, peace assures the victory of the Social Democratic party in about ten years. The war will bring either victory in two or three years or its absolute ruin for at least fifteen or twenty years."

When Engels wrote these words, he had in mind a situation entirely different from the one existing today. In his mind's eye, ancient Czarism still loomed threateningly in the background. We have already seen the great Russian Revolution. He thought, furthermore, of a real national war of defense, of a Germany attacked on two sides, on the East and on the West by two enemy forces. Finally, he overestimated the ripeness of conditions in Germany and the likelihood of a social revolution, as all true fighters are wont to overrate the real tempo of development. But for all that, his sentences prove with remarkable clearness, that Engels meant by national defense, in the sense of the Social Democracy, not the support of a Prussian Junker military government and its Generalstab, but a revolutionary action after the example of the French Jacobins.

Yes, Socialists should defend their country in great historical crises, and here lies the great fault of the German Social Democratic Reichstag group. When it announced on the 4th of August, "In this hour of danger, we will not desert our fatherland," it denied its own words in the same breath. For truly it has deserted its fatherland in its hour of greatest danger. The highest duty of the Social Democracy toward its fatherland demanded that it expose the real background of this imperialist war, that it rend the net of imperialist and diplomatic lies that covers the eyes of the people. It was their duty to speak loudly and clearly, to proclaim to the people of Germany that in this war victory and defeat would be equally fatal, to oppose the gagging of the fatherland by a state of siege, to demand that the people alone decide on war and peace, to demand a permanent session of Parliament for the period of the war, to assume a watchful control over the government by parliament, and over parliament by the people, to demand the immediate removal of all political inequalities, since only a free people can adequately govern its country, and finally, to oppose to the imperialist war, based as it was upon the most reactionary forces in Europe, the program of Marx, of Engels, and Lassalle.

That was the flag that should have waved over the country.

That would have been truly national, truly free, in harmony with the best traditions of Germany and the international class policy of the proletariat.

The great historical hour of the world war obviously demanded a unanimous political accomplishment, a broad-minded, comprehensive attitude that only the Social Democracy is destined to give. Instead, there followed on the part of the parliamentary representatives of the working class a miserable collapse. The Social Democracy did not adopt the wrong policy—it had no policy whatsoever. It has wiped itself out completely as a class partly with a world conception of its own, has delivered the country, without a word of protest, to the fate of imperialist war without to the dictatorship of the sword within. Nay more, it has taken the responsibility for the war upon its own shoulders. The declaration of the "Reichstag group" says: "We have voted only the means for our country's defence. We decline all responsibility for the war." But as a matter of fact, the truth lies in exactly the opposite direction. The means for "national defence," i.e., for imperialistic mass butchery by the armed forces of the military monarchy, were not voted by the Social Democracy. For the availability of the war credits did not in the least depend upon the Social Democracy. They, as a minority, stood against a compact three-quarters majority of the capitalist Reichstag. The Social Democratic group accomplished only one thing by voting in favor of the war credits. It placed upon the war the stamp of democratic fatherland defense, and supported and sustained the fictions that were propagated by the government concerning the actual conditions and problems of the war.

Thus the serious dilemma between the national interests and international solidarity of the proletariat, the tragic conflict that made our parliamentarians fall "with heavy heart" to the side of imperialistic warfare, was a mere figment of the imagination, a bourgeois nationalist fiction. Between the national interests and the class interests of the proletariat, in war and in peace, there is actually complete harmony. Both demand the most energetic prosecution of the class struggle, and the most determined insistence on the Social Democratic program.

But what action should the party have taken to give to our

opposition to the war and to our war demands weight and emphasis? Should it have proclaimed a general strike? Should it have called upon the soldiers to refuse military service? Thus the question is generally asked. To answer with a simple yes or no, were just as ridiculous as to decide: "When war breaks out we will start a revolution." Revolutions are not "made" and great movements of the people are not produced according to technical recipes that repose in the pockets of the party leaders. Small circles of conspirators may organize a riot for a certain day and a certain hour, can give their small group of supporters the signal to begin. Mass movements in great historical crises cannot be initiated by such primitive measures. The best prepared mass strike may break down miserably at the very moment when the party leaders give the signal, may collapse completely before the first attack. The success of the great popular movements depends, aye, the very time and circumstance of their inception is decided, by a number of economic, political and psychological factors. The existing degree of tension between the classes, the degree of intelligence of the masses and the degree or ripeness of their spirit of resistance—all these factors, which are incalculable, are premises that cannot be artificially created by any party. That is the difference between the great historical upheavals, and the small show demonstrations that a well-disciplined party can carry out in times of peace, orderly, well-trained performances, responding obediently to the baton in the hands of the party leaders. The great historical hour itself creates the forms that will carry the revolutionary movements to a successful outcome, creates and improvises new weapons, enriches the arsenal of the people with weapons unknown and unheard of by the parties and their leaders.

What the Social Democracy as the advance guard of the class conscious proletariat should have been able to give was not ridiculous precepts and technical recipes, but a political slogan, clearness concerning the political problems and interests of the proletariat in times of war.

For what has been said of mass strikes in the Russian Revolution is equally applicable to every mass movement: "While the revolutionary period itself commands the creation and the computation and payment of the cost of a mass strike, the leaders of the Social Democracy have an entirely different mission to fill. Instead of concerning itself with the technical mechanism of the mass movement, it is the duty of the Social Democracy to undertake the political leadership even in the midst of a historical crisis. To give the slogan, to determine the direction of the struggle, to so direct the tactics of the political conflict that in its every phase and movement the whole sum of available and already mobilized active force of the proletariat is realized and finds expression in the attitude of the party, that the tactics of the Social Democracy in determination and vigour shall never be weaker than is justified by the actual power at its back, but shall rather hasten in advance of its actual power, that is the important problem of the party leadership in a great historical crisis. Then this leadership will become, in a sense, the technical leadership. A determined, consistent, progressive course of action on the part of the Social Democracy will create in the masses assurance, self-confidence and a fearless fighting spirit. A weakly vacillating course, based upon a low estimate of the powers of the proletariat, lames and confuses the masses. In the first case mass action will break out 'of its own accord' and 'at the right time'; in the second, even a direct call to action on the part of the leaders often remains ineffectual."

Far more important than the outward, technical form of the action is its political content. Thus the parliamentary stage, for instance, the only far reaching and internationally conspicuous platform, could have become a mighty motive power for the awakening of the people, had it been used by the Social Democratic representatives to proclaim loudly and distinctly, the interests, the problems and the demands of the working class.

"Would the masses have supported the Social Democracy in its attitude against the war?" That is a question that no one can answer. But neither is it an important one. Did our parliamentarians demand an absolute assurance of victory from the generals of the Prussian army before voting in favour of war credits? What is true of military armies is equally true of revolutionary armies. They go into the fight, wherever necessity demands it, without previous assurance of success. At the worst, the party would have been doomed, in the first few months of the war, to political ineffectuality.

Perhaps the bitterest persecutions would have been inflicted upon our party for its manly stand, as they were, in 1870, the reward of Liebknecht and Bebel. "But what does that matter," said Ignaz Auer, simply, in his speech on the Sedanfeier in 1895. "A party that is to conquer the world must bear its principles aloft without counting the dangers that this may bring. To act differently is to be lost!"

"It is never easy to swim against the current," said the older Liebknecht, "and when the stream rushes on with the rapidity and the power of a Niagara it does not become easier. Our older comrades still remember the hatred of that year of greatest national shame, under the Socialist exception laws of 1878. At that time millions looked upon every Social Democrat as having played the part of a murderer and vile criminal in 1870; the Socialist had been in the eyes of the masses a traitor and an enemy. Such outbreaks of the 'popular soul' are astounding, stunning, crushing in their elementary fury. One feels powerless, as before a higher power. It is a real *force majeure*. There is no tangible opponent. It is like an epidemic, in the people, in the air, everywhere.

"The outbreak of 1878 cannot, however, be compared with the outbreak in 1870. This hurricane of human passions, breaking, bending, destroying all that stands in its way—and with it the terrible machinery of militarism, in fullest, most horrible activity; and we stand between the crushing iron wheels, whose touch means instant death, between iron arms, that threaten every moment to catch us. By the side of this elemental force of liberated spirits stood the most complete mechanism of the art of murder the world had hitherto seen; and all in the wildest activity, every boiler heated to the bursting point. At such a time, what is the will and the strength of the individual? Especially, when one feels that one represents a tiny minority, that one possesses no firm support in the people itself.

"At that time our party was still in a period of development. We were placed before the most serious test, at a time when we did not yet possess the organization necessary to meet it. When the anti-socialist movement came in the year of shame of our enemies, in the year of honour for the Social Democracy, then we had already a strong, widespread organization. Each and every one of us was strengthened by the feeling that he possessed a mighty support in the organized movement that stood behind him, and no sane person could conceive of the downfall of the party.

"So it was no small thing at that time to swim against the current. But what is to be done, must be done. And so we gritted our teeth in the face of the inevitable. There was no time for fear. . . . Certainly Bebel and I . . . never for a moment thought of the warning. We did not retreat. We had to hold our posts, come what might!"

They stuck to their posts, and for forty years the Social Democracy lived upon the moral strength with which it had opposed a world of enemies.

The same thing would have happened now. At first we would perhaps have accomplished nothing but to save the honor of the proletariat and thousands upon thousands of proletarians who are dying in the trenches in mental darkness, would not have died in spiritual confusion, but with the one certainty that that which has been everything in their lives, the International, liberating Social Democracy, is more than the figment of a dream.

The voice of our party would have acted as a wet blanket upon the chauvinistic intoxication of the masses. It would have preserved the intelligent proletariat from delirium, would have it more difficult for imperialism to poison and to stupefy the minds of the people. The crusade against the Social Democracy would have awakened the masses in an incredibly short time.

And as the war went on, as the horror of endless massacre and bloodshed in all countries grew and grew, as its imperialistic hoof became more and more evident, as the exploitation by bloodthirsty speculators became more and more shameless, every live, honest, progressive and humane element in the masses would have rallied to the standard of the Social Democracy. The German Social Democracy would have stood in the midst of this mad whirlpool of collapse and decay, like a rock in a stormy sea, would have been the lighthouse of the whole International, guiding and leading the labor movements of every country of the earth. The unparalleled moral prestige that lay in the hands of the German Socialists would have reacted upon the Socialists of all nations in a very short time. Peace sentiments would have spread like wildfire and the popular demand for peace in all countries would have hastened the end of the slaughter, would have decreased the number of its victims.

The German proletariat would have remained the lighthouse keeper of Socialism and of human emancipation.

Truly this was a task not unworthy of the disciples of Marx, Engels and Lassalle.

Chapter VIII

In spite of military dictatorship and press censorship, in spite of the downfall of the Social Democracy, in spite of fratricidal war, the class struggle arises from civil peace with elemental force. From the blood and smoke of the battlefields the solidarity of international labor arises. Not in weak attempts to artificially galvanize the old International, not in pledges rendered now and here, now there, to stand together after the war is over. No, here, in the war, out of the war, arises, with a new might and intensity, the recognition that the proletarians of all lands have one and the same interest. The world war, itself, utterly disproves the falsehoods it has created.

Victory or defeat? It is the slogan of all-powerful militarism in every belligerent nation, and like an echo, the Social Democratic leaders have adopted it. Victory or defeat has become the highest motive of the workers of Germany, of France, of England and of others, just as for the ruling classes of these nations. When the cannons thunder, all proletarian interests subside before the desire for victory of their own, i.e., for the defeat of the other countries. And yet, what can victory bring to the proletariat?

According to the official version of the leaders of the Social Democracy, that was so readily adopted without criticism, victory of the German forces would mean unhampered, boundless industrial growth for Germany; defeat, however, industrial ruin. On the whole, this conception coincides with that generally accepted during the war of 1870. But the period of capitalist growth that followed the war of 1870 was not caused by the war, but resulted rather from the political union of the various German states, even though this union took the form of the crippled figure that Bismarck established as the German Empire.

Here the industrial impetus came from this union, in spite of the war and the manifold reactionary hindrances that followed in its wake. What the victorious war itself accomplished was to firmly establish the military monarchy and Prussian junkerdom in Germany; the defeat of France led to the liquidation of its empire and the establishment of a republic. But today the situation is different in all of the nations in question. Today war does not function as a dynamic force to provide for rising young capitalism the indispensable political conditions for its "national" development. Modern war appears in this role only in Serbia, and there only as an isolated fragment. Reduced to its objective historic significance, the present world war as a whole is a competitive struggle of a fully developed capitalism for world supremacy, for the exploitation of the last remnant of non-capitalistic world zones. This fact gives to the war and its political after effects an entirely new character. The high stage of world-industrial development in capitalist production finds expression in the extraordinary technical development and destructiveness of the instruments of war, as in their practically uniform degree of perfection in all belligerent countries. The international organization of war industries is reflected in the military instability, that persistently brings back the scales, through all partial decisions and variations, to their true balance, and pushes a general decision further and further into the future. The indecision of military results, moreover, has the effect that a constant stream of new reserves, from the belligerent nations as well as from nations hitherto neutral, are sent to the front. Everywhere war finds material enough for imperialist desires and conflicts; creates new material to feed the conflagration that spreads out like a prairie fire. But the greater the masses, and the greater the number of nations that are dragged into this world war, the longer will it rage. All of these things together prove, even before any military decision of victory or defeat can be established, what the result of the war will be: the economic ruin of all participating nations, and, in a steadily growing measure, of the formally neutral nations, a phenomenon entirely distinct from the earlier wars of modern times. Every month of war affirms and augments this effect, and thus takes away the expected fruits of military victory for a decade to come. This, in the last analysis, neither victory nor defeat can alter; on the contrary, it makes a purely military decision altogether doubtful, and increases the likelihood that the war will finally end through a general and extreme exhaustion. But even a victorious Germany under such circumstances, even if its imperialist war agitators should succeed in carrying on the mass murder to the absolute destruction of their opponents, even if their most daring dreams should be fulfilled—would win but a Phyrric victory. A number of annexed territories, impoverished and depopulated, and a grinning ruin under its own roof, would be its trophies. Nothing can hide this, once the painted stage properties of financial war-bond transactions, and the Potemkin villages[1] of an "unalterable prosperity" kept up by war orders, are pushed aside. The most superficial observer cannot but see that even the most victorious nation cannot count on war indemnities that will stand in any relation to the wounds that the war has inflicted. Perhaps they may see in the still greater economic ruin of the defeated opponents, England and France, the very countries with which Germany was most closely united by industrial relations, upon whose recuperation its own prosperity so much depends, a substitute and an augmentation for their victory. Such are the circumstances under which the German people, even after a victorious war, would be required to pay, in cold cash, the war bonds that were "voted" on credit by the patriotic parliament, i.e., to take upon their shoulders an immeasurable burden of taxation, and a strengthened military dictatorship as the only permanent tangible fruit of victory.

Should we now seek to imagine the worst possible effects of a defeat, we shall find that they resemble, line for line, with the exception of imperialistic annexations, the same picture that presented itself as the irrefutable consequence of victory: the

---

1. **Potemkin villages:** Gregory Alexandrovich Potemkin (1724–1791) the most outstanding personality of the time of Catherine the Great, and said to have been Catherine's lover, was authorized by the Empress to organize "New Russia" in the South. He brought old ports up to date, set up new villages and founded Ekaterinoslav ("Catherine's Glory"). His critics alleged that his villages were cardboard fronts, built to deceive the Empress when she toured the area.

effects of war today are so far reaching, so deeply rooted, that its military outcome can alter but little in its final consequences.

But let us assume, for the moment, that the victorious nation should find itself in the position to avoid the great catastrophe for its own people, should be able to throw the whole burden of the war upon the shoulders of its defeated opponent, should be able to choke off the industrial development of the latter by all sorts of hindrances. Can the German labor movement hope for successful development, so long as the activity of the French, English, Belgian and Italian laborers is hampered by industrial retrogression? Before 1870 the labor movements of the various nations grew independently of each other. The action of the labor movement of a single city often controlled the destinies of the whole labor movement. On the streets of Paris the battles of the working class were fought out and decided. The modern labor movement, its laborious daily struggle in the industries of the world, its mass organization, are based upon the cooperation of the workers in all capitalistically producing countries. If the truism that the cause of labor can thrive only upon a virile, pulsating industrial life applies, then it is true not only for Germany, but for France, England, Belgium, Russia, and Italy as well. And if the labor movement in all of the capitalist states of Europe becomes stagnant, if industrial conditions there result in low wages, weakened labor unions, and a diminished power of resistance on the part of labor, labor unionism in Germany cannot possibly flourish. From this point of view the loss sustained by the working class in its industrial struggle is in the last analysis identical, whether German capital be strengthened at the expense of the French or English capital at the expense of the German.

But let us investigate the political effects of the war. Here differentiation should be less difficult than upon the economic side, for the sympathies and the partisanship of the proletariat have always tended toward the side that defended progress against reaction. Which side, in the present war, represents progress, which side reaction? It is clear that this question cannot be decided according to the outward insignias that mark the political character of the belligerent nations as "democracy" and absolutism. They must be judged solely according to the tendencies of their respective world policies.

Before we can determine what a German victory can win for the German proletariat we must consider its effect upon the general status of political conditions all over Europe. A decisive victory for Germany would mean, in the first place, the annexation of Belgium, as well as of a possible number of territories in the East and West and a part of the French colonies; the sustaining of the Hapsburg monarchy and its aggrandizement by a number of new territories; finally the establishment of a fictitious "integrity" of Turkey, under a German protectorate, i.e., the conversion of Asia Minor and Mesopotamia, in one form or another, into German provinces. In the end this would result in the actual military and economic hegemony of Germany in Europe. Not because they are in accord with the desires of imperialist agitators are these consequences of an absolute German military victory to be expected, but because they are the inevitable outgrowth of the world-political position that Germany has adopted, of conflicting interests with England, France and Russia, in which Germany has been involved, and which have grown, during the course of the war, far beyond their original dimensions. It is sufficient to recall these facts to realize that they could under no circumstances establish a permanent world-political equilibrium. Though this war may mean ruin for all of its participants, and worse for its defeated, the preparations for a new world war, under England's leadership, would begin on the day after peace is declared, to shake off the yoke of Prussian-German militarism that would rest upon Europe and Asia. A German victory would be the prelude to an early second world war, and therefore, for this reason, but the signal for new feverish armaments, for the unleashing of the blackest reaction in every country, but particularly in Germany. On the other hand a victory of England or France would mean, in all likelihood, for Germany, the loss of a part of her colonies, as well as of Alsace-Lorraine, and certainly the bankruptcy of the world-political position of German militarism. But this would mean the disintegration of Austria-Hungary and the total liquidation of Turkey. Reactionary as both of these states are, and much as their disintegration would be in line with the demands of progressive development, in the present world-political milieu the disintegration of the Hapsburg monarchy and the liquidation of Turkey would mean the bartering of their peoples to the highest bidder—Russia, England, France, or Italy. This enormous redivision of the world and shifting of the balance of power in the Balkan states and along the Mediterranean would be followed inevitably by another in Asia: the liquidation of Persia and a redivision of China. This would bring the Anglo-Russian as well as the Anglo-Japanese conflict into the foreground of international politics, and may mean, in direct connection with the liquidation of the present war, a new world war, perhaps for Constantinople; would certainly bring it about, inescapably, in the immediate future. So a victory on this side, too, would lead to new, feverish armaments in all nations—defeated Germany, of course, at the head—and would introduce an era of undivided rule for militarism and reaction all over Europe, with a new war as its final goal.

So the proletariat, should it attempt to cast its influence into the balance on one side or the other, for progress or democracy, viewing the world policies in their widest application, would place itself between Scylla and Charybdis. Under the circumstances the question of victory or defeat becomes, for the European working class, in its political, exactly as in its economic aspects, a choice between two beatings. It is, therefore, nothing short of a dangerous madness for the French Socialists to believe that they can deal a death blow to militarism and imperialism, and clear the road for peaceful democracy, by overthrowing Germany. Imperialism, and its servant militarism, will reappear after every victory and after every defeat in this war. There can be but one exception: if the international proletariat, through its intervention, should overthrow all previous calculations.

The important lesson to be derived by the proletariat from this war is the one unchanging fact, that it can and must not become the uncritical echo of the "victory and defeat" slogan, neither in Germany nor in France, neither in England nor in Austria. For it is a slogan that has reality only from the point of view of imperialism, and is identical, in the eyes of every large power, with the question: gain or loss of world-political power, of annexations, of colonies, of military supremacy.

For the European proletariat as a class, victory or defeat of either of the two war groups would be equally disastrous. For war as such, whatever its military outcome may be, is the greatest conceivable defeat of the cause of the European proletariat. The overthrow of war, and the speedy forcing of peace, by the international revolutionary action of the proletariat, alone can bring to it the only possible victory. And this victory, alone, can truly rescue Belgium, can bring democracy to Europe.

For the class conscious proletariat to identify its cause with either military camp is an untenable position. Does that mean that the proletarian policies of the present day demand a return to the "status quo," that we have no plan of action beyond the fond hope that everything may remain as it was before the war? The existing conditions have never been our ideal, they have never been the expression of the self-determination of the people. And more, the former conditions cannot be reinstated, even if the old national boundaries should remain unchanged. For even before its formal ending this war has brought about enormous changes, in mutual recognition of one another's strength, in alliances and in conflict. It has sharply revised the relations of countries to one another, of classes within society, has destroyed so many old illusions and portents, has created so many new forces and new problems, that a return to the old Europe that existed before August 4, 1914 is as impossible as the return to prerevolutionary conditions, even after an unsuccessful revolution. The proletariat knows no going back and can only strive forward and onward, for a goal that lies beyond even the most newly created conditions. In this sense, alone, is it possible for the proletariat to oppose, with its policy, both camps in the imperialist world war.

But this policy cannot concern itself with recipes for capitalist diplomacy worked out individually by the Social Democratic parties, or even together in international conferences, to determine how capitalism shall declare peace in order to assure future peaceful and democratic development. All demands for complete or gradual disarmament, for the abolition of secret diplomacy, for the dissolution of the great powers into smaller national entities, and all other similar propositions, are absolutely Utopian so long as capitalist class rule remains in power. For capitalism, in its present imperialist course, to dispense with present-day militarism, with secret diplomacy, with the centralization of many national states, is so impossible that these postulates might, much more consistently, be united into the simple demand, "abolition of capitalist class society." The proletarian movement cannot reconquer the place it deserves by means of Utopian advice and projects for weakening, taming or quelling imperialism within capitalism by means of partial reforms. The real problem that the world war has placed before the Socialist parties, upon whose solution the future of the working class movement depends, *is the readiness of the proletarian masses to act in the fight against imperialism.* The international proletariat suffers, not from a dearth of postulates, programs, and slogans, but from a lack of deeds, of effective resistance, of the power to attack imperialism at the decisive moment, just in times of war. It has been unable to put its old slogan, war against war, into actual practice. Here is the Gordian knot of the proletarian movement and of its future.

Imperialism, with all its brutal policy of force, with the incessant chain of social catastrophe that it itself provokes, is, to be sure, a historic necessity for the ruling classes of the present world. Yet nothing could be more detrimental than that the proletariat should derive, from the present war, the slightest hope or illusion of the possibility of an idyllic and peaceful development of capitalism. There is but one conclusion that the proletariat can draw from the historic necessity of imperialism. To capitulate before imperialism will mean to live forever in its shadow, off the crumbs that fall from the table of its victories.

Historic development moves in contradictions, and for every necessity puts its opposite into the world as well. The capitalist state of society is doubtless a historic necessity, but so also is the revolt of the working class against it. Capital is a historic necessity, but in the same measure is its grave digger, the Socialist proletariat. The world rule of imperialism is a historic necessity, but likewise its overthrow by the proletarian international. Side by side the two historic necessities exist in constant conflict with each other. And ours is the necessity of Socialism. Our necessity receives its justification with the moment when the capitalist class ceases to be the bearer of historic progress, when it becomes a hindrance, a danger, to the future development of society. The present world war has revealed that capitalism has reached this stage.

Capitalist desire for imperialist expansion, as the expression of its highest maturity in the last period of its life, has the economic tendency to change the whole world into capitalistically producing nations, to sweep away all superannuated, precapitalistic methods of production and society, to subjugate all the riches of the earth and all means of production to capital, to turn the laboring masses of the peoples of all zones into wage slaves. In Africa and in Asia, from the most northern regions to the southernmost point of South America and in the South Seas, the remnants of old communistic social groups, of feudal society, of patriarchal systems, and of ancient handicraft production are destroyed and stamped out by capitalism. Whole peoples are destroyed, ancient civilizations are levelled to the ground, and in their place profiteering in its most modern forms is being established. This brutal triumphant procession of capitalism through the world, accompanied by all the means of force, of robbery, and of infamy, has one bright phase: It has created the premises for its own final overthrow, it has established the capitalist world rule upon which, alone, the Socialist world revolution can follow. This is the only cultural and progressive aspect of the great so-called works of culture that were brought to the primitive countries. To capitalist economists and politicians, railroads, matches, sewerage systems and warehouses are progress and culture. Of themselves such works, grafted upon primitive conditions, are neither culture nor progress, for they are too dearly paid for with the sudden economic and cultural ruin of the peoples who must drink down the bitter cup of misery and horror of two social orders, of traditional agricultural landlordism, of super-modern, super-refined capitalist exploitation, at one and the same time. Only as the material conditions for the destruction of capitalism and the abolition of class society, can the effects of the capitalist triumphal march through the world bear the stamp of progress in an historical sense. In this sense imperialism, too, is working in our interest.

The present world war is a turning point in the course of imperialism. For the first time the destructive beasts that have been loosed by capitalist Europe over all other parts of the world have sprung with one awful leap, into the midst of the European nations. A cry of horror went up through the world when Belgium, that priceless little jewel of European culture, when the venerable monuments of art in northern France, fell into fragments before the onslaughts of a blind and destructive force. The "civilized world" that has stood calmly by when this same imperialism doomed tens of thousands of heroes to destruction; when the desert of Kalahari shuddered with the insane cry of the thirsty and the rattling breath of the dying; when in Putumayo, within ten years forty thousand human beings were tortured to death by a band of European industrial robberbarons, and the remnants of a whole people were beaten into cripples; when in China an ancient civilization was delivered into the hands of destruction and anarchy, with fire and slaughter, by the European soldiery; when Persia gasped in the noose of the foreign rule of force that closed inexorably about her throat; when in Tripoli the Arabs were mowed down, with fire and swords, under the yoke of capital while their civilization and their homes were razed to the ground.[2] This civilized world has just begun to know that the fangs of the imperialist beast are deadly, that its breath is frightfulness, that its tearing claws have sunk deeper into the breasts of its own mother, European culture. And this belated recognition is coming into the world of Europe in the distorted form of bourgeois hypocrisy, that leads each nation to recognize infamy only when it appears in the uniform of the other. They speak of German barbarism, as if every people that goes out for organized murder did not change into a horde of barbarians! They speak of Cossack horrors, as if war itself were not the greatest of all horrors, as if

2. Putumayo, a tributary of the Amazon in Columbia was the scene of atrocities against the local population when English rubber interests enslaved and killed thousands.

In China, a combined European task force led by the Germans, avenged the death of the German Count Waldersee at the hands of a Chinese soldier in 1899. The Kaiser had personally exhorted the troops to "emulate the Huns," and they did.

the praise of human slaughter in a Socialist periodical were not mental Cossackdom in its very essence.

But the horrors of imperialist bestiality in Europe have had another effect, that has brought to the "civilized world" no horror stricken eyes, no agonized heart. It is the mass destruction of the European proletariat. Never has a war killed off whole nations; never, within the past century, has it swept over all of the great and established lands of civilized Europe. Millions of human lives were destroyed in the Vosges, in the Ardennes, in Belgium, in Poland, in the Carpathians and on the Save; millions have been hopelessly crippled. But nine-tenths of these millions come from the ranks of the working class of the cities and the farms. It is our strength, our hope that was mowed down there, day after day, before the scythe of death. They were the best, the most intelligent, the most thoroughly schooled forces of international socialism, the bearers of the holiest traditions, of the highest heroism, the modern labor movement, the vanguard of the whole world proletariat, the workers of England, France, Belgium, Germany and Russia who are being gagged and butchered in masses. Only from Europe, only from the oldest capitalist nations, when the hour is ripe, can the signal come for the social revolution that will free the nations. Only the English, the French, the Belgian, the German, the Russian, the Italian workers together, can lead the army of the exploited and oppressed. And when the time comes they alone can call capitalism to account for centuries of crime committed against primitive peoples; they alone can avenge its work of destruction over a whole world. But for the advance and victory of Socialism we need a strong, educated, ready proletariat, masses whose strength lies in knowledge as well as in numbers. And these very masses are being decimated all over the world. The flower of our youthful strength, hundreds of thousands whose socialist education in England, in France, in Belgium, in Germany and in Russia was the product of decades of education and propaganda, other hundreds of thousands who were ready to receive the lessons of Socialism, have fallen, and are rotting upon the battlefields. The fruit of the sacrifices and toil of generations is destroyed in a few short weeks, the choicest troops of the international proletariat are torn out by the life roots.

The bloodletting of the June battle laid low the French labor movement for a decade and a half. The bloodletting of the Commune massacre again threw it back for more than a decade. What is happening now is a massacre such as the world has never seen before, that is reducing the laboring population in all of the leading nations to the aged, the women and the maimed; a bloodletting that threatens to bleed white the European labor movement.

Another such war, and the hope of Socialism will be buried under the ruins of imperialistic barbarism. That is more than the ruthless destruction of Liege and of the Rheims Cathedral.[3] That is a blow, not against capitalist civilization of the past, but against Socialist civilization of the future, a deadly blow against the force that carries the future of mankind in its womb, that alone can rescue the precious treasures of the past over into a better state of society. Here capitalism reveals its death's head, here it betrays that it has sacrificed its historic right of existence, that its rule is no longer compatible with the progress of humanity.

But here is proof also that the war is not only a grandiose murder, but the suicide of the European working class. The soldiers of socialism, the workers of England, of France, of Germany, of Italy, of Belgium are murdering each other at the bidding of capitalism, are thrusting cold, murderous irons into each other's breasts, are tottering over their graves, grappling in each other's death-bringing arms.

"Deutschland, Deutschland uber alles,"[4] "long live democracy," "long live the Czar and slavery," "ten thousand tent cloths,

3. In August 1914, the fortress of Liege in Belgium was bombarded by heavy German siege guns. In September, the Cathedral of Rheims, where every French King from Clovis to Louis XVI had been crowned, was shelled.

4. **Deutschland über alles:** Germany above everything. From a song by Heinrich Hoffmann von Fallersleben (1798–1876): "From the Maas up to the Memel; From the Etsch up to the Belt; Germany, Germany above everything; Above everything in the world." Originally written as a reflection of the desire for German national unification, it became later a military marching song, a Junker and imperialist anthem.

guaranteed according to specifications," "hundred thousand pounds of bacon," "coffee substitute, immediate delivery" . . . dividends are rising—proletarians falling; and with each one there sinks a fighter of the future, a soldier of the revolution, a saviour of humanity from the yoke of capitalism, into the grave.

This madness will not stop, and this bloody nightmare of hell will not cease until the workers of Germany, of France, of Russia and of England will wake up out of their drunken sleep; will clasp each others' hands in brotherhood and will drown the bestial chorus of war agitators and the hoarse cry of capitalist hyenas with the mighty cry of labor, "Proletarians of all countries, unite!"

THESES IN THE TASKS OF
INTERNATIONAL SOCIAL DEMOCRACY

A large number of comrades from different parts of Germany have adopted the following theses, which constitute an application of the Erfurt program[1] to the contemporary problems of international socialism!

1. The world war has annihilated the work of forty years of European socialism: by destroying the revolutionary proletariat as a political force; by destroying the moral prestige of socialism; by scattering the workers' International; by setting its Sections one against the other in fratricidal massacre; and by tying the aspirations and hopes of the masses of the people of the main countries in which capitalism has developed to the destinies of imperialism.

2. By their vote for war credits and by their proclamation of national unity, the official leaderships of the Socialist Parties in Germany, France and England (with the exception of the Independent Labor Party) have reinforced imperialism; induced the masses of the people to suffer patiently the misery and horrors of the war; contributed to the unleashing, without restraint, of imperialist frenzy, to the prolongation of the massacre and the increase in the number of its victims, and assumed their share in the responsibility for the war itself and for its consequences.

3. This tactic of the official leaderships of the Parties in the belligerent countries, and in the first place in Germany, until recently at the head of the International, constitutes a betrayal

---

1. **Erfurt Program:** Drafted by Kautsky and adopted at the German Social Democratic Congress, Erfurt 1891, replacing the Gotha program.

of the elementary principles of international socialism, of the vital interests of the working class, and of all the democratic interests of the peoples. By this alone socialist policy is condemned to impotence even in those countries where the leaders have remained faithful to their principles: Russia, Serbia, Italy and—with hardly an exception—Bulgaria.

4. By this alone official Social Democracy in the principal countries has repudiated the class struggle in war time and adjourned it until after the war; it has guaranteed to the ruling classes of all countries a delay in which to strengthen, at the proletariat's expense, and in a monstrous fashion, their economic, political and moral positions.

5. The world war serves neither the national defense nor the economic or political interests of the masses of the people whatever they may be. It is but the product of the imperialist rivalries between the capitalist classes of the different countries for world hegemony and for the monopoly in the exploitation and oppression of areas still not under the heel of capital. In the era of the unleashing of this imperialism, national wars are no longer possible. National interests serve only as the pretext for putting the laboring masses of the people under the domination of their mortal enemy, imperialism.

6. The policy of the imperialist states and the imperialist war cannot give to a single oppressed nation its liberty and its independence. The small nations, the ruling classes of which are the accomplices of their partners in the big states, constitute only the pawns on the imperialist chessboard of the great powers, and are used by them, just like their own working masses, in wartime, as instruments, to be sacrificed to capitalist interests after the war.

7. The present world war signifies, under these conditions, either in the case of "defeat" or of "victory," a defeat for socialism and democracy. It increases, whatever the outcome—excepting the revolutionary intervention of the international proletariat —and strengthens militarism, national antagonisms, and economic rivalries in the world market. It accentuates capitalist exploitation and reaction in the domain of internal policy, renders the influence of public opinion precarious and derisory, and reduces

parliaments to tools more and more obedient to imperialism. The present world war carries within itself the seeds of new conflicts.

8. World peace cannot be assured by projects Utopian or, at bottom, reactionary, such as tribunals of arbitration by capitalist diplomats, diplomatic, "disarmament" conventions, "the freedom of the seas," abolition of the right of maritime arrest, "the United States of Europe," a "customs union for central Europe," buffer states, and other illusions. Imperialism, militarism, and war can never be abolished nor attenuated so long as the capitalist class exercises, uncontested, its class hegemony. The sole means of successful resistance, and the only guarantee of the peace of the world, is the capacity for action and the revolutionary will of the international proletariat to hurl its full weight into the balance.

9. Imperialism, as the last phase in the life, and the highest point in the expansion, of the world hegemony of capital, is the mortal enemy of the proletariat of all countries. But under its rule, just as in the preceding stages of capitalism, the forces of its mortal enemy have increased in pace with its development. It accelerates the concentration of capital, the pauperization of the middle classes, the numerical reinforcement of the proletariat, arouses more and more resistance from the masses; and leads thereby to an intensified sharpening of class antagonisms. In peace time as in war, the struggle of the proletariat as a class has to be concentrated first of all against imperialism. For the international proletariat, the struggle against imperialism is at the same time the struggle for power, the decisive settling of accounts between socialism and capitalism. The final goal of socialism will be realised by the international proletariat only if it opposes imperialism all along the line, and if it makes the issue: "war against war" the guiding line of its practical policy; and on condition that it deploys all its forces and shows itself ready, by its courage to the point of extreme sacrifice, to do this.

10. In this framework, socialism's principal mission today is to regroup the proletariat of all countries into a living revolutionary force; to make it, through a powerful international organization which has only one conception of its tasks and interests, and only one universal tactic appropriate to political action in

peace and war alike, the decisive factor in political life, so that it may fulfil its historic mission.

11. The war has smashed the Second International. Its inadequacy has been demonstrated by its incapacity to place an effective obstacle in the way of the segmentation of its forces behind national boundaries in time of war, and to carry through a common tactic and action by the proletariat in all countries.

12. In view of the betrayal, by the official representatives of the socialist parties in the principal countries, of the aims and interests of the working class; in view of their passage from the camp of the working-class International to the political camp of the imperialist bourgeoisie; it is vitally necessary for socialism to build a new workers' International, which will take into its own hands the leadership and coordination of the revolutionary class struggle against world imperialism.

To accomplish its historic mission, socialism must be guided by the following principles:

1. The class struggle against the ruling classes within the boundaries of the bourgeois states, and international solidarity of the workers of all countries, are the two rules of life inherent in the working class in struggle and of historic world importance to it for its emancipation. There is no socialism without international proletarian solidarity, and there is no socialism without class struggle. The renunciation by the socialist proletariat, in time of peace as in time of war of the class struggle and of international solidarity, is equivalent to suicide.

2. The activity of the proletariat of all countries as a class, in peace time as in war time, must be geared to the fight against imperialism and war as its supreme goal. Parliamentary and trade union action, like every activity of the workers' movement, must be subordinated to this aim, so that the proletariat in each country is opposed in the sharpest fashion to its national bourgeoisie, so that the political and spiritual opposition between the two becomes at each moment the main issue, and international solidarity between the workers of all countries is underlined and practised.

3. The center of gravity of the organization of the proletariat as a class is the International. The International decides in time of peace the tactics to be adopted by the national Sections on the

questions of militarism, colonial policy, commercial policy, the celebration of May Day and finally, the collective tactic to be followed in the event of war.

4. The obligation to carry out the decisions of the International takes precedence over all else. National Sections which do not conform with this place themselves outside the International.

5. The setting in motion of the massed ranks of the proletariat of all countries is alone decisive in the course of struggles against imperialism and against war.

Thus the principal tactic of the national Sections aims to render the masses capable of political action and resolute initiative; to ensure the international cohesion of the masses in action; to build the political and trade union organizations in such a way that, through their mediation, prompt and effective collaboration of all the Sections is at all times guaranteed, and so that the will of the International materializes in action by the majority of the working-class masses all over the world.

6. The immediate mission of socialism is the spiritual liberation of the proletariat from the tutelage of the bourgeoisie, which expresses itself through the influence of nationalist ideology. The national Sections must agitate in the parliaments and the press, denouncing the empty wordiness of nationalism as an instrument of bourgeois domination. The sole defense of all real national independence is at present the revolutionary class struggle against imperialism. The workers' fatherland, to the defense of which all else must be subordinated, is the Socialist International.

GLOSSARY OF NAMES

Adler, Victor (1852–1918) Founder and leader of the Austrian Social Democracy; member, International Socialist Bureau; after 1906, Reichstag deputy. During war, a defencist. 1918, bourgeois Minister of Foreign Affairs.

Auer, Ignaz (1846–1907) Bavarian Social Democrat, Secretary German Social Democracy from 1875, reformist, Reichstag Deputy.

Bebel, August (1840–1913) Marxist of worker origin. Co-founder with Wilhelm Liebknecht of the German Social Democracy 1869. In Reichstag from 1867. Sentenced with Liebknecht to two years' imprisonment for treason (opposition to Franco-German War) in 1872. Leader of the German SD and the Second International in prewar years.

Berchtold, Leopold, Count (1863–1942) Landowner, industrialist, richest man in Austria. Austro-Hungarian diplomat: Paris 1894, London 1899, St. Petersburg 1906. Foreign Minister 1912. Completely under militarist heel. Author of the ultimatum to Serbia, July 19, 1914. Resigned, 1915.

Bernhardi, Friedrich von, General (1849–1930) Prussian Cavalry General. Militarist. As twenty-year old cavalry officer, was first German to ride through the Arc de Triomphe, 1870. Author: *Germany and the Next War*, 1911.

Bethmann-Holweg, Theobald von (1865–1921) Chancellor of the German Empire and Prime Minister of Prussia 1909–1917; succeeded von Bulow. Removed on the demand of the Crown Prince, Hindenburg and Ludendorff and dismissed by the Emperor, July 11, 1917. Replaced by Georg Michaelis (1857–1936).

Bismarck, Otto Eduard von (1815–1898) Unified Germany under Prussia and the Hohenzollerns; dominated the German and European political scene from 1862. First Chancellor of the German Empire. Dropped by Emperor Wilhelm II in March, 1890.

Blanc, Louis (1811–1882) French petty bourgeois socialist; Member, Provisional Government 1848; emigrated to England August, 1848; opposed the Paris Commune.

Bonaparte Dynasty Began with **Napoleon I,** (1769–1821) France's post-revolutionary General and Emperor from 1804 to 1815; ended with **Napoleon III,** (1808–1873), (Louis Bonaparte) nephew of Napoleon I, Emperor from 1852 to 1870.

Bourbon Dynasty Began with the accession of Henry IV to the throne of France in 1589; ended with the fall of Louis Philippe in 1848.

Bulow, Bernhard von Heinrich, Prince (1849–1929) German Foreign Secretary 1897; Chancellor 1900–1907; Count 1899, Prince 1905; Ambassador to Italy 1914.

Causidierre, Marc (1808–1861) Participant Lyons Insurrection 1834; Prefect of Paris Police from February 1848 and suppressed June 1848 uprising.

Cecil, Robert (1864–1958) Conservative British MP from 1903; Minister of Blockade 1916–1918; Under Secretary of Foreign Affairs 1918; Nobel Peace Prize 1937.

David, Eduard (1863–1930) German Social Democrat. Reichstag Deputy from 1903; Revisionist. In World War I a Majority Socialist, i.e., a supporter of the imperialist war. Minister without Portfolio 1919–1920. First President of the National Assembly 1919.

Favre, Jules (1809–1880) French lawyer. Minister of Foreign Affairs 1870–71. Helped crush Paris Commune.

Franz Ferdinand (1863–1914) Archduke of Austria and heir to the Habsburg Throne. Assassinated with his wife Sophie at Sarajevo.

Frederick III (1831–1888) Hohenzollern Crown Prince, son of first German Emperor, married daughter of Victoria of England, father of Kaiser Wilhelm II. Reigned for three months in 1888.

Golz, Colmar Freihen von der (1843–1916) German Field Marshal. Helped reorganize Turkish Army 1883–1895. The Ottomans gave him the title "Pasha." Despite his training the Turks were pushed out of Europe in the Balkan Wars. Died in command of Turkish forces. Author: *Nation in Arms,* 1883.

Grey, Sir Edward (1862–1933) Liberal MP 1885–1916. One of the authors of the Triple Entente. Foreign Secretary 1905–1916. Played part in the Balkans Wars, and Peace 1914. Ambassador to USA 1919–20.

Haase, Hugo (1863–1919)   Lawyer of Jewish origin. German Social Democrat. Member International Bureau; Reichstag Deputy 1897–1918. Succeeded Bebel as leader of SD Reichstag fraction 1913. Opposed voting for war credits within the Party, but succumbed to Majority decision, and made Reichstag statement on behalf of the Party supporting credits and the war. Founder and leader of the Independent Social Democratic Party 1916. Minister of Foreign Affairs and Colonies in Ebert's Coalition, November 1918. Resigned December 29, 1918. Shot on steps of Reichstag by Monarchist officer.

Hapsburg Dynasty   Ancient feudal ruling family, taking its name from the "Habitschburg" (Castle of the Hawk) of Alsace. Began with a few acres in Swiss Alsace. In 1282 Rudolph (1218–1289) was elected King of the Holy Roman Empire of 400 feudal baronies. The Hapsburgs ruled over an empire of many nations, and never could keep them unified. 1806 title of Holy Roman Emperor was abandoned. After the Ausgleich of 1867, the Hapsburgs ruled over Austria-Hungary. With the Austrian Revolution, Emperor Karl abdicated on November 12, 1918.

Hamid, Abdul II (1842–1918)   Sultan of Turkey 1876–1909. Overthrown by the Young Turks.

Hohenstauffen Dynasty   A theocratical dynasty in Germany which succeeded the Salian dynasty in 1138 and was overthrown by the Popes who were Italian Princes and consistently fought the Hohenstauffen. The line began with Conrad III and ended with Conrad IV in 1254.

Hindenburg, Paul von Beneckendorf and von (1857–1934)   Prussian militarist. Fought in war against France 1870–71. General 1903. Retired 1911. Recalled at beginning of World War I. Victor at Tannenberg (1914) and Masurian Lakes (1915) against Russia. Later Field Marshal. Succeeded Social Democrat Ebert as President 1925. Coexisted with Hitler from 1932 till his death.

Hohenzollern Dynasty   Frederick of Hohenzollern, Burgrave of Nuremburg was made elector of Brandenburg in 1415. To 1609 Brandenburg was a barren region between Middle Oder and Middle Elbe. 1618, Dukedom of Prussia (a Polish fief since 1466) devolved on Frederick William of Brandenburg, "the Great Elector." Rose after Peace of Westphalia 1648, with the help of France and England who backed the Protestant rulers against the Roman Catholic rulers of Austria. With the help of Bismarck, the dynasty emerged as principal power in the North German Federation. After the victory against France, the King of Prussia became Emperor of Germany. Dynasty ended with abdication of Kaiser Wilhelm II, November 9, 1918.

Jacobi, Johann (1805–1877) Prussian bourgeois democrat, known for his honesty and consistency. Presided at a meeting at Koenigsberg protesting annexation of French territory. Arrested for this reason and held a prisoner of state at Lotzen.

Jacobins Members of the Jacobin Club, the most radical party during the French Revolution. As they occupied the highest seats in the Convention, they were also called the "Mountain."

Jaures, Jean Auguste (1859–1914) French Socialist leader. Founder and editor *L'Humanite* 1904–1914. Right Winger. Leading figure and orator in the second International. Anti-Militarist. Assassinated by French officers on the eve of the war, July 31, 1914.

Junkers Descendants of the Teutonic knights who settled on the East bank of the Elbe since 1225. Large landowners, they kept the area undeveloped and under feudal control. Militarists.

Kaclerovic, Trisa (1879– ?) Lawyer. Founder Serbian Social Democracy. Parliamentarian 1908–1921. Founder Serbian Communist Party, then formed Independent Labour Party. Anti-militarist. Voted against war credits in parliament. Attended Kienthal Conference.

Kautsky, Karl (1854–1938) German Social Democrat. Theoretician of the German Social Democracy and the Second International. Author of the Erfurt Programme. Pacifist-Centrist during the war. Later Right Winger in Independent Social Democratic Party. Subsequently rejoined the Social Democracy. Died in exile.

Krupp, Alfred (1812–1887) Big German industrialist, munitions manufacturer and steel tycoon. Began with father's iron forge and converted it into the first Bessemer steel plant. In 1871, at founding of German Empire, was leading industrialist. Son, **Frederick Alfred Krupp** (1854–1902), was a personal friend of the Emperor.

Lassalle, Ferdinand (1825–1864) German working class leader and contemporary of Marx. His followers later helped to found the German Social Democracy, constituting one of its wings.

Laptchevic (1864– ?) Serbian Social Democrat, parliamentarian and anti-militarist. With Kaclerovic opposed war credits in Parliament, 1914.

Liebknecht, Wilhelm (1826-1900) Friend of Marx, founder and leader of the German Social Democracy. Reichstag Deputy. Jailed for opposition to Franco-Prussian War.

Lloyd-George, David (1863–1945)   Welsh M.P., Premier of Great Britain 1916–1922.

Manteuffel, Edwin von (1809–1885)   In October 1849, as Prussian Home Secretary, was strong man behind the Brandenburg Cabinet. September 1850, on death of Brandenburg, became Premier of Prussia.

Nevski, Alexander (1218–1263)   Russian Prince, hero and saint. Victor over the Swedes, Neva 1240. Grand Duke of Kiev, Novgorod and Vladimir.

Nicholas I (1876–1855)   Romanov, Emperor of Russia 1825–1855.

Rohrbach, Paul (1869–   )   German journalist and semi-official commentator on military affairs.

Romanov Dynasty   Founded 1613, by Michael Romanov, grandfather of Peter the Great. Ruled Russia till the February Revolution, 1917.

Saladin, Sultan (1171–1193)   Turkish ruler. Captured Jerusalem 1187.

Thiers, Louis-Adolphe (1797–1877)   French historian, Premier 1836, 1840. President French Republic 1871–73. Crushed the Paris Commune.

Troelestra, Pieter Jelles (1860–1932)   Helped found the Dutch Social Democracy. Member States General 1897–1925; Right-Winger. Member International Socialist Bureau. Defencist during the war. Retired from politics 1925.

Wrangel, Ernst, Count (1784–1877)   Prussian General. Real power behind the throne in 1848.

71 72 73 74   12 11 10 9 8 7 6 5 4 3 2 1

hARPER ⚡ ꙅORChBOOKS

† The New American Nation Series, edited by Henry Steele Commager and Richard B. Morris.
‡ American Perspectives series, edited by Bernard Wishy and William E. Leuchtenburg.
α History of Europe series, edited by J. H. Plumb.
§ The Library of Religion and Culture, edited by Benjamin Nelson.
‖ Researches in the Social, Cultural, and Behavioral Sciences, edited by Benjamin Nelson.
⊻ Harper Modern Science Series, edited by James R. Newman.
° Not for sale in Canada.
+ Documentary History of the United States series, edited by Richard B. Morris.
# Documentary History of Western Civilization series, edited by Eugene C. Black and Leonard W. Levy.
ʌ The Economic History of the United States series, edited by Henry David et al.
¶ European Perspectives series, edited by Eugene C. Black.
** Contemporary Essays series, edited by Leonard W Levy.
* The Stratum Series, edited by John Hale.